Raging Desire

Raging Desire

MONYA LOYA

RAGING DESIRE

This book is written to provide information and motivation to readers. Its purpose is not to render any type of psychological, legal, or professional advice of any kind. The content is the sole opinion and expression of the author, and not necessarily that of the publisher.

Copyright © 2019 by Monya Loya

All rights reserved. No part of this book may be reproduced, transmitted, or distributed in any form by any means, including, but not limited to, recording, photocopying, or taking screenshots of parts of the book, without prior written permission from the author or the publisher. Brief quotations for noncommercial purposes, such as book reviews, permitted by Fair Use of the U.S. Copyright Law, are allowed without written permissions, as long as such quotations do not cause damage to the book's commercial value. For permissions, write to the publisher, whose address is stated below.

Printed in the United States of America.

ISBN   978-1-64552-031-3   (Paperback)
ISBN   978-1-64552-032-0   (Digital)

Lettra Press books may be ordered through booksellers or by contacting:

Lettra Press LLC
18229 E 52nd Ave.
Denver City, CO 80249
1 303 586 1431 | info@lettrapress.com
www.lettrapress.com

ACKNOWLEDGMENTS

I want to thank Abagail Allen and Brianna Parker for supporting and helping me as I wrote this book.

AUTHOR BIO

Even though she had a rough life, Monya became an accredited artist selling her artwork all over the world; including having her work hang in the Blue Room of the White house in Washington, D.C. and in a doctor's office in Uvita, Costa Rica. She has a flare for color and design helping her in her everyday life. Her caring, nurturing way uplifts those around her. She has an excitement for life even when it doesn't go as planned always looking for the positive in all situations and the good in all people. Her sincerity and honesty can always be counted on. She is very knowledgeable and helpful no matter what the situation and always strives to help others without asking for anything in return. Her patience, understanding and compassion for all others is how she lives her life and shares with the world.

Dear Reader,

Family and the desire to have a loving relationship is at the heart of my story. They say only good things come to those who wait. This book depicts how constant poor life choices can be turned around and bad occurrences become great events.

After almost 30 years of abuse, neglect, hardships, loss of my daughter, and almost losing my son, I chose to turn my life around. I made some sacrifices and changes by the age of 45 and moved to Florida for a new start, which is where I currently live.

The waterfall in this book is fictional however, there are many picturesque waterfalls throughout the world. Like the one my grandmother used to take us to when we were kids in the Adirondack Mountains located in Canajoharie, N.Y. I encourage you to take in the sights of some of them when you can, they are magnificent and breathtaking.

While the names of places in this book are real and the scenery as described, the occurrences within them are mostly fictional, loosely based on true events. Some of these places can be found all over the world like the beauty found in Quepos, Costa Rica.

Although my life was rough growing up and during my early adult years, I have always found good and forgiveness within myself and others to weather any storm sent my way. I have always bounced back learning many life's lessons along the way.

I hope this book helps someone who seemingly has no hope wondering 'Why me' like I did, to realize there is always a way. There is a light at the end of the tunnel and there is help. You can do it but you have to begin the process yourself. It's the old adage, only those who help themselves can be helped. You must take the first step. When you respond to a negative event in a positive way, you are far more likely to guarantee a more positive outcome!

Enjoy and God bless!
Monya Loya

CHAPTER 1

GROWING UP WAS rough. We just moved from Schenectady, NY, U.S.A. to Sturgeon Falls, Ontario, Canada this past summer and we don't know anyone. There are four of us plus my mom and dad. My name is Chloe and I am eleven years old and I am the eldest. From oldest to youngest my siblings are Christina (Chris) age nine, Rheanne (Rea) age six, and Rose age two.

I am in grade six and it's not until the first week of school before my two sisters and I make any friends. We live just under a mile away from the school so the bus won't pick us up; thus the three of us have to walk to school. By the second week Chris knows everyone and Rea is like me, only a few friends. It is around this time this one boy makes himself known to us.

Attractive, cute, neat yet tidy is this quite tall boy. His slender, muscular build with shiny, short chestnut brown hair highlights his bluish-green eyes. Watching him in the school yard this past week I can tell he has a pleasant personality, is good natured, sociable and independent. He is clearly disciplined and self-confident as his friends look up to him, like he is the head of their clan.

Now, he walks across the courtyard and past me at recess making sure that I notice him. He follows me around when we have school functions such as track and field and my sister sees him following us sometimes on our way home.

One day he passes by with two of his friends. I overhear him say, "She is shockingly beautiful with her long straight brown hair, ivory skin, high cheekbones and soft green eyes. She is extremely attractive and I need to get to know her. Find out her name for me."

His friends nod as they look at me smiling. At first I am not sure they are talking about me; my eyes are brown-green, my skin is slightly tanned and I don't think I have high cheekbones, to me they are normal.

We have been in school for a month now and I still don't know who this boy is or why he is following us. Chris and I discuss it in great lengths on our walks home. She has told me of how she thinks he has been watching her during recess and school events so she isn't sure if he is following me or her.

One day she decides to find out so we walk slower than normal until he is not very far from us. She stops, turns and very bluntly asks him why he has been following us for the past month. He blushes and points to me. By this time she has walked up to him and is now standing in front of him. Rea and I have stayed back where we were and are far enough away that we can't hear what they are saying.

Within minutes both Chris and the boy walk towards us. "This is Josh and he's been following us all this time because he likes you." she says looking at me.

I blush because I never had anyone like me before and really didn't know what to say. He walked with us for a bit and during this time we found that he lives in the total opposite direction as us and it takes him almost two hours to get back home. He has been getting in trouble so now he lies to his parents telling them he is going to a friends' house so he doesn't get into trouble by following us. We also find out that he is in grade seven.

It isn't long before we become friends and do everything together. By the time summer comes, we have become the best of friends. My dad has left us and it's not long before my mom becomes a drunk. She is never home, always at the bars, and leaves me at the age of twelve, to care for my three younger sisters. My dad never visits us nor does he let us go and visit with him. He has a girlfriend now and it seems he has moved on with his life as though we didn't even exist. Mom tells us he doesn't love us because we are girls and he wanted boys.

By the time summer is over, my mom finds a boyfriend who is an alcoholic. His name is Brock and they met at the bar where my mom frequents.

A FEW YEARS have now passed and my dad rarely sees us or even talks to us. Brock is now our step dad and he and I fight all the time. I do what I can to protect my sisters from him because I don't like him. You see, Brock is a very mean drunk, which seems to be all the time. Through grade eight,

Josh is in high school and even though we can't see each other during the day, he tries to keep me busy and away from home as much as possible.

Josh has a new set of friends and he and I aren't together as much as we used to be; however, we do remain best friends. Although he tries to help me, my step-dad still finds time to abuse me. He hits me or pushes me down when things don't go his way, whether or not it is my fault; and, even if I wasn't home when it happened.

Now that grade school is behind me and high school is ahead of me, I only hope everything gets better. I pray that from here my home life changes and becomes more desirable.

I am in high school now and, Josh and I do almost everything together again. During my high school years, things get worse. Brock drinks all the time now and in his stupors, becomes more callous, beating me more often. I try to stop him but he is far stronger than I am and everything that I try does not work. I decide to take a self-defense class so I can use the moves on him; however, he is so strong that I don't impose any harm to him.

Summer is now here and grade nine is over. Josh has just got his motorcycle license and has gone down to see his cousins in Toronto for the weekend. My mom won't allow me on the bike yet so I stay behind. Chris convinces me to attend a party held by one of her friends across town. It is a Saturday night so I go.

We have been here for two hours now and I am not having much fun. I decide to leave but my sister isn't so she stays. It's almost midnight and with my mom and Brock at the bar, she doesn't answer the phone when I call. It is almost four miles from here to home and I now have to walk.

I leave the party and decide to walk through down town thinking it might be safer than taking the shortcut through the woods. At the end of town, the street lights are out from kids throwing rocks at them and breaking the bulbs, making it very dark. As I pass by the alley between the hardware store and Movie Theater, a large dark figure appears out of the shadows.

I can't make out any details of the dark figure. He just stands there as though he is just watching me. Getting spooked by the scene I walk faster hoping to make it to the theater. If I make it there, I can duck inside and try to get a ride. *I am almost there. Just a few more steps,* I think to myself. Then I feel it. His hand grabs me from behind and forces me to the ground.

Standing in front of me now, he is wearing a hooded jacket with a ski mask covering his face. He pulls me up and forces me into the alley.

With my right arm held behind my back and his left arm across my chest with his hand clasped tightly over my mouth, he rushes me to the back of the alley. I am then pushed towards the back wall where three other large dark figures dressed in similar clothing emerge from the shadows. As they come towards me, so does the darkness; as if the rippled shadows cling to their figures.

They tie a scarf around my mouth so I can't scream. Pulling and clawing at me, I am defenseless as they throw me to the ground and tear my clothes off. Panic grips me for I am almost certain my impending death is upon me.

Two of them hold my arms down, another sits on my legs while the fourth forces himself inside me as he clamps his hands around my throat. One at a time, they take their turn thrusting inside of me, forcing their way in. I am bleeding, can hardly breathe and my entire body goes numb. All I can do is cry and pray that they will soon stop and let me go. Two of them get their kicks out of hitting me every time I make a noise or try to stop them. I am punched in the arm or stomach and slapped across the face. It seems to last for a very long time. I do not move letting them do what they want. The more I struggle the harder they hit me and the more they pounded on me.

After a while, voices are heard from a distance and they are getting closer. Leaving me there, the four guys jump up and run from the alley. The people walking across the street see them run from the alley. Knowing it is an odd sight, they decide to see what they were running from.

There I am. Lying on the cement covered in bruises and blood. My eyes are swelled shut, my throat hurts and I am gasping for air. My stomach feels like it is on fire and so do other parts of my body. There is blood all around me but we don't know where it is coming from. They find me and thinking I am close to dead call 911. I am taken to the hospital where I spend the night.

While at the hospital they spend almost three hours taking small rocks, sand and gravel that is imbedded into my back. I lay here slightly on my stomach with the nurses changing medicated towels they laid over my back.

By morning I am able to lie on my back lightly, the swelling on my lip and eyes has gone down and from the medication the doctor gave me, I really don't have any pain either except for the burning sensation in my stomach. It turns out that I was stabbed three times in the stomach; I was so out of it by then, I didn't even know that had happened. I spend the day under close watch and am kept doped up on meds so I sleep most of the day away.

It is now Sunday morning and after all the reports are done and tests have been taken, I am released. My mom takes me home. On our way home I make my mom promise not to tell Josh what has happened and she makes Brock do the same. I have not slept with Josh or anyone for that matter because up until this happened, I was a virgin. That afternoon Josh gets home from Toronto and calls. Not wanting to talk to him yet my mom tells him I went to my dad's and should be home after dinner.

The next two days I avoid Josh and my friends. My mom tells them that I came home sick with the flu from my dad's. By Wednesday I have stopped crying and pull myself together. Most of the bruises are going away and the ones that are left, I can cover up with make-up or clothing.

That afternoon, Josh stops by to see how I am. I am scared but have to try to act normal. It isn't hard for me to show that I am really glad he is home but I have a hard time hugging and kissing him. I do my best but he knows me too well and by dinner asks me what is wrong. I tell him I just am not up to par yet from the flu. He accepts that, even though I can tell he doesn't believe me.

School starts in three weeks and I can't wait. The less I am home the better, I should be healed by then and hopefully Josh won't know what happened. The rest of the summer is really hard. When Josh wants to go out with everyone, I have to go too because it would be out of the norm if I didn't, and if I stayed home he would know something was wrong.

Going made me really nervous. I didn't know who the four guys were and I didn't know who, if anyone, knew it was me that it happened to. It was in all the papers and all over the news, so I knew it was only a matter of time. However, because of my age and I didn't give permission, my picture and name were left out of the media.

Summer is now over and we are back in school. It isn't long after school starts when Josh moves away and only tells me he is moving the night before. Without even a phone call or a good bye, he leaves. I don't know where he is going, if he makes it there safely or how he is. I never see or hear from him again and I am devastated.

My step-dad decides to take advantage of the situation and frame of mind that I am now in and starts to console me. At first, I think he is trying to become my friend so we don't argue as much. He says he is trying to make it easier on my mom. He tells my mom he will look after me when she is at work. It's not long before bad becomes worse and I just want to die.

It begins with him talking to me and giving me the odd hug. I don't hug back and hardly say a word to him, simply put, I don't like him. I never have and until now I thought the feeling was mutual. After a week of this, he progresses to putting his arm around me and patting my back when we talk.

This soon changes. He begins to sit beside me and rub his hand up and down my thigh, then my neck like he is giving me a massage. I am now back at school and hope it will soon stop. It doesn't. He continues becoming more aggressive. It all makes me very uncomfortable so I try to stop him by telling him I don't like it and want him to stop. He gets mad and picks up the pace.

When I am at the table doing homework he will come up behind me and rub my neck working his way down my back. His hands run across my shoulders then down my arms. Then he pushes me forward, lifts my top, undoes my bra and rubs his hands all over my bare back. When he does this he says how nice I feel and tells me things he wants to do to me and doesn't stop until someone comes in. If I move to stop him, he pushes me against the table so I can't move. When someone comes in the door, he pulls my shirt down quickly pretending like he is helping me with my homework.

I am always a pack of nerves at home and this makes it worse. When I try to tell my mom what is going on, he would walk in and I have to change the subject quickly. The one time I was able to tell her, it was like she didn't believe me and puts it off that it is from the rape I went through and never questions it.

One night Chris is out with friends and Rea and Rose are in bed. I go into the basement which is where my bedroom is. I put on some music and start to draw at my desk. After a few minutes, I hear a noise and look up to see he is standing in my doorway with his hands behind his back and a grin on his face.

"What do you want?" I ask as I continue with my drawing.

"It's time you become a woman." showing me his 10-gauge shot gun.

With his pants unzipped, he walks up to me, grabs my arm and forces me onto my bed telling me I am going to learn how to give oral sex to a man and be good at it.

"You will practice on me until you get it right!" he says with the gun in one hand and putting his hand on the back of my head. He then forces his penis into my mouth and forces his way in and out. He doesn't stop until he comes no matter hard I fight and try to push him away.

When he is done he smacks me across the face a couple of times and tells me next time not to put up a fight or it will be harder. He then holds the gun to me and threatens that if I say anything to anyone, they will never find my body. "They will believe you ran away looking for Josh." he tells me.

I am terrified, hurt and don't know what to do. I promise him I won't say anything as I am now afraid for my life.

He does this to me every night for the next two weeks. Every time I try to fight him off or push him away I get bruises all over from him hitting and punching me. However, he is clever because he makes sure to hit me where the bruises can be covered up.

It is a Wednesday night and my mom is at work while my sisters are in bed. It is ten p.m. and I am in my room studying for a test. Brock comes down the stairs. Hearing him I stand up hoping to be able to stop him from doing anything. It doesn't work. He tries to force me to my knees. He pushes on my head so hard I scream because my neck hurt really bad and I can't move. My sisters come running down the stairs when they heard me scream and sees that Brock is helping me up the stairs. He tells them to watch Rose so he can take me to the hospital.

When they ask what happened, he tells them he doesn't know, just that he heard me yell and by the time he got to my room I couldn't move. On our way to the hospital he tells me that I had better go along with his story if I know what's best for me. When we arrive at the hospital, he tells the doctor and nurses I was at the park and fell off the jungle gym.

The nurses and technicians take x-rays which show the extent of the injuries I really have; we are told that I have really bad whiplash. They put a collar on my neck and say that I have to be very careful on how I move for the next couple of weeks. They give us some pills that I have to take three times a day for a week.

When I am released, we get into the car and he tells me to stick to that story and tell my mom the same thing or next time it will be much worse. We stop to pick my mom up from work on the way home and he tells her the same story. I agree with him and don't say anything different. She believes us and he smiles.

I am scared to death of what the worse could be so I did what he said. I lay in my bed thinking that if he can hurt me like this, and this easily with no remorse, maybe he would kill me like he says. If it got to that point, what would happen to my sisters; I couldn't let that happen.

Oral now turns into actual sex acts. It got to where I didn't want to be home at all anymore. I try several times to tell my mom but she never listens to me. Scared if I left he would do this to my sisters, I stay. I am hoping I will be able to protect them from this horrific ordeal.

I find out much later in life that they too suffered the same thing from him and none of us ever knew it was happening to the other.

This continues through grade eleven at least four times a week; which are the days my mom is at work. I had quietly been taking Jui Jitsu classes to learn how to protect myself and get out of certain situations. During one of my classes, I am thrown over a shoulder learning a practice technique when I am hurt really bad and brought back to the hospital.

While there, I tell the nurse that I don't want Brock in the room with me. She notices how I act around males, agrees with me and tells the doctor. The doctor has some orderlies come and get me saying they are going to do an MRI and x-rays on my neck. I thought they were doing tests around my injuries and so did Brock; which is what the doctor was hoping for. He waits in the room while I am getting the tests done.

Once I am away from him and on a whole different floor, I am badgered with question after question about my life at home and the bruises and scars I have on my body from the technicians as they do the tests. They keep on until I can't keep it in anymore and I break down telling them everything. I even tell the stories I have had to tell throughout the past year to cover the bruises and why and even how I tried to tell my mom with no luck.

I am kept for two days under observation and my mom and step dad are not allowed to see me. They want to investigate and do further testing, and then question them, but they don't know it yet. I know once they are questioned, I am doomed. Scared out of my mind not knowing what he is going to do me once he finds out I told, I try to take my life by injecting air into the I.V. tubing. It didn't work. As soon as I put the needle in the end of the tube, all kinds of beeps and sounds started coming from the machine and they all came rushing over.

I am then restrained and put under suicide watch. If nothing else, I am safe for three more days as when you are put on suicide watch, it is an automatic three day hold. During this time, they ask why I did that so I tell them how he threatened me and I would rather die by my hand than his. The next morning my siblings are taken to children's aid and my mom and Brock are taken in for questioning. They are there for two days then released and my siblings are allowed to go back home with them.

Once I am released and back home, my mom treats me like I an outsider. I have to shop for and cook my own meals, do my own dishes and laundry and am even kept away from my sisters. My mom, hospital staff and police don't press charges on Brock. The doctor and nurses say they did all they could do when they reported it to the police. The police say at my age I must have done something to deserve the beating or, because I didn't like Brock, I only added the sex abuse to get back at him. My mom simply doesn't believe me and tells me she won't have Brock arrested and thrown in jail without proof.

Brock gets away with it without so much as a slap on the hand. After a couple of weeks, and unable to take it anymore, I decide to leave. I am now on my own having to deal with all this alone, knowing that my mother thinks I am a liar. She has disowned me now and took it a step further. She tells my sisters, that if she finds out they are talking to me, they too will be thrown out and disowned.

I am literally alone in this cruel world. Now what do I do? Where do I go? Who can I trust?

Life has to be better than this, isn't it?

CHAPTER 2

A FEW YEARS have gone by since my ordeal and I am in swimming, Karate and Jui Jitsu. They help me to focus giving me something to do and keeping me occupied. After winning many competitions, I find myself in yet another relationship.

He has been great and we get along as well as Josh and I did. Jake is his name and he is three years older than me. He is a handsome man with broad shoulders, a muscular chest, narrow waist and long legs. Being an athletic person with biceps of steel, his is on the wrestling team winning several of his competitions. We complement each other really well.

After two years of courting and six months of living together he asks me to marry him. We have a small intimate wedding held in a small chapel with celebrations in the basement. There is a total of fifty-two guests including the six who are in our wedding party. The day goes well and we all seem very happy.

Our wedding night seems to change everything. He becomes this giant monster turned from a soft gentle spirit and tells me that I can no longer have friends or go anywhere without his say so. "I now own you." he says.

"What do you mean, you own me?"

He holds the marriage license in his hand waving it in front of my face. "You are now mine and you will do as I say."

He then lays down the rules telling me I can no longer have friends or go out unless he is with me or approves of it. He then makes me quit Karate and Jui Jitsu. "For now you can stay with the swim team. They need you and they travel with my wrestling team so I will be able to keep an eye on you!"

I am floored. Until now I didn't think there were any issues. He knew from day one what I was into and the time I spent with each team. He always acted as though these were the things that drew me to him and I didn't want to quit any of them. These things were my salvation, my get away and now he is making me quit them!

"Why do I have to quit them? Our wedding shouldn't change any of our activities."

"No wife of mine will outshine me in strength or endurance!"

"What the hell are you talking about? That makes absolutely no sense! We aren't even on the same teams."

"Just do as I say or you will regret it!"

I am only five foot six weighing one-hundred and fifteen pounds, while he is six foot seven inches tall weighing a total of one-hundred and eighty-two pounds. He is very adamant and demanding, almost scary. This is a side of him I have never seen before nor did I think was even in him.

Scared of what he might do, I quit as he said. What was starting out to finally be a good life turns over night and I find myself in the same situation I have tried so hard to stay away from.

I endure a full year of abuse, neglect and followed everywhere I go, even for walks along the beach. I have no alone time nor peace as he or one of his friends always watches me. I feel like I am in prison now. If I do something he wasn't aware of and finds out later, even if it is just grocery shopping, I get slapped around and beaten by his hand or belt.

It's not long before he sells my car telling me that he or one of his friends will take me to and from work. He says this way he can keep a better eye on me. It is like he doesn't trust me and I don't know why. I have never given him any reason not to trust me in the entire three years we have been together. My family is allowed to call me but he listens to every conversation by holding the other phone to his ear, muting it so they don't know he is listening in.

When he is gone he takes the phone cord so I can't make or receive calls while he is gone. When I am asked how we are doing I have to say we are doing good and act like we are madly in love, when all I really want to do is run and hide.

One year into our marriage, he decides things need to change. He comes home after a night on the town with his friends, locks me in our bedroom telling me it is for my own good. The next morning he comes in with ropes in his hands. He ties me to the bed posts and ties a scarf around my mouth then takes all of our clothes out of the room.

"You will wear what I tell you to wear when I want you to wear it and nothing else!"

I am shocked and scared as I don't know why he is doing this or what he has planned. I want to scream but can't. He takes the scarf from my mouth and I scream as loud as I can. He backhands me across my face telling me to shut up.

"I won't do it!"

"Yes you will. You have no choice!"

"I don't think so!"

He storms out of the room slamming the door closed behind him and locking it leaving my hands tied to the bed. I scream and yell and call him every bad and foul name I can think of. After a while, I stop as my throat is getting sore from the yelling. He finally comes back in and says if I promise to behave, he will untie me. I nod my head and he unties my hands.

"Get some sleep, you are going to need it!" he tells me.

He leaves the room before I can ask what he meant by that. I crawl into a little ball under the covers and cry. *Why me – what did I do to deserve this?* I ask myself. I cry myself to sleep.

He keeps me there for several weeks with only a towel to shower with and two negligees' wear. It is winter time and it is very cold outside. He keeps the room at sixty-five degrees. All I have is the towel and couple thin blankets to try to stay warm. I am not tied and am free to move around as he only unlocks the door to bring me food or to let himself in for sex.

A few weeks pass when he comes in with two of his friends locking the door behind them. They have been drinking and have a bottle of beer in each of their hands and Jake has a six pack in his hands. He throws me onto the bed, tears the negligée I have on off and says, "Please my friends and do everything they tell you to do while I watch!"

There is no way I am complying with that. "No I am not going to do that!" I yell.

"Trust me you will do it and you WILL like it!"

He tells his friends that they have permission to slap and spank me if I struggle or don't do what they say. He also tells them if they need to hold me down and force their way in to do so.

I am now shocked and scared and am trying to get to the other side of the bed to get away from them.

They pull me back and do what they were told. Throwing me back down on the bed they hold me down taking turns. One holds me down while the other perform sexual acts on me. Then they take turns fucking me and shoving their cocks into my mouth. They pound me so hard with each thrust that my nose gets broke and one of my teeth is pushed through my upper lip; but, this does not stop them.

Putting me into several positions I feel like a pretzel. They spray cold water on me and rub ice cubes all over my tits and down my belly. They even shove a few into my ass as they pound on my pussy. They do the same to my pussy as they fuck me in the ass. If they aren't slapping me across the face or spanking my ass, Jake tells them to hold my ass in the air as he whips me with a flyswatter. During this entire time, they are all getting drunker on the beer.

This continues for almost three hours. When they are done, Jake tells me to take a shower and get as much sleep as I can because there won't be much of it. "You need to be ready at all times."

"I don't think so. This will never happen again!" I scream.

He smiles and says nothing as he takes every last piece of clothing leaving only the one towel. On his way out, he stops in the doorway and turns to me with a smile. "When me or my friends get horny, we will be coming in. I don't want them to waste any time getting what they want."

Before I can say anything, he is out the door locking it behind him. I am flabbergasted and scared. I am sore, bruised and bleeding and can't believe this is happening to me.

It turns out to be several times a day most days. I have lost track; track of time, track of days and whether it is day or night. I am so sore I can hardly move and when they come in, I am rubbed with Vaseline all over before starting just so their cocks slide easily. I am bleeding from cuts and ruptures and am bruised from head to toe. My throat is raw and my mouth is like one big cold sore. I have two black eyes from the broken nose which has not healed yet and I am one solid hickey from my neck to my nipples. I just want to die. There is very little time for sleep let alone to heal.

After what seemed like forever, I find myself alone. It has been a few hours since I have seen anyone and at least an hour since I have heard any noises. No one else seems to be in the house, or at least not that I can hear. I pick up a lamp from the bed side table, close my eyes and throw it through the bathroom window. It is very small but I know I can fit as I only weight ninety-two pounds.

It is still winter time and it is very cold outside, minus twenty with the wind chill. I climb out and slide down the snow bank with only the towel around me. Having nothing to wear and freezing, I try to make my way to the police station.

It is snowing and blowing and extremely cold. Being sore, tired and having very little strength, I collapse into a snow bank alongside the road. As I drift in and out of consciousness I hear cars drive by. I don't know how long I am here, it seems like forever and I am about to give up. As I pray to God to take me and put me out of my misery, I hear a car screech to a halt and doors slam. Next thing I know I am being picked up, wrapped in a blanket and laid into the back seat of a car.

Everything goes black again as I pass out before the car even begins to move. I wake up to find that I am in the hospital. I can hear the nurses and doctors around me talking but I don't know what they are saying and I can't even tell if they are talking to me or not. When I am consciousness enough for everything to be clear, I am asked a barrage of questions and put through many tests, just as I was a few years back. After they get all the results, I describe the guys who have done this and the police get involved. Within hours, he and his friends are arrested and put in jail.

My injuries are severe. My nose has to be rebroken so it can be set and heal properly. The hole in my upper lip is beginning to heal and some of the swelling in my face is starting to go down. I have two cracked ribs and my vocal chords are severely bruised. They won't know the full extent of the damage until I am fully healed. I have a sprained wrist and am covered in bruises from head to toe. From my neck to my nipples is a great concern to the doctor because of all the blood that was brought to the surface from their sucking. Then there is the fear that I might lose some of my toes and fingers to frostbite that began to set in.

Being outside in the cold as long as I was, frost bite could have been worse but the doctor says it is still bad. The nurses are treating my hands and feet in efforts to save them. It doesn't look good for me; yet all I can think about is *'why me?'* After a couple of weeks in the hospital and almost recovered I am allowed to go home. I go home and pack my things and move in with my dad and step-mom.

It takes almost three months for me to completely heal and six months before we go to trial. During trial it comes out that one of his friends doing this now was one of the four guys who raped me and left me for dead back in high school. They all get 30 years but the one gets 60 years to life. Although I feel a bit relieved, I don't feel safe. If one of those guys have made their way back into my life and done it to me twice, now I have to wonder where the other three are. Will they find me and do it again?

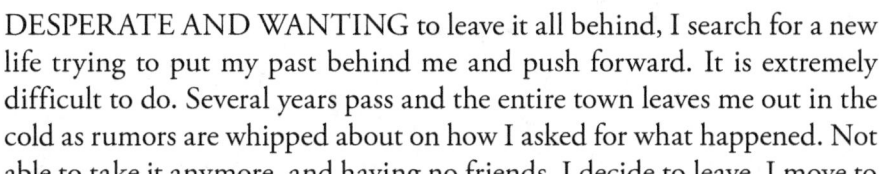

DESPERATE AND WANTING to leave it all behind, I search for a new life trying to put my past behind me and push forward. It is extremely difficult to do. Several years pass and the entire town leaves me out in the cold as rumors are whipped about on how I asked for what happened. Not able to take it anymore, and having no friends, I decide to leave. I move to Hamilton, far away from this place.

CHAPTER 3

I AM HERE not quite a year when I meet Zak, my son Dylan's father. We are together for twelve years. The last ten of those years are spent enduring sexual, emotional, financial, mental and physical abuse. More than most can endure and still be sane. It is so bad a child is miscarried and another barely survives. Doctors have put me on medications for depression, and I am put on suicide watch for a month.

What I thought was only happening to me turns out to be happening to my son as well. After several years I finally convince Zak to let me take a job driving a school bus. I tell him that with a bunch of kids on the bus who would I tell anything to. He reluctantly agrees. The second year in my son ends up on my bus route.

During our times alone from the last drop to home he tells me stories of what his dad says and does when he comes home from school before I get home. He tells me that he stays in his room all the time because he can't stand his dad and is telling me this because he wants us to leave. I know he is telling me the truth because he knows things he shouldn't. I tell him I have to plan it and we will talk. Dylan and I talk every day of what we will do, how and when.

Dylan's thirteenth birthday is this weekend so I tell him that we will make final plans after his birthday. "Okay but I don't want to wait." he says.

I explain to him about the laws and how we have to do things right or he will be right back in our lives. "When he goes I don't want any chance of him coming back." He agrees.

After my son's birthday party, is when I realize the full extent Zak has really hurt Dylan. Looking for him for ten minutes, I open the door to the attic and see that he is hanging from the rafters. Screaming and crying I yell his name as I climb on the chair to get him down. He is barely breathing and unconscious but he is alive.

I call 911 and he is hospitalized for three weeks. While in there he tells the psychiatrist that he tried to kill himself because he just can't be around his dad anymore. He tells him stories of what he has done to him and to me and says that he doesn't want to live if he has to stay in the same house as him.

When the doctor tells me this, I explain to him what we were planning and how and when. He tells me that Zak is the reason and absolute cause of this. I agree to have him arrested.

The doctor files the reports he needs to file with the police and I stay the night at my sister's house. The next day, the police call me to go in and give them a statement. Zak is arrested shortly thereafter.

When I get the call saying he has been picked up and will remain in holding until his court date, my sister and I pack up our things and move my stuff to her place. It will only be temporary until Dylan is out of the hospital and we decide what we want to do.

I then post our home for sale on the real estate market and hold a sale selling most of our furniture. My sister doesn't need any of it and I really don't want the memories they hold for me.

Zak is now in jail awaiting trial and Dylan is finally released from the hospital.

A month passes and our house finally sells. Zak has gone to court and is sentenced to 25 years with no chance for parole.

After twenty years of abuse and neglect, left for dead twice, the loss of my daughter and almost losing my son to suicide, we move. We decide to move far away to start a completely new life. My son moves with some of his friends to Manitoba to begin his college career and I move to Florida; both to start a new life.

CHAPTER 4

WE MEET ON a beach in Anna Maria, Florida. I moved here eight months ago and found a job almost immediately. I now have a week off, as it is our slow season, so I head up to Anna Marie Island to spend the week on their beautiful white sandy beaches.

For me, the beach is the ultimate cure to my problems. All of my obligations suddenly ease; all problems resolve and my stresses melt away.

I rent a small kitchenette at the Sunrise Garden Resort. Not a spectacular room but with a constant view of the ocean and walk out through the patio doors onto the beach, it was just what the doctor ordered. The first two days are very relaxing; and, how could it not be. I wake up every morning with a cup of my favorite coffee in hand sitting on a white sandy beach watching the sun rise.

As I sit here, the breeze graces my face as I am in awe to the most beautiful sunrises I have ever seen. Breath taking views of cloudless night skies as they receive streaks of gold rays from the rising sun, met by the deep blue ocean. Looking along the horizon you catch glimpses of dolphins jumping as they swim along their life's' path. The skies now turn many colors from dark blue to golden rays of light shimmering along the horizon. As the sun peeks, what seems like hours takes only minutes and, I am lost in the beautiful colors of the skies which is many shades of oranges, purples and blues. Then all at once, a cloudless endless sky of the most beautiful cerulean blue is in front of me.

I awoke this third day early and decide that after the sun rises I will drive to the west side of the island and spend the day there. I want a change of scenery and this way, I will be able to watch the sun set tonight as well. What seems to be a great day for me would become one to remember. Little do I know just how special it will be.

After watching the sun rise, I change into my bikini, pack a few things and head for the west side. Driving my red two-door, 1969 Ford Mustang

GT convertible with Boss 302 engine and fast back, with the top down, I take in all the sights and sounds of the island. I feel like a bird flying free, drifting endlessly in the wind, seemingly without a care in the world. I know I am close now as the heat of the suns' rays is stronger now as they stream across my face. The hustle and bustle of families as they head to the beaches for the day is now upon me and the smell of the salt water is in the air.

I find a parking spot beside a black and light brown Jeep Wrangler with its top down. Little do I know the significance of this! I gather my things and walk onto the white sugar sand. Finding myself a cozy spot on the beach close to the water, I lay out my blanket, set upon it my cooler, bag and towel, and take my seat. It is perfect.

As I sit rubbing on some sun screen, I lay back and spend the rest of the morning basking in the sun soaking in its rays and seeing all the sights of the endless summer Florida has to offer. Children building sand castles along the ocean's edge, couples in love walking hand in hand up and down the white sands, and to my right a volleyball tournament is under way. Men and women are jogging two by two along the coastline in efforts to keep their figures and to my left young teens are chasing each other into the water and splashing around.

As I lay here turning from my back to my stomach watching as all the events of the day unfold, I soon am at the point where my body can no longer take the rays of the now blistering sun high in the sky. I look to the water and it is calling to me, enticing me, as though it is waving to me, daring me to jump in. I get up and run to the endless pool of cool bliss and dive into the crashing waves head first.

The water is warmer than thought but lends a relief to my hot sun drenched skin. I swim a few laps back and forth fighting the waves and when my arms feel like lead weights, I float peacefully among the waves. I can hear the laughter of the children as they frolic in the water and build their castles. Looking up the coastline, I notice two men, both tall, slender, muscles popping out everywhere wearing only tight bathing shorts. They are jogging along the water's edge slowly headed my way.

Mesmerized by the two of them as they get closer, I am unaware of the impending waves soon to break over me. Crash! A monstrous wave engulfs me. Its' force knocks me into the sandy bottom then tosses and turns me every which way it can before letting me go.

As I stand, I notice I now face the ocean. Turning slowly hoping no one seen it happen, the two guys are now in front of me. They slow their pace and watch me with smiles on their faces.

As I slowly walk to the shore, I watch them as they jog away from me. Standing there for a moment smiling at them, another wave comes from behind taking me out at my knees. Next thing I know I am on my hands and knees at the water's edge. I stay for a second to determine if I am hurt and when I realize I am fine, I begin to laugh. I can't believe this has happened and I find myself thinking about the laughter my son would have if he was here.

In my peripheral vision I notice the two men are running towards me. "Oh my God, are you ok?" they ask as they approach me.

"Yes I am fine."

They help me up.

Very tall, very attractive, athletically toned sculpted body with short straight chestnut brown hair, he looks no older than mid-thirties and he is the first man to reach me. His bright blue-green eyes lure me in with his long lashes and expressive look, they pull me in like a fish being reeled in on a line.

Quite tall, good-looking, thin toned body with wavy medium-length blond hair, describes the other man that is with him. He appears no older than mid-thirties as well with his grayish blue eyes, long lashes and bright smile.

"Thank you for helping me." I reply.

"You are welcome, we are just glad you are okay." says the second man.

"Ya we wouldn't want a pretty lady like yourself to be hurt on this beautiful day." says the other man.

I thank them again trying not to blush as they both smile and start back to their run.

Suddenly, they stop as the brown haired man grabs his friends' arm and stops. Turning his head to look back at me, he stares at me for what seems like forever. I too am frozen in my spot. *Why is he staring at me like that?* I ask myself.

He whispers something to his friend then begins to walk back towards me. "Chloe?"

CHAPTER 5

TRUE LOVE MAKES you more of who you are not less. This was our love; the kind of love everyone thought would last forever, then reality hit.

Our love started with the 'love at first sight' syndrome. We first meet when I am in grade six. I moved that year from New York to Sturgeon Falls. I was only twelve and in grade six and he was thirteen in grade seven. We saw each other for the first time at recess. He was walking across the courtyard as I stood at the fountain with my sister and one girl whom I just made friends with. He was the most gorgeous boy I had ever seen. Light brown hair, only slightly taller than me, thin yet muscular build, arms of steel and a swagger walk. As he got closer, his eyes sucked me right in, ice blue in color, as though enticing me to learn more about him. His name is Josh.

We are now high school sweethearts. We have been going to the monthly school dances. Although we have been dating for the past couple of years, I still go with my friends and sit with them and he would do the same. We both feel it gives the dance a completely different feel. For every slow song and every other fast one, he comes and gets me to dance as if it is the first time he is asking me. On the slow dances, he holds me very close to him. You can't put a piece of paper between us if you wanted to, that's how close we are. On the fast songs, he keeps about three steps away from me but always close enough that when he reaches out to take my hands there is no stretching.

We are inseparable, doing everything together. He meets me outside every class to walk me to my next class even though he knows he will get in trouble for being late for his. He takes care of me and my needs before his no matter what. If I am sick, he is always there to make sure I am okay and even helps me with my homework so I don't get behind when I start to feel better.

This past summer he got his motorcycle license and with the occurrences this past summer, my mom allows him to pick me up every morning on his bike and we ride to school. It is during this time that it seems like there is just the two of us and we are free. With the wind blowing around us and my arms around him, holding him, feeling him, I feel nothing but complete happiness and completely safe.

Josh is a boy who, even at the age of fifteen, puts others he loves first before himself. Everyone says we are the perfect couple that will last forever. It is true what they say, you must be friends first before you can be lovers or it won't work. I truly believe this because this is how Josh and I started out.

It is spring time and the school is having their yearly spring dance this coming Friday night. The day is here and Josh is acting funny. He is different somehow but I can't put my finger on it. Something is off about him. Riding to school, he seems distant. During the day, he doesn't walk me to my classes or even sit with me at lunch. It is as though he is ignoring me, like I did something wrong or we had a fight and he is mad. None of these things happened so I don't know what is wrong or why he is acting like this.

As the day comes to an end, Josh waits for me outside with his bike rather than walks me to my locker and then out with me. He greets me with a quick peck on the cheek and we drive off. During the ride home, I ask him if everything is okay, he doesn't answer. We arrive at my house, I get off the bike. "Can you meet me at the dance rather than go with me tonight? There is something I have to do first." he asks.

"Sure, but what's wrong?"

Not giving any explanation, he gives me a kiss and drives off. I can't help but wonder what is going on with him and why he is acting so strangely.

After dinner I walk to school with my sister and her friends all the while wondering what is wrong with Josh. We get to the school and I sit with my sister and her friends. Within a short time, some of my friends come and join us. The dance has already started and Josh is nowhere to be seen.

After about five songs, I walk up to his friends. "Have any of you seen or heard from Josh?"

"He is on his way. He had to do something for his dad before coming here." Rick replies. "Thank you." I reply and sit back down.

Before long, Josh shows up but doesn't seem to be in too good of a mood. Two songs later a slow one plays. I am sitting with my back to where he is sitting. Wondering why he hasn't come to me and let me know he is here, I don't really pay attention to what anyone is saying. My sister is the one who tells me he is here.

Then all at once, there he is, standing in front of me with his hand out for me to dance with him.

As we are dancing, I ask him what's wrong. "Nothing!" he expresses very curtly.

Saying nothing back as I am in shock he spoke to me like that, he brings me in close to him. As we dance, I try to pull away from him a bit, so I can look at him in the eyes and see if I can get him to talk. He holds me so tight and close to him that at times I can hardly breathe. It is as though it would be the last song we would ever dance to. When the song is over, he goes back and sits with his friends like everything is normal.

I stand here for a moment just looking at him. I don't understand. I go back to where I was sitting worried and upset. It is all I can do not to cry. *'I can't think of anything I have said or done to make him be like this.'*

Not being able to take it anymore, I stand up. As I turn, there he is again, standing in front of me as though he knew I would stand at that very moment.

I stare at him not knowing what to say or if I should even move. He walks up to me, puts his arms around me, kisses me as if he has never kissed me before and then leads me to the dance floor. All without saying a word, he looks deep into my eyes. I can tell something is wrong just by the way he is looking at me. He just holds me close, as if it is the last time he will ever see me. None of this makes any sense. I have to find out what is going on with him.

After the song is over, he starts to walk away as he always does but I stop him. I tell him I want to talk to him and after a few minutes of convincing him we needed to talk or I was leaving, we go to the landing in stairwell #2 and sit on the windows' ledge.

After a few minutes, I ask him to look at me. He doesn't saying, "I can't or I will lose it."

"What do you mean you will lose it?"

Not answering me, I lay out the day's events. "Again I am going to ask you, what's wrong? You haven't been acting like yourself and you have treated me like an acquaintance rather than your girlfriend all day. Did I do something wrong or are you mad at me for something?"

He looks at me with tears in his eyes. "No baby, you didn't do anything wrong. I just don't know how to tell you this and I wasn't sure I was even going to tell you."

He starts to cry so I put my arms around him.

"It's okay. You can tell me anything. What can be so bad that has you this upset? Did something happen to your mom or dad?"

"No. Something is going to happen but not to them."

"What is it then?"

"I won't be able to see you anymore after tonight."

"What? Why?"

Not really answering my questions he says, "Well, it's because of that, I tried to remove myself from you all day and when that didn't work, I tried to make you mad at me and not want to be around me. That didn't work either so I tried to pretend that you meant nothing to me but I can't do that either because you mean everything to me."

Okay so now he really isn't making any sense. What could possibly happen that would affect us and he wouldn't be able to see me anymore? I had to know.

After sitting for a few minutes just holding each other, I let him regain his composer. "So what is so bad that you don't want to tell me? You know you can tell me anything right?"

He doesn't move and won't let go of me. "I know, and we talk about everything. This is different. Something is going to happen. I can't stop it or change it and I really don't want it to happen."

He then moves away from me and sits on the stairs so he is a good six feet away.

"What is going to happen that will stop you from seeing me anymore? None of this is making any sense, Josh. What's going on?"

"I am moving away this weekend. My parents only told me about it yesterday when I got home from school."

I am in shock. All I can do is sit here and stare at him. He stands up and comes up to me. Putting his arms around me, he looks deep into my eyes and asks, "Did you hear what I said, I am moving without choice this weekend, far away?"

My eyes have teared up as I look into his eyes. "Yes I heard you and I can't believe it! I won't believe it!"

"I know, I am having a hard time with it myself."

"How can this be? Why?"

"I don't know the reason. My mom told me that dad was being transferred. It makes no sense to me with the job he has but they also said I had no choice but to move with them."

"I can ask my mom if you can stay with us at least until the end of the school year. Your parents like my mom and step dad and it is only a couple months away. By then you will be sixteen and they can't tell you what to do. Then we can figure out what to do. At least it will give us time."

"I love the idea, but what if she says no or what if your step dad talks to my parents and they say no?"

"I don't want to think that."

"Me either but what if it does?"

After a few minutes of bantering back and forth, we decide to have tonight together. Tomorrow morning we will talk to our parents and see what they say. That would be our first step then pray and hope that both parents say yes.

We spend the rest of the dance together, sitting together, dancing every dance and just being with each other. At the end of the night, he drives me home and we sit in the driveway for a few hours just talking hoping the night wouldn't end. He promises he would see me later this afternoon before he leaves. He then kisses me and hesitantly, I get out of the car and go into the house.

THAT WAS THE last time I saw Josh. He left later that morning without even saying goodbye. I am heartbroken. I barely got the words out to tell my mom what was happening when my step dad walks in and says that they were already gone.

I am so upset and devastated that I didn't want to go to school or go out with friends. I did nothing but lie in bed and cry. My mom would make me eat dinner at the table and sit for a couple of hours to watch TV with them but for the next week, I did not do much else.

She made me go back to school after a week even though I didn't want to. I would always look and wait for him between classes, at lunch and even after school. I finished school that year and passed but barely. My marks went from straight A's to C's and D's. The day Josh left was the day I died and didn't care what happened.

A FEW YEARS have passed now and I have not heard anything from Josh. I never knew where he moved to and didn't even know if he made it safely or not. He never called me, wrote to me or even came to visit me when he was in town for his grandmother's funeral.

Josh was the love of my life and now he was gone from my life for what seemed to be forever. Everyone at school said we were the 'Grade School' sweethearts that would last forever. We were together for six years before he left.

I spend the next five years trying to find myself and salvation. Every time I dated someone, I compared him to Josh and the love that we shared. If he didn't measure up, he was gone. After living with four guys and dating several others, I realize that it just is not going to happen so, I settle for the next man that comes into my life.

That is when I found Zak, my son's father. I spent the next fifteen years miserable and dedicated my life and time working to support, care for and raise my son the best I could.

He is now my ex-husband. Zak abused me, mistreated me and after fifteen years, losing my daughter because of the abuse, and almost losing my son to suicide because of him, I kick him out.

It takes my son two months to recover and during his recovery I sell the house and move us into my sister's house eight hours away. It's a hard decision to make because Dylan's' entire life was spent in the same house, going to the same school with the same friends and all his family on his dads' side lives there.

For his better mental health and life, the doctor said if I don't move him out of this town, I may not be so lucky next time and might find my son dead. There was no question at this point, I move us.

While I am packing to move, a headline in an article in the paper catches my attention. It reads, "WHAT WILL MATTER". It is a short article that says:

Someday it will come to an end and all things collected, whether treasures or baubles will pass on to someone else. There will be no more surprises, minutes, hours or delays. The wealth, fame and power you had will shrivel to irrelevance and it won't matter what you owned or what you were owed. Your hopes, ambitions, plans and to-do lists will expire and the wins and losses that seemed important will fade away.

HOW WILL THE VALUE OF YOUR DAYS BE MEASURED?
WHAT WILL MATTER?
It is not what you bought BUT what you built
It is not what you got BUT what you gave
It is not your success BUT what your significance
It is not what you learned BUT what you taught.

Living a life that matters does not happen by accident or chance –
IT HAPPENS BY CHOICE!

This is when I decide that we both need a new life, a completely new start. My son wants to go away to Manitoba with some friends for University and I need a change too. Maybe this time, I will find my salvation. If nothing else at least have a better life and now that my son is starting his life, we both can be happier now. So, we move again!

I help my son pack his things and send him off on a plane to Manitoba. It is the third hardest day of my life. Josh moving away from me nine years ago was the first, having to hospitalize my son due to suicide attempts was the second and now, sending him away to school. I know he will be alright and I will see him again. However, watching him fly off without me leaves me with an empty feeling once again.

Now it's my turn. I sell what I can't move with me, rent a U-Haul truck, load my things and drive off to begin my new life. After four days of driving across the country I am finally in Florida. I soon see the sign:

WELCOME TO ORLANDO
POPULATION 250,160

Davenport is less than sixty miles away and in one-hour, I will be home.

CHAPTER 6

"YES." I ANSWER, "Do I know you?"

He smiles from ear to ear, looks over his shoulder to his friend who is now walking towards us and says, "This is her Chase!"

"Excuse me!" I sneer, "Who am I?"

Just looking at me with a smile, Chase says, "Wow, in the flesh and she doesn't even know".

"Please sit down and I will explain." he says.

"Wait a minute. I know that voice. And those eyes, I've seen them before." The voice sounded eerily familiar to me but I can't put my finger on from where or who he is.

He sits down beside me as his friend Chase kneels in front of us. "This is going to be good."

"Go back to the game Chase. I will meet you there in a bit."

Chase shakes my hand. "It's really nice to finally meet you." He stands and jogs back to the volleyball game.

"Now." he says looking at me, "Figure out who I am yet?"

"No, but I know I have met you somewhere before. There is something very familiar about you."

"Let me tell you a story. It's a short one and see if you can figure out who I am then."

Agreeing he begins.

"There once was a boy who seen this shy, skinny girl. She was new in town and he instantly fell in love with her. He did everything for her and went everywhere with her, anything to be with her. Until one day, when things change and he moves away."

Then it hit me. I grab his arm to stop him. "Oh My God, Josh?" I ask shocked.

Nodding his head yes I lunge forward and give him the hardest and longest hug I have ever given anyone. I can't believe it, he is here and I don't want to let him go.

It has been more than twenty-five years since I graduated high school, and thirty years since I have last seen Josh. My mom moved to Florida two years ago to take care of my grandmother and I visited her last summer. I really liked it here so I moved.

I now live here, well in Davenport, Florida for almost a year and love it. Always warm summer weather, sun almost every day, and no one to know me so I can start over. It is the best life could offer. Now it offers even more. With the white sandy beaches, swimming with the dolphins, and jelly fish, and now Josh, it couldn't be better.

"Oh my god it is you. I can't believe you are here?" I state.

Well my eyes start to tear up and I am speechless. My heart is pounding, hands are sweating, and butterflies fill my stomach as my mind goes blank, just like it did when we were in high school. After all these years, there he is in front of me for the third time in my life. Thinking of the old adage, third time is a charm I quickly realize that I had better not make the same mistakes I did thirty years ago because I don't want him to walk out of my life again.

For the next few minutes, we just sit here. We are both in disbelief that of all places in the world and of all the people there are, we would be sitting here together in one of the most beautiful places on earth.

He begins by telling me about his life the past thirty years. "As weird as this sounds, I suffered a lot of abuse from my ex-wife when she became a drug addict and alcoholic. Her constant infidelities and the way she treated our children was not a life I had hoped for."

He then explains how while he was at work, his kids would starve or have to fend for themselves; they were only four and six years old; because she wouldn't cook or care for them. His work took him away for three days at a time.

"When I would come home, I would have to cook dinner because she would be out of it."

"Out of it, what do you mean by that?"

"She would be drunk and passed out or so high on whatever drug she took that day, she didn't even know where she was."

"Wow that's horrible. How can she do that?"

"I don't know. She got in with the wrong crowd. Anyway I tried for five years to get her clean before things got too bad. And I tried to work things out. Nothing worked so finally, I left. I had to leave his kids behind but I told them I would always be there and it wouldn't be long until they were with me."

"And were you?"

"Yes, I seen them every day and had them at my apartment more than they were at their moms. That was two years ago. Last year I went after her for custody and in fact, just won my case last month for full custody of my kids."

"Wow that's great!"

"Ya. It took longer than I wanted but I got it. I am picking them up to move with me in one week and that's why I am here."

"I don't get that. You are celebrating here in Florida before you get your kids?"

"Sort of. My friends and I have been visiting places to figure out where I want to live. We still live in Toronto but I don't want my kids to be brought up in a big city. Besides, they don't like the city."

"So where have you been?"

"Several different places. We went to Manitoba then, California, Texas, and Arizona. Florida is our last stop. After this trip, I will make a decision and when I pick up my kids, that will be the place we will move to."

"Do you have any idea of where you want to go?"

"Yes, actually I do. I condensed my list to two places."

"Cool. Well I hope it works out for you."

During the day, he is a construction worker operating big heavy machinery and was just recently promoted to assistant manager. At night, he will become the family man, a single dad raising two children on his own, 1 girl and 1 boy. The weekends will be their fun time consisting of fishing, camping, swimming, four wheeling, going to parks, car races, etc., the kind of fun I love to have.

It is now my turn so I tell him about the past thirty years of my life. First, because he knows Brock from our childhood years, I tell him about how he drank himself to death. I decide not to tell him about the rapes prior to him leaving back then or about me leaving home or why.

"Throughout my life I have gone through many years of sexual, physical and mental abuse, neglect, infidelity and hardships."

"By your ex as well?"

"Yes and by others too prior to him. It started in grade 12 and never really stopped."

"Oh. I am so sorry."

"It's okay. It wasn't your fault. Anyway, with my soon to be ex-husband, I tried for several years to make it work thinking that he was only doing these things to me, or that it was only a phase he was going through. Then I found out that he was doing these things to my son as well when he attempted suicide. This was the straw that broke my back."

"Wow, I am very sorry you had to go through all that." he says as he holds my hand.

"Thank you. I put my son in the hospital to deal with his issues and hopefully prevent any further suicide attempts, packed up our things and I left his dad. This was a year and a half ago. Last year my son graduated high school with honors and is now attending university in Manitoba to become a language arts teacher abroad."

"Wow that's great to hear. So everything is good with him now?"

"Yes. The psychiatrist told me I had to move him away from Sudbury or I may not be so lucky next time. When I questioned 'next time' he told me that if we stayed there, my son would try again and could succeed. It was stay and lose my son or move. I moved!"

"Wow, good for you."

"That is when I decided to start a new life and had the opportunity to move here to Florida. I sold my house and most of my things then moved here to help my mom with my grandmother six months ago. We now live in Davenport."

Me, a tall slender woman with long brown hair, fair skin with high cheek bones and thin lips I am a natural beauty where makeup does no justice. Green eyes create mystery about me yet I carry myself well. A strong woman who knows what she wants and gets it is how my friends describe me. By day, I am a gold certified framing expert. By night, an artist who sells and teaches water color and oil painting. Weekends are my time. I enjoy the outdoors and having fun with friends and family. Sitting by a campfire at night having a few drinks singing and telling stories or camping on the beach with swimming, games and fun in the sun is where I love to be.

Chase is now making his way back to us. "Josh, we are getting ready to leave for the restaurant. Are you still coming?"

Looking at me for a minute he replies, "Yes give me five minutes. I will be right there."

Chase smiles, turns and walks back to their other friends.

Josh looks back at me smiling. "How long are you going to be here?"

"I am here until after sunset then heading back to my motel."

"I will be back around seven to sit with you and watch the sun set. That is if you want me to."

"Of course I want you to. That would be great. I will see you then."

We stand up and give each other a hug. As he walks away, I walk over to the small restaurant that is just up the beach and get myself something to eat. I take it back to where I am sitting and eat in peace.

During dinner, as I watch the ocean's waves crash along the shore and the families with children still playing in the sand and swimming, I decide that if Josh did not come back then this was only a chance meeting and not meant for us to be together.

If Josh does come back then it is my sign that the third time is in fact the charm and I will tell him exactly how I felt about him thirty years ago, and how seeing him today makes me feel. *'I won't let him leave and I will look at him straight in the eye until I am finished then leave it up to God and fate for whatever should happen'* I think to myself.

I look at my phone and see it is only 5:45 p.m. so I decide to go for a quick dip before he comes back. Diving once again into the oceans' waves as they come crashing towards the shore then swimming a few laps, I decide to float letting the waves take me back to the shore.

Once back on shore, I sit on my blanket, close my eyes and focus on my surroundings. The laughter of the children as they runabout, the songs of the birds as they fly by, the crashing of the waves as they break on the shore, the parents calling to their children for dinner. As I do this, I say a prayer that Josh will come back and that this is our chance; our chance to be together, to be happy, have the perfect happy ever after.

It is now 6:55 p.m. and I feel myself start to get nervous. What if he comes back? What if he doesn't come back? I'm not sure how I will feel either way. I look around, first to my left, then to my right. Out of the corner of my eye, I can see a group of guys walking from the parking area towards the beach. I turn my head and there he is, Josh and his friends have actually come back.

As I watch him walk towards me, it is like a rekindled friendship set on fire. It is a feeling that fills me with warmth and vigor like nothing else ever has. I am happy. This man, who once gave me everything then left, is now back, shining a beacon of everything that is wonderful. This effect gives me comfort; the kind that says I can weather any storm as long as I am with him. It is like an energy field that fills you with a hot ball of life. I realize then that the love I had for him when we were young, I still had for him even after all these years.

I stand up as he approaches me. "Wow, you came back." I say with a smile.

"Of course." he replies, "I said I would."

He turns and asks his friends to leave us for a bit so we can talk. "I will call you when we are done."

They leave and we sit down. "Did you have a nice dinner?" I ask him.

"Yes. I actually made a decision while I was gone and my friends and I have decided to go out tonight to celebrate it."

"That's good. Can I ask if the decision was about where you and your kids are going to move to?"

"Yes, it was in fact."

"Well, before you tell me anything about your decision, there is something I need to tell you first."

He just looks at me with a bewildered look and nods.

I stand, tell him to put his legs out straight and then I straddle him sitting on his thighs so that I am facing him.

"What I have to say to you I should have said thirty years ago. I didn't say anything before dinner because I didn't want to persuade you in your decision, so I am glad you made your decision first."

"Okay that makes sense, I guess. So what is so important it can't wait until I tell you my decision?" he puts his arms around my waist.

I take a deep breath to get up enough courage, then I start.

"Thirty years ago we had a love that felt like a sun that would never darken. Our love made everything better, easier to handle, every song sounded sweeter and every moment we shared was filled with hope."

Josh opens his mouth as if he is about to say something. I put two of my fingers on his lips. "Please, just let me finish before saying anything."

He agrees and I continue.

I put my arms around his neck. "I loved you. The last night we spent together I wanted so badly to tell you then how I felt but every time I tried you would hold me close and wouldn't let me. Then you left without saying goodbye. I didn't know where you went, if you got there safely, nothing.

I spent a very long time getting over you, or so I thought. All these years every man I was with I compared to you, to us and the love we had. I never had butterflies in my stomach every time I saw any of them or felt weak in the knees. There was no sweating of the palms or mind going blank. I only got this with you, and today I realized that I still do. You have always had this effect on me back then and even now."

Smiling trying not to tear up, I caress his face with my hand. "When I realized it was you today, all these emotions came rushing back. The love I felt for you, the hate and heart break I went through when you left, and the feeling of belonging when you are near me. There's a fire within me that only seems to burn strongly when you are with me. Never have I felt this before except for when I was and am with you."

Now he has tears in his eyes and you can tell he is doing everything he can with everything he has to not let them out. He tightens his grip on me bringing me closer in to him.

"Josh, what I am saying is simple, I loved you from the first moment I saw you thirty-five years ago, I have never stopped loving you, I still love you and will always love you. You are and always will be here."

I take my hands, fold them together, and put them over my heart. "You are the love of my life, I knew it before and it is even more evident today."

I sit back a bit and pull away from him for a moment to take a breath. He wipes away the few tears that run down my cheeks with his hand as I tell him I am done. "Take from that what you will and do with it what you want."

As I start to get off him he pulls me close to him, "No, stay here. There's something I need to say to you now."

I take a deep breath and he begins. "When I left you thirty years ago it was the hardest thing I had ever done in my entire life. It wasn't a choice I made, it was made for me. However, that is the past. These past few years I did like you. Looked for true love and settled when I couldn't find it. I loved you then; so much so that I couldn't tell you because I couldn't bear the thought that you wouldn't say it back or didn't feel the same way."

I must have a shocked look on my face because he pauses and looks at me with a puzzled look. As I shake my head to let him know I am all right, he continues.

"Anyway, I realized about five years ago that I was looking for something that most likely was already gone. Until recently, I didn't realize the person I was looking for was you. You have always been in my heart and in my thoughts and I have missed you so much that at times I caught myself from calling my wife you."

Well I don't know how to react to that or what to say. I guess I'm not supposed to because he continues without hesitation.

"When you have a love that is so strong with a force that doesn't let go, you can't ignore it. I have tried for many years but have always come back to you. Now, as I said earlier, I had a decision to make and during dinner I made it."

Before I could say anything, he leans in and kisses me. I am in shock because I did not expect it. He pulls away even though I don't want him to stop.

"I have decided to move with my kids here to Florida so I can be with you. I don't want another minute to go by without you in it. We have lost too much time already; I don't want to lose any more."

I just sit here with my arms around him not sure what to say. The smile on my face diminishes slightly as I'm not sure how to feel. I am ecstatic, excited, happy yet nervous all at the same time. The feelings are so strong that I don't know if I can even move.

"Are you alright?" he asks.

"Yes, I am fine. I just did not expect you to say that."

"Would you like to go out and celebrate with me and my friends?"

Having nothing else to do and being able to be with Josh, I reply with a huge smile, "Absolutely. I would love to help you celebrate your decision."

I lean in and kiss him back.

He calls his friends over to tell them I will be going with them tonight. They are happy and excited and it is going to be the best night of my life. "Good. Now we will get to know the woman who has stolen Josh's heart many years ago." Chase remarks.

Josh then introduces me to his friends, Chase I already know. There are three others: Razor, Gabe and Austin.

"We have heard so much about you throughout the years Chloe. Josh's wife was always upset because your name always came up in many conversations." says Razor.

I smile looking at Josh as I know the feeling because I did the same thing with everyone I have been with since high school. "I will go with Chloe in her car so she knows where to go. We will follow you until we are at the bar and then we will go to her motel so she can change. We will meet you back at the bar." Josh says to his buddies.

They agree and we pack up my stuff and walk back to the parking lot.

Josh and I get into my mustang and they pile into Chases' Jeep Wrangler – yes, the same jeep I parked beside earlier today. We all head to the Island Time Bar and Grill along Gulf Road.

Luckily, it is only eight miles up the road from the motel I am staying at. It takes Josh and me forty minutes to get to the motel, change and arrive back at the bar.

CHAPTER 7

AS THE NIGHT ensues, we play pool, drink beer and sing karaoke. It is like old times all over again, like we stepped back in time to when we were teenagers. We used to do this type of stuff back then at the local club. Josh and I were long lost lovers but no one, other than his friends whom we are with, knows that we haven't been together for thirty years.

The bar tender remarks, "It's nice to see that true love still exists. How long have you all been together?"

We tell him our story and he is amazed that we found each other after all these years and the love we had for each other never died. He gives us free drinks the rest of the night. It is a blast and lasts well into the early morning hours.

We leave at two a.m. when the bar closes and decide to crash in my motel room for the night. We are all too drunk to drive anywhere else and it is extremely close. We leave our vehicles at the bar with their permission and walk to the motel. We pile in from the beach side so as not to disturb anyone else.

I have two double beds in the room with a pullout couch. Chase, Gabe and Razor lie across the one bed and pass out almost immediately, as they hit the bed. Austin falls into the couch and lays half on the floor and half on the couch, we leave him there. Josh and I take the other bed.

As he undresses to his shorts, I get undressed down to my bra and underwear. "Aren't you worried the guys will see you in that in the morning?"

"Not really. You saw more of me on the beach today in my bikini."

He nods in agreement, pulls back the blankets and motions for me to climb in. As I crawl into bed beside him and lay in his arms, he tells me how beautiful I am and how happy he is that he has found me once again. He then pulls away and leans up on his left elbow.

Putting his right arm around me he looks into my eyes. "I have wanted this for many years. You are the only woman I have ever wanted, then and now."

We kiss caressing each other for a while but never let it get too far. I stop him before it gets to the point where sex can't be stopped. "I don't want to have sex with you like this. I want it to be when we are alone, where we don't have to worry about anyone or anything else interrupting us. Just be there with each other, taking our time and feeling each other."

Although I can tell he is disappointed, he agrees. "We will have our time." he says kissing me again before he lies back down. He then puts his arms around me and we fall asleep.

Before I know it, morning is upon us and everyone is sitting at the table talking while Josh makes coffee. As I open my eyes, they all look at me and Chase says, "Well good morning sunshine."

I look over at him, smile and say good morning back. Josh comes over to me, sits down on the side of the bed beside me, gives me a kiss and asks how I am feeling.

"Other than a slight headache I am good." I tell him as I give him a kiss on the cheek.

I get up out of bed and go into the bathroom. When I come out Josh is standing in front of me with a coffee in his hand. Handing it to me he says, "Just cream if I remember correctly. You're sweet enough and don't take sugar. Right?"

"Wow, you remembered that after thirty years, impressive." I smile and thank him as I take the cup from him. I take a drink and say, "Perfect." and give him a quick kiss.

After we all wake up and have enough coffee in us, I pack my things and we go down to the desk in the lobby. Telling them I won't need the room anymore, I settle up and spend the next few days with Josh and his friends at Chases' apartment.

The daytime is spent mostly at the beach swimming, sun tanning, making castles, burying each other, playing volley ball, tossing a football around, etc. At night we go to bars playing pool, singing karaoke, and playing several drinking games.

Tonight we decide to go to the Monster Truck Jam at Raymond James Stadium in Tampa. "I love watching these trucks." I say as we walk to the stadium from the parking lot hand in hand.

"I knew that from your faceplace page." Josh replies.

Raging Desire

It takes us almost a half hour to get to our seats. We have good seats too, center stadium mid-way up. Where we sit, we can see the entire track, all the jumps and entrances too. It is a perfect night, low 80's with slight warm breeze, clear skies with three-quarter moon and many stars shining brightly high above us.

"So which one is your favorite?" asks Josh.

"Well, I have two." I reply, "Grave Digger and Big Foot. Yours?"

"Grave Digger and Maximum Destruction."

The next two hours are spent each of us rooting for our drivers. It is fun and very enjoyable. We root for the same driver when Grave Digger races but then against each other when Big Foot races against Maximum Destruction. When I win, he kisses me. When he wins, I kiss him. The others tease us but we don't care. At one point, I even kiss Chase on the cheek when my driver won over his in a joking manner. He is shocked and blushes as Josh, the others and I laugh. It is a great evening and it is very late by the time we get to bed.

It is now the next morning and I wake up in Josh's arms with his friends still passed out all over the floor. We are at Chases' apartment. It is a small place with one bedroom. Chase was gracious and gave Josh and me the bed while the rest of them passed out on the couch and floor in the living room.

While I make coffee, Josh begins to cook bacon for breakfast. Slowly the rest of them make their way to the kitchen and before long they are all awake and eating breakfast at the table.

Josh tells the guys today is going to be spent just him and me. He wants to spend one day just the two of us before he goes back to Toronto. They are okay with it saying they will meet us tomorrow morning for breakfast before they leave.

As the guys leave, Gabe smiles back at Josh then winks as he walks out the door. Josh wants to start the day at the beach like every other day however just him and me. This time, while we are there, rather than me watching couples walking hand in hand up the beach; we are one of them as others watch us. It is very different however feels very good.

Before leaving the beach, we decide to rent jet skis and have some fun on the water. It is exhilarating as we speed across the water at top speeds zig zagging back and forth and jumping each other's waves.

He is the most gorgeous sight I have ever seen. Blue ocean water dripping from his hair as it runs down his body like a free flowing waterfall.

The rays of the hot sun make his body glisten with bright lights as the water reflects off the water droplets on his body.

His powerful legs guide the jet ski as he circles me like a whale ready to pounce on its prey. Making waves and going fast enough, he creates a swirling motion in the water around me. As I jump the waves to show I can be relieved of his clutch, my jet-ski careens off a big wave straight into the air throwing me off into the water.

Rushing towards me and diving in Josh is frantic thinking I am hurt. As he swims to me, he realizes that I'm not in trouble, in fact I am laughing. "What is so funny?" he asks a little upset as he reaches me.

"That was fun." I reply realizing that he is not laughing with me.

He hugs me. "Oh my god I thought I hurt you. I am so sorry, I didn't mean to do that."

"It's okay Josh." I say looking at him bewildered. "It was my fault. I wouldn't have fallen off if I didn't try to jump your waves."

Looking at his face I realize it was not alright for him and I feel really bad about laughing now. His kiss is one that shows me just how much he really cares and how worried he was. I calm him down as we swim back to the jet-skis and he helps me back onto mine.

As he climbs back onto his he says, "Let's head back. It's getting to be mid-afternoon and there's still something I want to do with you today."

I say alright and we bring the jet skis back being careful not to be thrown off them.

We spend the afternoon at an Amusement park, as this is what he wants to do. "I want to go on every ride sharing each exhilarating and romantic experience with you. I want this day to be the best day ever so I have something to take back with me." he says as we park the car.

We start on the biggest wooden roller coaster here; it is called Blazing Saddles and it stands up to its name. With our hands clasped together throughout the entire ride, we scream with joy as we dip, turn and looped the loops.

There are rocket rides, swings, bumper cars, all the rides and games an amusement park would have with a few extras. We take a romantic boat ride. Like the Gondola's of Italy with the oar man and everything, the ride only takes fifteen minutes but it is the most romantic ride ever. We sit arm in arm, holding hands, kissing and taking in the sights as the ride slowly moves from one city to another.

It is now 5:30 p.m. so we decide to get something to eat. We drive around for a few minutes until he finds the perfect restaurant. We walk in to have two ushers show us to a romantic, two-person table across the room next to a bay window. The view outside is breathtaking, a garden with vibrant colors and luscious flowers all in full bloom. It is almost like they knew we were coming.

Holding hands, we gaze into each other's eyes not saying a word but knowing what the other is thinking, until our food arrives. We eat slowly, using the food to tease each other to create anticipation and build climax. Not only can you feel the electricity in the air but also you can see the passion, wants and desires we both share at this moment.

When we are finished and get back into the car, Josh turns, takes my hands and says, "This has been the most magical day I have ever spent with a woman. I want you and I know you want me but there is one more thing I have planned that I know you will enjoy before we call it a night."

Already feeling like I am ready to burst and grab him right then, I try to calm myself down. "Okay, what is it?"

"A surprise." he says leaning in to give me a kiss. He then sits back and starts the car.

He drives about a half hour holding my hand and caressing my face all the while I can feel his eyes undressing me, wanting me, calling to me; and I am doing the same thing to him. We arrive at a park but not like a playground park. This one has several grand stands and grassy fields everywhere you turn. We walk over to the third one where a band is setting up.

We stop. "Stay here for a minute, I will be right back." he says giving me a kiss and walks towards the stage.

I want to see what he is doing as I bob back and forth trying to see past the people who are already there. Losing sight of him only briefly I wonder what he is planning.

It isn't long before he comes back within my sights carrying some things in his arms. As he gets closer, I see he is holding a blanket with a bucket and some glasses. He hands me the bucket and glasses as he lays out the blanket and helps me down.

As I place the bucket beside me he sits with me and says, "I know this band, I used to play with them a few years ago. I brought you here because I love their music and it is a romantic place. I hope you like it too."

By this time, others have joined us and sit around on blankets as well. "This is perfect." I say with a smile.

He pours us a glass of white wine and as we take our first sip, the band begins to play. They play country music both fast and slow. We sit holding each other, with hands here and there precision; my body shivers with each touch.

After a few songs, the band stops playing. "For those of you who know us, we have a band member missing tonight." announces the main singer. "He is here in the audience with the love of his life. Let's try to get him up here and play a song with us."

Everyone claps and cheers as he says, "Come on up here Josh."

I look at him in amazement. He looks at me questionably. "Go." I tell him, "I would love to hear you play."

He gives me a kiss and goes up to the stage.

As he reaches the platform, the main singer says, "This song is for you, Chloe. Josh wrote it himself a few years ago and we had only played it during practice."

Shocked I sit up wondering what it is and listening closely. The beat of the music is that of a Shania Twain song that I absolutely loved, 'From This Moment"; however, the words are very different, very personal. They pull me in with the sound of the music, the rhythm and beat. The words say how he has felt about me all these years. They say how he lost me and hopes to find me again before his life is over. It is like something out of a fairy tale. They are words of romance, love, feelings, compassion and lust.

This is the first time anyone has ever done anything like this for me in my entire life. Not thinking it is possible, I fall even more in love with him. The song is beautiful and I can't help myself, I cry, as I am speechless.

After the song is over, everyone claps and watch him walk back towards me. He kneels down in front of me, takes my hands and helps me up. Without saying a word, he looks at me and leads me to the stage. We walk up the stairs as I wonder what he is up to.

When we get to the center of the stage he takes the microphone, and looks to the crowd. "This is Chloe, the love of my life." Everyone claps and there are even a few whistles. "There is something I need to say." Josh says as he turns back and looks at me.

"We had a love that lasted from grade seven until I moved away in grade eleven. We have not seen each other for thirty years until four days ago. The past four days have been the most wonderful time I have ever spent with a woman. Chloe, I love you. I always have and always will and when I saw you on the beach, I knew that love was still there, even after all these years. I know I will be leaving soon but you know I will be back."

He pauses as he tries not to cry. I can't help it, tears roll down my face as he says this. You can tell by the look on his face, the tears in his eyes and the trembling in his voice he is nervous.

"Chloe," he continues getting down on one knee, pulls out a small box from his pants pocket, and asks, "I don't ever want to go through life without you in it again. Will you wait for me to return and do me the honor of becoming my wife?"

Well I don't hold back. I begin to cry as I can't believe what has just happened. The man I love and have loved all my life is not only back in my life for the past week but has now asked me to marry him.

Hardly able to speak, "Yes." I mutter, "I will marry you".

With tears running down both of our faces, we are hardly able to contain ourselves. Josh stands up and we embrace as everyone claps and cheers.

We don't stay at the park for very long. With the excitement of what just happened, we get into the car and drive off. Josh says he has already booked a room for us to spend the night, saying it is somewhere out of the way. "It's a place where we can be alone without any interruptions and without any expectations."

It only took us fifteen minutes to get to this place. We walk in, he signs us in and we go up to the room. Josh unlocks the door and I walk in ahead of him.

As I put my purse on the table to the right of the door, Josh closes the door, grabs my arm and immediately backs me up against the door kissing me feverishly. He lifts my gauzy skirt and starts touching me everywhere while I tug furiously at his shirt pulling it over his head. He slams me against the wall and I am lost to his insistent embrace. His kisses are like anesthesia; I feel numb, lost and I wouldn't change a thing.

He leads me to the bed and we fall into it laughing. To my surprise, we don't dive into the clawing, breathless, animalistic passion one might expect of two long lost lovers who just got engaged. Instead, Josh slowly progresses with hand-here, mouth-there precision as we undress each other slowly.

Eyes open and watchful now, he runs his fingers over my skin and softly kisses my mouth before initiating the most tender, connected sex of my life. I wrap my legs around him with ease; he grabs me in all the right places. We move together in a soft, syncopated rhythm that I have never experienced before. Comfort and intimacy are immediate and beautiful. I feel safe. When I'm struggling to hit my peak, he whispers in my ear, 'give it to me baby, I want to feel you.' and after a few minutes climax is released.

He rolls over with me on top of him and starts thrusting upward, encouraging me to grind my way for more. My heart is pounding, my hair is wet with sweat, and my body is tingling everywhere. Collapsing to the bed, I am literally panting with pleasure as he kisses his way down my breasts and belly. He starts licking me my clit very softly until I scream, "Oh my god!" all the way to the end of yet another orgasm.

He climbs on top of me and thrusts a few hard pushes burying himself deep before blowing all of his cum inside me.

When we are done, we are sweat covered and sex flushed, visibly rocked. The sex is fueled by a detached, energetic fury. It is raw sex--the kind you can have with a lover only when there is nothing else but love. We are free to be selfish, and in being selfish, we are both completely satisfied.

After taking a shower and cooling off, we lay back in bed holding each other. A few minutes pass before Josh says, "I have something to tell you."

Not liking the way he says that, I get nervous and pull myself up so I can face him. "What is it?"

"You know I am leaving tomorrow to go back to Toronto."

"Yes."

Although I knew it was inevitable and I know he is coming back, it still hurt to hear it. I don't want to deal with him being gone again out of my life, he must sense this. Holding my head, he looks deep into my eyes.

"It will only be for thirty days. I will be back I promise. I don't want to lose you ever, I love you and I will marry you."

I start to cry as I start to feel like I am losing him again. I hear the words he is saying, but this all brings back what happened thirty years ago. The only difference this time is he is saying good bye where he left without saying good bye the first time.

"I know you will be back." I say as I try to stop crying. "This time I know it is only temporary but I can't help but feel the same sense of loss I felt thirty years ago."

He holds me close to him and says it's nothing like then. He will be back and while he is gone, he will call me every day.

"There won't be a day that will go by where you won't hear from me," he says. "I promise."

I look at him and smile then we kiss. We lay back down, and as I lay here wanting to remember how it feels to be with him and looking at my ring, we fall asleep.

It is morning now and we wake up late. Rushing to leave we meet the guys for breakfast. All I want to do is hold him and never let him go. We then head out to the airport so Josh, Gabe and Austin won't be late for their plane. I stand there trying not to cry as Josh says good-bye to his friends Chase and Razor who live here in Florida.

He then comes to me and promises he will call when he lands, every morning when I wake up and every night before going to bed, it will be his voice I hear. I tell him I will hold him to that promise and hope that the next month goes by fast. We embrace and kiss very hard and long. Then he walks away from me and into the airport.

As I stand here feeling empty, Chase and Razor come up beside me, put their arms around me and Razor says, "It's okay you know, he will be back soon."

Looking at him, I reply, "I know."

I still can't help feeling the same emptiness I felt years ago when he left.

"If you need someone to keep you company while he is gone, let us know. We will be happy to spend time with you. Besides I promised Josh I would keep my eye out for you and keep you safe until he returns." says Chase.

Keep me safe? From what? I look at him. "Thank you, I think. I do have to get back to Orlando though because I am due to be back to work tomorrow morning."

"Will you have lunch with us before you head back?"

I agree and we eat lunch at a small restaurant not far from the airport before I head back home.

During lunch, we make plans for the next two weeks as I know my hours at work only two weeks at a time. During our days off, I will go to their place and hang out, or they will come to mine. When possible, I will Skype with Josh so we have face time and give his kids a chance to get to know me before meeting in person.

I am hoping that by keeping busy with my job, Chase and Razor, and talking with Josh and his kids every day, it won't be too long before he returns to me.

CHAPTER 8

ON MY WAY home I stop at my mom's to tell her how my week went. Before getting out of the car, I take my ring off and put it in my pocket. I want so surprise her and this is one surprise I know she will love. When we were kids she loved Josh, he was one of very few who was allowed to come to our house when she wasn't home. Her words, 'he was the son she never had.'

I begin by telling her where I stayed and how I simply walked out of the room onto the beach, the sunrises I seen and showed her some pictures I took of them along with the dolphins. I tell her how I spent most of the time on the beach sun bathing and relaxing.

"I have some news for you though and I think you will be as shocked as I was."

She looks at me with one eye brow up and makes a grunt noise "huh".

"Well, the third day there, I went to the other side of the island just for a change in scenery. That afternoon, I was swimming among the waves when I noticed these two guys jogging along the waters' edge. As I got back to the shore, they were in front of me. Before I could say or do anything a large wave took me out at my knees and they came rushing over to make sure I was alright."

Well my mom gave me an inquisitive look. "Nothing unusual about that." she says.

"Wait, I'm not done. The voice of the one guy was very familiar to me, but I couldn't place him. At least not right away. Then he looked at me and said, 'Chloe is that you?' Bewildered I said yes and asked who he was."

By now, my mom has stopped playing her computer game and is looking at me in suspense. "So who is he?"

"You will not believe it when I tell you but I have pictures to prove it." I reply. "Josh Joduin."

I am right she can't believe it. I show her the pictures of him and us that I had taken and then proceeded to tell her that I spent the last five days with him.

"So how did that go? Did you talk at all about what happened back then and did you tell him what leaving did to you?"

"Yes we did. We spent the entire first day and evening talking about just that and then told each other what we have done the past thirty years."

"Well I hope that if anything happens between the two of you this time," she says a bit irritated, "that as adults it is handled better."

Not sure how to tell her that we are engaged and he is moving here I tell her that after a couple of days being together we both realized that we still love each other as we did back then even after all these years. I also tell her that he is divorced from his wife and just recently got full custody of his kids.

"They are all moving here at the end of the month." I tell her smiling from ear to ear.

Shaking her head she says, "Okay, that is a good thing. I can see that you are happy about it."

"There's something else too."

"What, are you pregnant?" she asks jokingly.

"No!" I reply, "But he plays in a band and the other night in front of the entire crowd he called me up on stage. Being shy like I am I went up but slowly."

My mom at this point was laughing, "I would have loved to see that."

"Anyway, while up there, he, ummm...." I hesitate and put my hand in my pocket. I pull out the ring but hid it in my hand. "Well, he asked me to marry him and I said yes." I say showing her the ring.

The ring is one of the most beautiful rings that either of us has ever seen. It is a chocolate diamond three stone setting in a 10K rose gold 5.0 mm manganite band. Its' elegant shades from the palest brown to deepest cognac depending on how the sun hits the setting, gives this ring an elegant look showing off their radiant hues.

To my surprise, she is happy and actually cries. "Oh my God. You mean I am finally going to have one of my daughters happy and a son-in-law worth-while."

"Ya I guess." I reply with a chuckle.

I then tell her that he wants to talk to her. I give him a call via Skype. He is still on the plane heading home. She congratulates us and says she is elated that we finally found our way back to each other and he will finally be a part of this family.

During the next month, I talk to Josh and his kids every day via Skype. It's a face time online program where you see who you are talking to as though you are in the same room even if you are across the world. It helps me to realize that my worries and what I felt when Josh left were for nothing because this is real and he will be back.

A month has gone by since Josh left to go back home and he has called me every day since he left. He will be here in two days with his kids and wants me to pick them up at the airport.

Six weeks ago, I was looking at life rather grimly. My future was bleak at best with no one to love and never to feel love. Alone with only a few friends that would come and go; a life, where my days were spent at work, nights alone watching TV and weekends were spent at the beach, just to get some sense of belonging to something. How quickly things change.

I'm on my way to the airport now; my life now has meaning and purpose. I have a sense of belonging and feelings of love. I am beginning a new life, a happy and complete one with the one man I cherish most in this entire world. In less than twenty minutes we will be together forever.

I arrive at the airport pick-up gates and there he stands with his two kids. He is beaming like the happiest person on the face of this earth. His kids are jumping and bouncing with excitement not able to contain the joy they too are feeling. His kids and I get along really well. They called me every day for the past three weeks when they got home from school. They would tell me when they were there and even Skype me to help them with their homework even if their dad was home.

The girl, Paige is nine years old. She is three foot five inches tall, medium build with long blonde hair and the same ice blue eyes as her father. She is wearing a green and white dress with red running shoes. She is a unique individual and Josh lets her be herself. What she wants to wear she does and how she wants to act, she does, with exceptions of course.

The boy Ethan is twelve years old and somewhat larger. He is five foot seven inches tall, taller than I am, medium build but you can tell he works out. He has short brown hair also with the same blue eyes as his father. He is wearing knee length red and black shorts, a red and white Nike wife beater shirt and red and black shoes.

Josh believes in raising his kids to be themselves without trying to mold them into something they aren't or won't be happy with. This comes from his upbringing, which I knew but am happy about because that is how I raised my son as well. He says that this was one area that he and their mom argued about because she grew up with rules, a very strict household and believed that the kids should be raised the same.

As I get out of my car, the kids run to me latching on as though I am a long since seen relative. Josh leans over them, gives me a hug, a kiss, and says, "Boy did I miss you. The kids and I are extremely happy to see you!"

I can tell they are and I am just as happy to see them. "Promise me you will never leave me again, ever." I say.

He promises and then tears his kids away from me. As they get into the back seat, Josh put their suitcases in the trunk and we all get in to start our new lives together.

That night Josh and I talk about my job schedule and whether I can take the next few days off until they are settled. He wants us to get to know each other again, even more so for the kids. I tell him all I have to do is call in sick. "I very rarely call in sick. So, when I do they know I am so they won't suspect anything."

Happy that I said I would do that, we spend the night holding each other and rekindling our love picking up where we left off a month ago.

The next morning, we awoke to whispers just outside our door. Josh gets up and opens the door to have both kids fall into the room. We laugh. I get up telling them I have to make a quick phone call and they have to be quiet.

As I call work to tell them that I am sick and wouldn't be in for a few days, the three of them have piled into the living room beside me. I hang up the phone, turn to them and ask, "Who wants to spend the day at the beach?"

Very excited Josh and I dress into our swim suits and then we all jump into the car and head to the store. The kids need bathing suits and I want to get some beach toys such as tubes, rafts, pails and shovels, etc.

The kids change into their new bathing suits in the bathroom of the store and we head to the beach. It is over an hour away. As we get closer, we stop at the grocery store and pick up some snacks, drinks, a cooler, ice and some lunch items. We spend the day at the beach along the west coast of Florida. It is a great day and all of us have lots of fun.

The rest of the week is spent together doing 'family' things. I bought some paint and Josh helps the kids repaint their bedroom to what they want. We spend time at the fair, shopping, and signing the kids up for school, which is just down the street. Things are going well and we all get along as if we have been together forever.

CHAPTER 9

IT HAS NOW been two months since Josh and the kids moved here and life could not be better. The kids love their school and have made many new friends already. Ethan is on the football team as a quarterback. He has practice five times a week and usually a game on the weekends. So far their team has won three of their first seven games. He's having fun and loves it. Paige, to everyone's surprise, is on the track team. Right now she only practices twice a week and every Saturday morning. Their first track meet is in October, which is only two weeks away, in Miami. It will be perfect as Ethan has a game in Miami that same weekend. Needless to say we will be very busy and are very proud of both of them and love it.

We are now getting ready to head to Miami this weekend. The kids will be on the buses with their teams and several parents will be following in their vehicles. The track team will begin their competitions early Saturday morning at eight a.m. while the football team will have their first game Saturday afternoon at three p.m.

The drive will take five and a half hours. The buses will be leaving tomorrow, Friday afternoon. The kids will be home from school soon so we are packing and getting ready. Josh and I will be leaving tonight to spend some alone time in Miami before the busy weekend begins. Paige and Ethan will be spending the night with their grandma. We will be taking most of their stuff with us in the jeep. When they get home, we pack the car and go to dinner at Apple Bees before taking the kids to my moms.

It is now 6:30 p.m. and we are on our way to Miami. Although it's been a long day, we are very excited. This will be the first time Josh and I will be alone since he and his children moved here. We are taking the convertible Jeep Wrangler Sport. With its' 3.6 L V6 engine, 16 inch wheels and roomy interior it is the best vehicle for beach driving.

We hold hands on the drive there. As it gets dusk, we are only an hour away when he says, "I want to make tonight a date night for us."

Raging Desire

"What do you have in mind?"

"Well, we missed the sunset on the beach but I was thinking, once we have everything unloaded and in the room, we could take the top off this jeep and drive around, and see what's here."

"Okay. It sounds like a great idea."

We are staying at the Villa Vizcaya Motel. It is in the center of town and has its own museum, a mansion and several gardens. There are many sculptures and even an Italian Renaissance-style villa; all of which is breathtaking on its' own. I can't wait to see the rest of what the town has to offer.

It is still early so we drive slowly taking our time to soak in the sights. Water with beaches are all around us as we drive down interlocking stone roads throughout town. The roads are lined with many shops; from surfing, gifts and things, beach wear and accessories, food and drinks, clothing and odd & end stuff. We pass by a sign that directs us to the Bay Harbor Islands; another to the Coral Gables; one for the Everglades and another to the Miami Shores.

We go to the Historic Overtown to learn about the town's history and culture. We park at the edge and decide to walk it. This town used to be a Northwest Black area, one with civic pride and lots of culture. There are colorful murals of African American Heroes, Lyric theater once known as Little Broadway where Patti Labelle and Aretha Franklin played and landmarks dating back to 1913.

While we are here we also learn about the other places around Miami, some being the signs we seen on our way here. As we walk back to the jeep and drive along the beach corridor, we discuss what we learned and what our thoughts are. As we drive along we come across an outside Tiki Bar with live music, so we stop. As we sit at a table with bar stools, order a drink with some appetizers, we plan what we will do tomorrow before the kids arrive.

We look at the information we picked up about Miami hot spots. The Everglades is a subtropical wilderness where we can take a one hour air boat tour. Coral Gables is a city of its own nestled in a cove with fountains and windy roads where we can snorkel to explore the bays' underwater gardens. Bay Harbor Islands is the fourth largest harbor in the continental U.S. where we can take a three-hour boat excursion able to eat lunch while viewing the 450 islands throughout the harbor. Once planned we put away the literature and spend the next couple of hours singing, dancing and drinking enjoying the evening, just the two of us.

The night is whimsical, romantic and fun. The evening planned at the hotel is even more romantic. The room is laced with white and orange rose petals and candles are lit everywhere. The setting leads to lots of copulation as neither of us holds back. It is a night I never want to forget.

He presses my lips to his, and they're searing hot. I want to reach the top with him. He lets go to unzip his jeans. He grabs me by the waist of my skirt and yanks it, breaking the elastic. He pulls me away and tosses me onto the bed.

Looking up at his face, I feel myself get wet. It came from inside and I could feel the muscles flowing, giving out that liquid. Josh smiles down at me, so I guess he could feel it too. He turns me over and I crumble with anticipation. Hard and steady on the back of my head, I could feel his fingers tangle in my hair. It is a good feeling; and, I get wetter.

Turning back over I crawl forward. Straddling his chest instead of his hips, my flesh of satin is nearly in his face. He can't do it. He can't resist. He shifts down and kisses me from my thighs as he moves in closer. It's not long before his tongue touches that special spot. My thighs tighten around his face as I gasp. I don't pull back.

The sounds we make – laughter mixed with pure pleasure. We are not shy in letting the other know how much we like what the other is doing. It doesn't take much before I give in and let the juices flow.

"That isn't fair!" I say.

He doesn't answer me. He looks up, stops and smiles as he moves back up. I slide down until my thighs are around his knees. Leaning in I kiss him. First his lips, then down his chest, then all the way to his stomach. I don't stop. He has no idea how incredibly wonderful he is about to feel. I am going to make it somewhat fair.

I wrap my lips around the head of his shaft. He doesn't pull back. Then I move up and down sucking as I do this. He arches his back and makes noises as his fingers tangle in my hair once again.

He takes hold of my face, forcing my release and rolls me onto my back. Our eyes meet, and that beautiful stillness descends upon us. Even though he is not inside me yet, my whole body is trembling as though we are one.

Raging Desire

Locked into his gaze, I take a breath as he kisses me. With the taste of myself mingled with him on my lips, I let out the breath I held. My chest rises as I release it. My body shifts as Josh presses his shaft into me. Pleasure came over us as he moves in and out slowly and methodically. We look into each other's eyes when all at once, I come. As I gasp, he kisses me and makes one last thrust before he comes inside of me.

We don't look away from each other. He soon moves onto his back and I roll into him. We are sexually rocked and satisfied. It took a lot out of us and it isn't long before we fall asleep.

It is early the next morning now and we are finally up. We have breakfast in one of the restaurants within the villa before heading to the Everglades. The air boat ride takes us through a sub-tropical wilderness where wild Flamingoes live. While touring the many preserved eco systems and viewing places where Native American Tribes once called home, we drive through crocodile and alligator habitats.

We then drive to the Bay Harbor Islands where we board the boat and take our seats along the rail. As we tour the islands, drink coffee and eat lunch, we see dolphins as they swim and jump alongside the boat. At one point the captain stops the boat and tells us to look out to our left. When we do we see a group of humpback whales, some with babies swimming in the distance. It is a beautiful and wondrous sight.

It is now almost two p.m. as we head to Coral Gables for our snorkeling adventure. It is gorgeous under the water; not something you would expect to see at the bottom of the ocean. There are coral reefs with many coral polyps of diverse shapes and species. There are colonies of multi-colored living organisms and plants giving home to the lobsters and fish that call this home. We swim around taking in the beauty nature has made when we are told it is time to get back to the surface. It seems like we just began this adventure when in fact is has been an hour and half.

We head back to the hotel as we are an hour away now and the buses are due to arrive in hour and half. We arrive fifteen minutes before the kids when chaos ensues. Sixty-five kids excited and in Miami can be a hair-raising experience. From then we join the group going where they go and eating where they do.

That afternoon we are given a tour of the theater where the track and field meet will be held then the fields where the football games will be played. After dinner we leave letting them to plan the weekend with their teams and we head back to our hotel room. It's been a long day and we are both tired. We lie down and before we know it, we are both fast asleep.

The next morning we meet the teams for breakfast. Paige will be competing in the long jump, javelin and relay race today; as luck would have it all three of her competitions are held during the morning. This allows us all to attend Ethan's first football game at three p.m.

Paige's first competition is the long jump. There are ten girls competing. Each competitor will run down a runway and jump as far as they can from a wooden board that is built flush with the runway into a pit filled with finely ground gravel or sand. The distance they jump is measured from the edge of this board to the first break in the sand. They will each have two tries of which the longest of each jump will be recorded. The girl with the longest jump will win.

Paige will be jumping in the sixth position. The first three competitors have jumped the farthest length of 2.4 meters. The fourth competitor has recorded 3.2 meters after two jumps. The next competitor jumps a length of 3.0 meters even.

It is now Paige's turn. She stands at the start line. She takes a minute then takes off. Her first jump is 3.1 meters. She walks back to the start line and looks at me as she passes by. I smile and mouth to her *'You Got This'*.

She smiles back, nods and takes her place at the start line. She takes a deep breath and starts her second run attempt. She hits the board and takes off into the air. When she lands she falls forward allowing her to get the maximum distance. We hold our breath. Her second jump is 3.75 meters. So far she has the longest jump.

The next three competitors take their turn. The longest has recorded a jump length of 3.4 meters. Now it's the last competitors turn. She takes her first jump recording a distance of 2.9 meters. We are all standing here and I am thinking that Paige has this in the bag.

She takes her second jump. This jump is far. I hold my breath. She has jumped a total length of 4.0 meters. This put her into first place with Paige getting second. For her first time in a track and field meet and this being her first competition, she did really well and we are very proud of her.

We now have ten minutes to head over to her second competition of the day – Javelin. As we walk over she questions me on how well she really did.

"Paige you did really well sweetie. We are very proud of you. Second place is very good and nothing to be ashamed of."

Raging Desire

"Okay. But I really thought I had it until she made her last jump."

"We did too but that proves you can't count your chickens before all the eggs have hatched."

"Hey. That saying makes sense to me now. Thanks."

"You're welcome. Now let's put that behind us and focus on the javelin. Okay?"

She agrees as we arrive at the field where the javelin is being held. Javelin is a spear that is thrown from a predetermined point. At the other end of the field there are white lines with flags that mark different distances. Once the javelin is thrown it sticks into the ground. The distance is then measured from the throw line to where it hits the ground. The one with the farthest distance takes the trophy.

There are twenty girls in this competition. Paige will be the third girl to throw. The first two girls have thrown a distance of fifteen feet and twelve feet respectively. Paige is now up. She grabs the spear at the grip, takes four steps towards the throw line and throws it as hard as she can. It flies through the air like a low gliding airplane. It sticks into the ground almost like it is buried deep into the earth's crust. They measure the distance. Paige has thrown the javelin a total of twenty-six feet. The record for this age group is twenty-eight feet.

The rest of the girls take their turns throwing the javelin. The longest distance among them was twenty-one feet. Paige took first place in this competition. After the competition is complete, one of the officials walks up to Paige. They talk to her for a couple of minutes when we are then waived over. They want to give Paige another throw. "She was so close to getting the record we want to give her a chance to break it."

Josh asks her if she wants to try. "Yes. Of course I do."

All three officials take their positions. One at the throw line, one at the end of the field and the third is half way down the field. Paige takes her position and grips the spear. She takes a deep breath and this time takes five steps towards the line. She reaches it and throws it as hard as she can. It flies through the air like a bird gliding in the wind. It seems like it is flying in slow motion, it just keeps going and going.

Then all at once it comes down with a thud and sticks into the ground. We are holding our breath as the officials take their stance and begin to measure the distance. All three then convene in mid-field. You can tell they are talking among each other and looking at the distance meter recorder.

They are now walking back towards us. They smile as they head to the microphone. "Ladies and Gentlemen, may I have your attention."

Everyone settles down and faces the men. "We have an announcement to make. The javelin record was set six years ago. We are pleased to announce that today that record has been, not just broken but shattered."

They pause. Looking over at us as we are hugging Paige they say, "Paige Joduin, can you please join us on stage."

Paige looks at us and we encourage her to go up. She reaches the podium and we can tell she is really nervous. "This young lady just shot a distance of thirty-one feet in Javelin shattering the old record of twenty-eight feet. Congratulations young lady, you now hold the record."

Everyone claps as she is handed a red ribbon, a plaque and a trophy. As she walks back to us she is accompanied by one of the officials. "I wanted her to show you the plaque and trophy but she can't keep it right now. We will get the correct spelling of her name and have it put on them and then we will send them to her school where she will then be given them back."

We say okay, take some pictures of her with these items and the official before he takes them away.

"I am very proud of you honey."

"Thanks dad. I can't believe I did that."

"I don't know why. Chloe is always saying we can do stuff like this." Ethan says. "Maybe we should listen to her more often. She was right. You did it little sister and I am proud of you too."

Hugging her brother she thanks him and then turns to me. "Ethan is right. You are always saying we can do these things we just have to think positive. When I threw my second javelin, I thought of that before I threw it."

"See. All you have to do is have faith and do your best and it will always work out. This works for other things too."

She hugs me and we all walk back to the school. There is almost two hours before Paige's last competition – the relay race; and an hour and half before Ethan's football game begins. We decide to have a quick bite to eat before Josh and Ethan have to leave.

As they leave I give Josh a kiss and hug Ethan. "Paige and I will be there before half time. Be safe and kick some butt. You got this. You are good at this. Just believe in yourself."

"I will Chloe. Thank you." He then looks towards Paige. "Good luck sis. You are a fast runner. You will do great in the relay race."

She thanks him and they leave for the football field. We head out to the track as they have just announced that the relay race will begin in twenty minutes and she needs to meet with her teammates and coach before they begin. I give her a kiss and hug and tell her I love her and am proud of her. She jogs to her team mates in the middle of the track and I take my seat in the stands.

The relay race consists of a three-person team and there will be a total of ten teams racing against each other. There will be three heats. Five teams will race against each other in the first and second heat. The winning team of both heats will then race against each other. Each runner will run a distance of one-third of a mile carrying a baton, before passing it onto the next runner as they reach them.

Paige's team – Hillsboro Tigers - will be running the first race. This is a good thing because if her team wins, it will give them time to rest before having to race again. Not something the winning team of the second race will have.

Paige is running the second leg of the three man race. Her coach says the slowest runner is in the first leg, the fastest is the second leg to make up for the slowest giving the third runner a chance to win. Because Paige and Samantha are both equally fast, they tossed a coin to see would run the second and third leg. Brianna will run the first part. They will be running right in the middle of the track, in lane number three.

They all take their places. The official yells, "Ready. Set." Then he shoots the flare gun and the race is off. Brianna is doing really well. She is second in the race and only behind by a couple of steps but the next runner is on her heals. As she gets to Paige, she fumbles the baton but Paige is able to catch it and begins her leg. As she reaches Samantha the baton is passed and she is almost even with the other runner who was in first to this point.

As they round the last corner the sprint is on. They run as fast as they can until they cross the finish line. It is a photo finish. We can't tell who crossed over the line first, Samantha or Diane, the other runner from the Ybor Grishom team. We are standing now in our places, with breaths held as we wait for the announcement.

"By a half a step, the winner is Samantha from Hillsboro Tigers."

We are ecstatic. Paige's team won the race. Now they can rest for about ten minutes while the other five teams race against each other. The official yells again, "Ready. Set." Then he shoots the flare gun and the second race is off. It is a close race. The winner of the second race is Jefferson County. They are given five minutes before the final race starts.

Everyone has taken their place and I have move from sitting in the bleachers to standing at the start/finish line. In this race Paige and Samantha have changed positions and Paige will be running the final leg of this race.

The official makes his announcement. "This will be the final race. The winner of this race will take home the trophy."

He holds the gun into the air and then yells once again. "Ready. Set." He then shoots the flare gun and the final race is off. It is a very close race. As Samantha reaches Paige with the baton she is in first but the other racer is right on her backside. They round the third turn and they are neck and neck. They remain this way until they complete the fourth turn. In the last stretch the other runner pulls away from Paige only slightly but enough that Paige can't catch her. Their team placed second in what is one of the best relay races I have seen in a very long time.

Now that all of Paige's competitions are over and she has received all of her ribbons, we get some water and head over to the football field. We are a bit longer than we thought we would be but at least we will be there before the end of the game.

We arrive at the field and it takes us almost twenty minutes to find Josh. I take note of the score board. Ethan's team is down by four points. They are in the fourth quarter and Josh tells us that with only ten minutes left to the game, Ethan's team needs to get a touchdown and then kick the ball through the goal posts to win the game.

Although there was only ten minutes left to the game, it takes almost forty-five minutes to play out. Each team has called time outs and swapped players on and off the field. The last play has begun. Ethan's team is right before the goal line. Their play is great and the linebacker has the ball in his arm jumping over the two guys in front of him. They flip him into the air and as luck would have it, he lands across the goal line tying up the game.

It is now the kicker's turn on Ethan's team. If he can kick the ball between the goal posts, they will win the game. If he doesn't they will have to play another fifteen minute quarter or until a team wins by a field goal.

As we have been doing all day, we are once again on pins and needles holding our breath. He lines ups. He steps twice before kicking the ball. From our angle it looks like the ball will be short of the goal posts. As

Raging Desire

we begin to think that the game is not over, the ball just reaches over and between the goal posts. Ethan's team has won the game.

We are very proud of both of our kids. They have both done very well today in all their competitions and games.

The next day is very different. Josh spends the morning and part of the afternoon with Ethan at the football field for his game and I am at the track and field meet with Paige for her competitions. Today she is in Shot Putt at 10:00 a.m. then a three-mile triathlon at 12:30 p.m. Ethan's first football game is at 9:30 a.m. and if they win, their second game will be at 6:00 p.m.

Josh has agreed to video tape the game for me and Paige. I have agreed to do the same thing for Paige's competitions. Paige is tired this morning. After yesterday's competitions, she didn't get much sleep last night from all the excitement. As a result she placed in the top five in her Shot Putt competition and did not receive any ribbons. She is okay with this because she is more worried about the three-mile triathlon.

Today's triathlon consists of a one-mile bike ride followed by a half-mile swim completed with a mile and half run. Boys and girls will be running side by side but winners will be announced for both girl and boy divisions based on their placement across the finish line. There are a total of seventy-five kids competing in this race and there will be a special gift for the school that has all their competitors cross the finish line first.

Josh has called me during Ethan's half time break just as Paige began her triathlon. I tell him how she did saying that she is not upset over it. He tells me that Ethan's team is behind by twelve points and they are now at half time.

"Okay baby. The game is about to start back and I want to record it for you and Paige. I can't tape and talk at the same time, the phone won't let me."

"Okay baby I understand. Paige and I will be over when she is done her race. The first runners should be coming across the finish line in about a half an hour."

"Okay. I love you."

"I love you too."

We hang up the phone. Twenty minutes pass by and the first group of runners can be seen coming up the street. There are eight boys and four girls in the first group, none of which Paige can be seen. Five minutes later there is another group coming up the street. This group consists of ten girls and three boys. Still, there is no sign of Paige.

Paige has told me that all she is worried about is finishing the race. She doesn't care if she even finishes last just as long as she finishes. As I am thinking of this, there is another group coming up the street. There are quite a few kids with a good mix of boys and girls in this group.

I look into the crowd of kids. Ten boys and four girls pass by me when I see her. She is in the middle of this group. If she crosses the finish line last in this group she will not only finish the race but won't be last like she thought. Either way she is a winner to me and her father.

She crosses the finish line placed forty-second out of seventy-five. It is a great finish. She is flushed and out of breath, falling to her knees as she crosses the finish line. I go up to her and give her some water to drink while I pour some over her head to try to cool her off. After five minutes she stands and we walk to the school.

She gets some fruit to eat and then drinks a glass of orange juice before we walk over to the football field. As we arrive Ethan's game is over and they are walking out. Paige runs up to her dad and tells her all about her day. Ethan comes up to me giving me a hug and tells me they did not win so he won't be playing in the game at 6:30 tonight.

Although he is a bit upset he is okay. "I was getting kind of tired anyway." he says.

Everything is over by four p.m. Sunday afternoon and even though everyone is tired and exhausted, there is a lot of energy still flowing. Paige has won two bronze medals and one silver medal, Ethan's team won second place and overall their school has ranked third in track and field and increased from fifth to fourth place overall in football. It was a great weekend and lots of fun but I for one will be glad to get home.

We have Paige and Ethan come back with us in the jeep. Before heading home we take the kids to the beach. It's only seven p.m., one hour before the sun is due to set so we swim and play in the water for an hour. As dusk rolls in we dry off and sit to watch the beautiful red and orange hues stretch across the horizon as the sun dips downs beyond the water's edge. We change from our bathing suits, get into our car and head home. It is a quiet ride home.

Being the busy weekend it was, the kids fall asleep in the back seat quickly. I sit beside Josh with my head on his shoulder and holding his hand the whole drive home. Once we arrive, we decide to unpack the car in the morning and we all fall into our beds.

We all sleep in and allow the kids to stay home from school today. The next month has us all over the state of Florida for one or the other. Sometimes they both have games and competitions in separate directions. It is taxiing and sometimes frustrating but like most families, we get through it.

In the end, Ethan's football team is second in the entire league heading into their last game of the season —the game that will determine who is the best. It will be the winner of two of three games and it's a winner takes all. They will be playing to have their team's name put on the trophy, their team picture in the local papers and the winning team will also receive $15,000 for uniforms and equipment. This game is scheduled for the first week of December which is a month away, giving them time to practice.

Paige is done with her track and field meets and competitions now making our lives a little easier. She and her team did very well this year. In total Paige herself received, four gold medals, six bronze medals, two silver medals and one trophy. Her team placed second overall resulting in their picture showing in the local papers, a trophy with the schools' name on it which is displayed in their showcase, and $5,000 for new equipment and uniforms.

Both Josh and I are very proud of the kids. Not only are they doing well on their teams, they are also doing well in school. Both are on the honor roll. Ethan has a grade point average of 3.2 and Paige has a grade point average of 3.6.

CHAPTER 10

IT IS NOW November 21st and it is my forty-fifth birthday. Not having said a word to Josh or the kids, I assume they don't know what today is. It is Saturday and I wake up alone, Josh is already up and I can hear him and the kids in the kitchen. I lay here for a moment before getting up letting them have their time together.

I go into the bathroom. When I come out Josh and the kids are standing there with a tray of food, coffee and two cards. As I stand here not knowing what to say, they sing happy birthday to me. I am to say the least, surprised. "Wow, you did this for me?" I ask wiping away the tears.

"We made you breakfast in bed for your birthday." the kids say then ask why I am crying.

I get back into bed because they want to give breakfast to me in bed. "Because I am happy. No-one has ever done this for me before, not even my own son. And, I can't believe your dad remembered my birthday."

He smiles, leaves for a minute and grabs his coffee and the kids' juice they had already poured and we all sit on the bed eating breakfast.

After I read the cards the kids made me Josh pulls out this small box from behind his back, "Here baby Happy Birthday." he says giving me a kiss.

"What's this?"

"Open it and see."

I un-wrap the box and open it. Inside could not have been a better gift. On top there are two gold round key rings that attach yet separate. On one, it says she's mine on the front and on the back has my name on it. The other says he's mine on the front with his name on the back.

"This gift is for both of us, so we will always be connected. Go ahead there's more in there." So I remove the key rings and give him his and set mine aside.

Under this is another wrapped item, so I un-wrap it. It is a handmade necklace with bracelet the kids made themselves for me. They were beautiful and had all of my favorite colors – ruby red, emerald green and burnt orange all tied together with white to give it an elegant look. Paige helps me put them on.

Under this is an envelope. I open the envelope and inside is a gift certificate for one free spa day at Marilyn Monroe Spa in Orlando Florida.

"It is good for two people and consists of full body massages, hot rock therapy, mud bath, facials, and even includes a manicure and pedicure." Josh says.

So now I'm crying again. "I love everything. This is more than I ever wanted. The three of you are the best. I love you all very much."

The kids give me a hug and a kiss, then run into the kitchen. Josh moves the tray, sits closer to me, and turns to give me a kiss.

"I love you very much. This is only the beginning; it is what you can expect for every special day for the rest of your life."

I smile as I wipe the tears away. "How did you know it was my birthday? I never said anything to any of you."

"If I told you that I remembered from when we were kids would you believe me?"

"I might and if that's the case I am amazed."

"Well to be honest, I knew it was in November but I called your mom and asked the actual date. I thought it was the 22nd so I wasn't far off."

I hug him. "The fact that you remembered the month is amazing to me and that you called my mom so you didn't miss it makes it that much more special. This shows me beyond anything that you truly do love me."

Just then, the kids come back in, stand beside the bed, and look at their dad. "Did you ask her?"

Josh shakes his head. "I'm leaving that up to the two of you."

I look at Josh and then the kids and ask, "What's going on?"

"We have a question for you."

Telling them it is alright, they can ask me anything Ethan starts. "Well you know about our past and what our mom was like."

Nodding my head, he continues, "You see it's like this. Paige and I both like you a lot."

Paige speaks up, "No we love her like she was our mommy." she says excitedly.

Shushing her Ethan speaks louder. "Like Paige said, we love you and we have been talking and, well ummm…" he stops, looks at his dad.

Josh nods his head.

"We want to know if we can call you mom." Paige blurts out.

"Well if it's alright with your dad." I respond as I look at him.

He is smiling from ear to ear in agreement. "Yes it is, we already talked about it."

I look back at Paige and Ethan. "Of course it's okay. I would love to be your mom." I put my arms out and they jump into them. It is the happiest day of my life and it has only just begun.

The rest of the day I am waited on hand and foot. They cook lunch for me, clean and let me stay in my art room to finish the painting I need to have done and out in two days. It is an enjoyable day.

We go out for dinner at the local Outback Steakhouse restaurant. We begin with chicken wings and quesadillas appetizers shared among the four of us. We are telling jokes and the kids are razzing each other as we eat. The main course is brought to us. Both boys ordered the outback sirloin steak which is a seared, quarter pound piece of meat with salad and potatoes. Both Paige and I order their world renowned chicken and rib platter. It comes with a quarter chicken barbecued and smothered in a zesty BBQ sauce, a half rack of baby back ribs that melt in your mouth, coleslaw and French fries.

During dinner we all discuss how the kids' football games and track meets are going as they are winding down for the winter months. Our desert is shared among us as it is a fourteen inch round salted caramel cookie skillet. It has pieces of white chocolate, almond toffee, caramel bits and pretzels baked into them smothered in a chocolate sauce.

After dinner we decide to go mini putting. Close by is a mini gulf place called the Putting Edge. The entire experience is glow in the dark and sounds like it would be loads of fun; and it was. Your balls glow and each golfer is given a different color ball with matching glowing putters. As you walk through putting from hole to hole, the walls are covered in glow in the dark painted murals. Each hole has its own theme: Under The Sea, Airspace, Planes, Cars, and one for each of the major holidays including Christmas, Easter and Halloween. It puts a whole new meaning to mini gulf and is an experience we recommend to anyone as it is a lot of fun.

We break into two teams, girls versus boys. Ethan bets Paige if they win she does his dishes and laundry for a week. Paige bets that if we win he does her dishes and cleans the bathroom for the next week. They both agree shaking hands then Paige looks at us asking what we are going to bet.

At first I tell her nothing it is only for fun; but then, Josh speaks up. "If we win I will clean the house and cook dinner for Chloe next weekend."

I smile saying I like that. I then say, "Well if we win, I will make your dad breakfast in bed and wait on him hand and foot next weekend."

Agreeing with that we shake hands and kissed on it then the game began.

It is 18 holes of putting fun. By the fourth hole, the boys are ahead by four and rubbing it in. By the tenth hole we are ahead beating them by six so we rub it in. Hole sixteen has us all tied up. Throughout every hole everyone makes noises and jinxes the putter and banter words back and forth to try to foil each other shots. At the 18th hole, we are tied at plus four a piece. This hole will determine the winners.

It is a par three hole. The hole begins atop a hill. You have to putt the ball into the hole which comes out at the bottom. If lined up right and has enough speed when it comes out, it goes into the hole at the bottom and you get a hole in one.

I have already taken my putt and made it in two putts, I missed the hole atop the hill on my first shot. Ethan has done the same except he didn't have enough speed and it fell short of the hole at the bottom, keeping it tied. So, it is up to Josh and Paige to break the tie. Josh takes his turn. He lines up the shot and misses the hole atop the hill. When the ball comes out at the bottom it falls short of the hole, thus he makes the putt in three shots.

It is now up to Paige. If she gets her ball in the hole in two shots, we win. She lines it up and takes her shot. She gets it in the top hole on her first try and we all hold our breath as we hear the ball roll down the hill through the pipe. It comes out at the bottom with just enough speed and strength that it goes into the hole. Not only did she win the game for us but she has gotten a hole-in-one getting a free game as well.

We decide to take the free game for another time. All the way home Paige nags Ethan bragging that we won. She is happy that she doesn't have to clean the bathroom for the next week or do the dishes. I am kind of excited myself as it will be the first time Josh has ever cooked for me.

The week goes by fast and the weekend is here. Paige and I sit around watching movies and watching the boys cook and clean. It is refreshing to see and have done because we are usually the ones doing it. I got breakfast in bed, we both had lunch served to us on trays in the living room and Josh takes us out for dinner. This was Saturday.

Sunday we were taken out for breakfast, and while the boys finish cleaning Paige and I work on our crafts. It is a joyous weekend.

CHAPTER 11

SUMMER HAS COME and gone and school is now back in session. One month passes and we are at the school's first track meet for the year. While in the gym, we over hear a group of teenagers talking. The one is telling his friends of a story his dad has told him over the summer of a rape case from when he was back in high school himself. He tells them that there is new evidence into the case. They have one of the guys in jail for a rape he did last year and they found the remains of another. There are still two at large.

He says, "My dad says he never knew who the girl was but she was messed up so bad they left her for dead; however, she survived. No one knows where the girl is now or how she is even doing."

Josh makes a statement to me remembering that he heard about that. "Wasn't that the summer I got my motorcycle license and went to visit my cousin?"

I nod my head. "Yes and I remember it like it happened yesterday."

The boys turn to us realizing we are talking about the same thing. "What do you know about it?"

"Well," I tell them. "I knew the girl that it had happened to. I don't know where she went or where she is now though. A year after the rape, her step-dad was arrested for raping both her and one of her sisters. She moved shortly after that and I haven't heard from her since."

"Wow. I thought my dad was just telling me a story. I didn't think it really happened."

"Well it did. You can believe your dad."

Just then his dad came over and got him and they left.

Josh is very quiet and different for the rest of the day. When I ask him if he is alright he says he is fine. He has been looking at me funny and not saying a whole lot. Usually he is full of come backs, jokes and the center of attention; but, today he is different. I wonder if he suspects something from what I told the boys.

That night when we get into bed he asks me why I never said anything to him back then.

"I promised her I wouldn't because she didn't want anyone to know. All she wanted to do was put it behind her and try to forget about it."

He sits here quietly looking at me as though he does not believe me. A few minutes pass. "I know Brock raped your sister and was jailed for it about a year after this girl was raped. Was it your sister this happened to?"

"No, it wasn't my sister that it happened to but we both know the girl that it did happen to."

After a few minutes and a couple more questions, he notices that I am trying not to cry. The tears well up and I turn away from him hoping he doesn't see it as I try to hold them back. He sees.

"Oh My God! It was you, wasn't it?" he starts to freak out.

"What makes you say that?"

"If I think back to when I got back and how you were acting, it all makes sense now."

I nod my head and the tears start to run down my cheeks. "I guess I should tell you what really happened."

He is now sitting at the end of the bed facing me. I tell him what happened with the rape by the four boys. He is furious. He walks up and down the floor at the end of the bed asking me why I never said anything. "You should have told me. You shouldn't have had to go through that alone! I thought we told each other everything?"

"I couldn't tell you. I didn't want you to treat me differently and I couldn't bear doing that to you and I really didn't know how to tell you."

"Your mom could have!"

"I made her and Brock promise not to."

He continues with the questions for about ten minutes not letting me get a word in edge wise. Then all at once, he stops. He stops talking and stops walking. He turns and looks at me with tears in his eyes.

He walks to my side of the bed still looking at me. Not saying a word he drops onto the bed. He wraps his arms around me and repeats over and over, "I am so sorry."

"It's okay." I keep telling him. "There is nothing to be sorry for, you didn't do any of it."

He starts to blame himself for what happened. "If I would have stayed home that weekend and not went off to my cousins' house then that would not have happened."

Trying to tell him he is wrong, he doesn't want to listen, so I state the facts to him.

"Look! Everyone can be blamed for what happened. You for leaving me that weekend; me for going to the party in the first place or for choosing to take that way home; my sister for not leaving with me or for letting her convince me to go to the party in the first place; and, my mom and Brock for going to the bar and not being home to answer the phone to pick me up. In the end, the only ones to really blame for what happened are the four guys who raped me, no one else."

Extremely upset he hesitantly agrees with me. We spend a good part of the night talking about this. Then I decide I should tell him everything. "There is something else I should probably tell you."

"Now what? It can't be any worse than that!"

"Just remember that I couldn't tell you this part because you weren't even around then."

"Okay, what is it?"

"Well, it's about Brock and what really happened."

I proceed to tell him how Brock raped me for years before attempting with my sister. I told him how he and my mom out casted me from the family and everything that he did.

Josh is now really mad. "I can't believe that. You and your mom are getting along so well. There's no way."

I tell him it's the truth and even tell him that tomorrow I will call my mom and he can hear it from her. We talked about all of this for a while then both agree that it is the past, and let it stay there.

"You know. There is some satisfaction in knowing that two of them will never do it again to anyone." I state

He asks if I know who any of them were and I tell him no. "The one that is in jail is there because I am the one who put him there."

"How?"

I tell him how it came about and what happened. "I don't want to try to find out who the others are. If they get caught because of other things, then they get what they deserve. I just hope that no one else went through what I did by their hands."

We left it at that and went to sleep.

IT TOOK A couple of weeks before Josh was able to actually let it go. We finally moved on not talking about what had happened anymore. We started living our lives again and he never told his kids about it.

It has been almost a year since our engagement so we set a date and begin our wedding plans. We decide to hold it on the very same beach where we found each other again and rekindled our love affair. The color scheme will be burnt orange, and royal blue – both of our favorite colors – offset by white for that elegant look.

Separately we will decide who will be in our wedding party and we have decided to write our own vows to each other. The date is set for October 6th, six weeks from now. Although it's going to be a small, intimate wedding, there isn't much time to plan it, so I get started on it right away.

We are living proof that love at first sight exists and it is now evident that I never found my soul mate all these years because Josh is my soul mate. We have been together ever since.

Until, that one dreadful day.

CHAPTER 12

IT IS NOW our wedding day and I couldn't be more nervous. It is the most honest, heartfelt, beautiful ceremony there ever was. It is an original ceremony that is truly meaningful and quite the tear jerker. It takes place on the most gorgeous beach on Anna Maria Island and scheduled to take place at sunset. Beautiful white sands, calm, blue ocean in the background, and the most beautiful sunset, as the back drop. It couldn't be more perfect.

One of the most magical moments during a wedding day is watching the bride slip into her dress, that first look into the mirror, the sparkle in her eyes, the bridesmaids' gasp and something that has been anticipated for so long becomes reality.

The moment I slip into my absolutely gorgeous dress is nothing short of magical. It is not the traditional dress as we both have been married before. It is a draped high-low dress, off white with emerald green lace and trim. My dress, hair, makeup, shoes - everything is perfect, I look absolutely stunning and I catch myself on a thought that I can't wait to see Josh's reaction.

With Paige as my maid of honor, my youngest sister a bridesmaid, my son giving me away it is perfect. Ethan is Josh's groomsman and Chase is his best man. His, soon to be our, grandson is the ring bearer and my youngest niece is our flower girl. The pictures just don't do the ceremony justice and I am ever so glad we capture it on film, both video and still.

Chairs are set three by three, twenty rows down each side with a six foot wide aisle separating them. For walking ease, a blue-green carpet runs the entire forty foot length of runway from the back to the front. As my son and I walk down the aisle to the front where Josh, Chase and Ethan are standing, everyone watches us. There are 120 guests all standing, some crying, most smiling, all seem in awe of me in my dress.

It takes thirty minutes until we get to the exchange of vows. As the bride, I am asked to go first. I take Josh's hands as I face him.

"Josh. We have known each other since grade school. Back then you were my rock, the only person I could really and truly trust. You were my one true love then and still are now. Even though we lost thirty years, the love we shared was never lost. I didn't know it was possible but I love you more now than I ever have. You are the love of my life, always have been and always will be."

I am hardly able to keep the tears from running down my face with great difficulty. Now it is Josh's turn. He doesn't let go of my hands.

"Chloe, the best thing to ever happen to me is you. You were in school and still are now. We may have lost thirty years but we found our way back to each other, and that's all that matters. You are my best friend, my lover, my soul mate. I love you now and forever."

So now I can't help it. I am crying. We exchange the rings and are pronounced husband and wife. He kisses me with the most passionate French kiss.

After the ceremony, everyone takes off their clothes down to their underwear and we all jump into the ocean for a celebratory dip just as the sun crests the horizon. A few of us stay and swim for a bit while others get out and start a fire in the make shift pit we made earlier in the sand. The rest of us slowly walk out and we all warm up by the fire. The night ensues with drinking, eating s'mores, hot dogs and marshmallows, talking and some of us singing. Shocked as some may have been but two of my sisters and I break out singing a few songs that we sang when we tried to get on American Idol a few years back.

During the night some walk hand-in-hand along the shore lit up by the light of the moon while others take a moonlit swim before hunkering down for the night. We have pitched tents along the beach and family by family, one by one we lay with our loved ones and go to sleep.

The next day we get a volleyball game going on the beach; it is my family against his. There are six to a team with each having two kids under the age of thirteen. The game will go to fifteen and we decide to have both grandmothers referee the game. There are four kids wanting to keep score so Amy age ten and Lucas age six will be score keeper for Josh's family and Johnny age eleven and Brenda age five will be our score keepers. A coin is tossed and his family serves first.

We rally the ball back and forth over the net between both families many times. After the first hour, Josh's family has twelve points and my family has eleven points. It is extremely hot outside and we have been drinking water and juice between serves. It is decided that should no team reach fifteen points in the next thirty minutes, the team with the highest score will win. Twenty minutes passes and Josh's family scores their fifteenth point just after we scored our fourteenth. Thus his team has won.

It was a very close game and we had lots of fun. Baking under the hot blazing sun, our skin is sweltering with little blisters as the cool water of the Atlantic Ocean calls us. It is very enticing and not able to take it anymore, I am the first to plunge into the turquoise beauty and cool bliss. The waves softly crash against my body as though it curls its fingers gently caressing as the wind ushers me gently towards the shore. The way the sun shines off the ripples in the water, its' golden light warps like twisted glass. It's not long before many others follow behind and before I know it, I am engulfed with people all around me. Some of the guys are jet skiing while the young kids are making sand castles along the waters' edge.

It is now time for Josh and I to leave as we have a plane to catch. He is taking me somewhere romantic for our honeymoon. Not saying where we are going, we say our goodbyes and leave.

THE GOLDEN HOT sun. Fine white sands. Blue-green water. Grass roof with full surround glass hut at the end of a long boardwalk overlooking the ocean in Fiji is where we are. It is a tropical paradise. Neither of us has ever been, so it is a new adventure for both of us and we are not disappointed. The staff is simply amazing. We instantly have a connection with the bar and restaurant mob. Many laughs ensued and we don't want to go back!

It is adventure packed, with everything from playing golf, to riding bikes and mopeds to cruises and just chilling out with massages. We wake up every morning to glorious sun rises surrounding us and end each night with beautiful sunsets in various venues.

It is perfect. Our life is perfect. Finally I have a life worth living, and am sharing it with my one true love. It is the last night of our honeymoon, before our return home and Josh looks at me with a very serious look on his face. "I have something I need to ask you."

I am not sure what to think of how he says that. "Okay, should I be worried?"

"No, but I've been thinking. Now that we are married and I have a good job, this is something I feel strongly about and have for a while."

"Okay. What is it?"

"I don't like the hours you have at your job. It's only part time now and you aren't very happy there. I would like you to quit your job, stay home with the kids and get back into your painting again."

I am shocked. I did not expect him to say anything like that. Not sure what to say I just sit here for a minute looking at him.

"Are you alright?" he asks me.

"Yes." I reply. "I just never expected you to say that. I'm not sure what to say. Quitting is not something I have ever done."

We discuss it for almost an hour and after making his case, I agree. "When we get back I will give my notice."

He wants to provide for the kids and me and wants me to be happy. I want him to be happy too and if me staying home with the kids and getting back into my art makes him happy, then that is what I will do.

Upon our return, I keep my promise to him. I go to work the following day and give my notice telling them I won't be back.

With that, I left and never look back, ready to begin our new life together.

CHAPTER 13

THAT WAS THREE years ago. We have a great life. Paige still lives at home ready to begin high school in the fall. Ethan still lives at home but is in his second year of college soon to graduate as an airline mechanic. His eldest daughter Eliza is now married and is due to have her second child in four months. My son is living with his now fiancée with their wedding date set for next summer.

All four children and their families get along really well. My son says he finally has a loving family with a brother, sisters and a dad who cares and spends time with him. His kids say they finally have a mom who helps them, cares for them and treats them with love and kindness; and they love their older brother.

Almost a year after our return from our honeymoon, the construction industry starts to take a dive. We struggle for almost two years, as his full time assistant manager job with DB Construction becomes a sporadic part time job and he still doesn't' want me to work.

Finally, unable to make it anymore, Josh decides to get his Commercial Driving License (CDLs) and become a truck driver. There is a demand for it right now. After looking into it he says he will only do it for one year as an over the road trucker then get a local job paying the same money but be home.

Over the road trucker means you are gone away from home for weeks or months at a time and then home for a week before you are gone again. It is not a life I want to live. I have an uncle who was a trucker, I grew up with kids whose father was a trucker, and the life they all led and the problems the parents had was not a life I wanted. For me, I did not want him gone for six to eight weeks or longer only to be home for a few days, then gone again, for an entire year. I hate being away from him for two days at a time now, being apart for that long will kill me.

We have already lost thirty years and only regained the last few back. However, he does it anyway saying it will only be for a year and together we will get through it. I don't like it and he knows it; however, he still does it anyway, saying there is no other option for him.

The first few months were extremely hard for all of us. Every night I would cry myself to sleep feeling lonely and empty without him by my side. He is on the road six to seven weeks at a time and when he does come home, he is only here four to five days then gone again. He isn't home long enough to do much as a family. He barely has enough time to get caught up on his sleep, do laundry and buy stuff to take back out and he is gone again.

Paige is upset all the time because her dad is never home anymore. She wonders if he is ever going to be around, as I am, or if our life as we know it now is how it will remain. I do everything I can to try to reassure her that this is only temporary. It's hard to do because although I know it is only for a year, it's hard to believe with the way our life is now. It's always in turmoil and I am bringing up a family of four on my own.

Ethan begins to rebel thinking that he can slack off because his dad isn't around to say anything. After a few months of arguing with him and his dad trying to talk to him, Ethan decides it is best for him to move out on his own so he can do what he wants without us imposing rules. He is after all, eighteen now and there is nothing we can do but let him go, so we do.

It is now almost Christmas time again and Josh is supposed to be home for Christmas, so Paige and I plan a party. We go all out on the decorations then pack the tree with gifts. Josh is like me, loves Christmas and Easter (I also love Halloween), so we go big. Ethan has agreed to come home for the holidays, his eldest daughter and her family will be here and so will my son and his soon-to-be wife. I also invite my mom and her new boyfriend. Along with family, we invite some of Josh's friends, Chase and Razor and our common friends Leila and Max.

Josh is now home, two days before Christmas, just in time for the surprise party I am holding for him. The party will be held tomorrow night, Christmas Eve. It will be a theme party – pot luck style Christmas Cocktails with food and karaoke. Paige and I are excited. Josh is not only home for Christmas but will be here for eight days rather than four.

It is now the night of the party and Josh knows something is up but doesn't know exactly what it is. As the guests start to arrive, he is surprised.

The first few are his friends and he thought they were simply here to welcome him home and wish him a Merry Christmas. It isn't until the others start to arrive that he realizes we are hosting a party in his honor.

Everyone brought his or her favorite Christmas cocktail rather than food. There is Candy Cane Martini's, Rum Butter Eggnog, Peppermint Cocoa with Baileys, Boiler Makers, Flaming Cosmos, Coffee Tonic's, Cherry smoothies with Vodka and Mimosa's.

I provide the food because as his friends, kids and I know all too well, Josh is fussy when it comes to food and I want to make sure we have things he will eat. We have finger foods like pigs in a blanket, chips and dip, veggie platters, pretzels, cookies, bars and other various deserts.

Karaoke is a bust full of laughs as well. We took the usual Christmas classic songs and did pop and country interpretations to them. Songs include All I Want for Christmas; Rudolph the Red Nose Reindeer; Silent Night; Chestnuts Roasting By an Open Fire; White Christmas; We Wish You A Merry Christmas and Joy To The World.

Everyone has a blast and enjoy themselves immensely. I can't remember the last time we had fun like this; it's almost like normal without a care in the world. The party lasts well into the wee hours of Christmas morning. Having got to bed at three a.m., it is hard getting up with the kids at seven a.m. We both have major hangovers and the kids are laughing at us. After everyone chips in to pick up and Josh and I have several cups of black coffee, we are finally ready to open the gifts.

It takes an hour for the kids to unwrap all their gifts. There were 54 in total between them. I bought Josh several things as well, mostly things for his truck and warm clothing while he is on the road driving in those dangerous conditions. Josh has bought me the most beautiful jewelry set I have ever received. The ring, necklace and earrings are set in 92.5 sterling silver settings including the bands, posts and chain. The mount is a large Citrine Stone (my birthstone) hexagon shaped. From the band up each of the six prongs holding the setting in place there are ten small Jade Green stones leading up to the Citrine Stone. It is the most elegant set I have ever received and I love it.

The rest of the day is spent with everyone trying on their clothing, the kids playing with their toys, Josh putting together some of the toys they got and me cooking dinner. Paige helps me in the kitchen throughout the day and I enjoy every minute of it. I do not want this day to end.

It is now eight p.m. and the kids are going to bed an hour earlier than usual because they are tired. We all have had a very long day. While Josh is turning off all the lights, T.V., computer and locking the door, I slip into the bedroom. I still have one more gift for him and have to put it on before he comes in. I go into the bathroom and get changed while waiting for him to join me in the bedroom.

When he comes in, I holler. "Baby, I have one more gift for you. Press play on the CD player and have a seat on the bed. I will be right out."

With a questionable, 'Okay,' he does as I asked and it's not long before I hear the music start to play. I chose a song that he and I both love. It is one that we danced to every time it played when we were in high school. It is, 'Waiting For a Girl Like You', by Foreigner.

"I'm on the bed waiting." he says excitedly.

I open the door. With one arm against the door jam, bent with hand on my head, the other is on my hip with one leg bent. I look at him and smile, his jaw drops. He sits straight up from his slouched position and moves as if to get up and come to me.

I take my hand off my hip and shake my finger at him. "No, stay there and let me come to you."

My outfit is a black and red fishnet garter chemise with lace hem and push up halter style top. It has an attached matching, thigh high fishnet stocking that leaves your partner breathless and wanting more. With the open bottom, result is a wide-open treasure cove as no undressing is required. The back is just covered with a single strap mid back with lace swooping up to meet the sides in a classy yet very inviting manner. Underneath I have on a cute and sexy Lycra G string that adds to the experience. I have on black sexy t-strap shoes, open toe, with rhinestones studding the strap. They have two-inch heels dressed in red fishnet finishing the outfit for the ultimate sex appeal. It is clearly designed for the all in sweet yet sexy persona I want to convey.

Josh is now sitting on the edge of the bed. I take a few steps into the room, turning as I walk so he can see the entire outfit. "Oh My God. This is the best present of all!" he says.

I now face him. He begins to stand. "No." I say, "Stay sitting. I have this all planned out. I just want you to sit there and enjoy this."

He sits back down on the edge of the bed with a huge smile from ear to ear and a twinkle in his eyes. I can tell he is very excited and wants to come to me bad; but he can't, I am coming to him instead, slowly.

As I walk, I sway my hips from left to right and do a little sexy dance to the music as I run my hands up and down my body feeling every curve. Only steps away from him I stop and grab hold of each side of my outfit and act as if I am going to pull it off. I stop, take three steps back and turn so my back is now to him.

Separating my legs shoulder width apart, I bend over and run my hands down the inside of my legs then back up the back and over my ass. I look at him through the opening in my legs as I do this and notice that he is getting more excited as every minute passes, hardly able to contain his self.

I stand and face him once again. I walk slowly towards him. As I approach him, I lean in still two steps away and kiss him letting him touch me with his hands but not able to pull me in. I remove his hands from my body and sit beside him laying him back down on his back.

Looking into his eyes, I unbutton his jeans. He pulls them off quickly. His fingers running through my hair then caressing my face, I lean in and kiss him. His hands are all over me now as I run my hands down his body to the bottom edge of his shirt. I sit up pulling him up with me; I pull his shirt off over his head revealing his trembling body.

"Are you alright?" I ask him.

"I am fine, just really excited is all. I am almost to my breaking point and can't take much more of this. I just want to jump."

Laughing I get on the bed and onto my knees straddling him. He takes me into his arms and not holding him back any more, we lose all control. We begin by performing oral sex on each other slowly. He brings to a climax that leaves me breathless and my body tingling all over. It's animalistic, passionate and extremely hot sex that last for almost two hours.

We lay on our backs to catch our breath. After a few moments, he mutters, "Wow! That was the best." with the largest smile I have ever seen on his face.

"I agree. It was the best I've ever had."

We cuddle and I run my hands up and down his body just feeling him. Just being with each other now, we fall asleep.

With the holidays now over and everyone gone back home, it is time for Josh to leave us once again. I hate it when he leaves; and it is harder this time. Having him home for this long helps us to get back to 'us' and now he is going to be gone again.

He promises that this is his last time he will leave us. "The next time I come home, it will be for good. I promise."

Paige cries as she hugs her dad. "Dad, please don't go. I want you here, home with us."

"I have to go baby girl but I will be back. I promise."

She lets go of him. "I love you dad." she says as she runs into her room and slams her door.

I put my arms around him as I fight back the tears myself. "I love you Josh. Very much. Please come back home to me in one piece."

"I always do and I promise. I love you too. Very much. You'll see, this time it will go by fast and I will be home before you know it."

"I hope so. I miss you so much when you are gone."

He kisses me, picks up his bags and walks out the door. This will be his last six week tour as an over-the-road truck driver.

Paige and I cry for a while and I try to lift her spirits throughout the time. I remind her that he will be home to stay very soon. It seems to work, for her anyway. For me, I miss him too much and can't wait for it to be all over.

This is when I hear someone in a television show I am watching say, "Be careful what you wish for because you might just get it."

Little did I know just how true this statement would be for all of us very soon.

CHAPTER 14

THE LAST FIVE weeks seem to take forever; it is the longest it has ever taken. Josh was wrong when he said it would be over quick. I guess the anticipation and knowing that he will be home soon and this time for good almost seems too good to be true.

The time is almost here for us to live our lives together. He is finally on his last leg. It will be the last time he will be away from us for any length of time. It has been a year since he started this job and when he comes home in less than two weeks, he has a job waiting here.

The new job will mean he will be gone for only three days and home three days at any given time. Not the best but it is much better than what he has been doing so it is acceptable. At least we will be together much more often. We are all excited by the news that his time away from us will soon be over. It is Valentine's Day the weekend he gets home and I have a special gift planned for him and the kids are planning a huge celebration for him as well.

Two days prior to him being home the kids are at their grandmothers getting ready for their surprise when I get a call. It is from Josh's head office. In the year he has driven for them the head office has never called me for any reason. When I see their name on the phone, my heart sinks and my eyes tear up. I pick up the receiver.

"Hello." I say in a shaky voice.

"Mrs. Allen?" says a deep male voice on the other end. "This is Malcolm and I am Josh's fleet manager." He pauses, "I'm afraid I have some bad news."

My heart sinks further fearing the worse but praying it isn't. Saying to myself, please God only let him be hurt but not badly, and I listen to what he has to say.

"Josh's truck hit some black ice on Widow's Ridge in the Rockies late last night. It spun out of control landing on its side and slid off the road.

It careened down the mountain side until it came to a complete stop at the bottom. He dropped 3,000 feet and there is nothing left to the truck." utters Malcolm. "It happened so quickly his death was instant and most likely did not feel anything."

My world comes crashing down around me and I can't believe what I just heard. The worse has happened and nothing matters, my heart stops.

"I am so sorry for your loss." he says and hung up the phone.

My life as I knew it is over, gone forever and there is nothing I can do. Feeling lost and depressed I drop the phone, sink to the floor and uncontrollably begin to cry. After almost an hour I gather myself together, sit on the couch and pick up the phone. I have to tell the kids and his mom what has happened.

As I sit here slowly dialing the phone number, I think to myself, *'How am I going to tell them? What do I say?'* Before I could finish dialing the last number, the door opens and in walks the kids and their grandmother. All are in tears and I know in an instant they have already heard the news. We all sit on the couch holding each other for hours reminiscing about the good times we have had with Josh.

Before we know it the sun is rising again as it is the next morning. My mother-in-law Olivia makes coffee while the kids go and change their clothes. I just sit here, in shock. I can't believe it and don't want to believe that this has happened. I can't move, it's all I can do to drink my coffee.

The next week is spent making arrangements to have Josh's remains sent home with all his belongings for what they could gather from the crash site. The companies' investigation team kept them until they completed their investigation and autopsy. They now are preparing to have him shipped home. Shipped home, what a thought. He is coming home for good but not how we wanted.

I am in shock and disbelief that this is happening, to me, to us. I am numb all over, it all seems like a dream. I feel dizzy, nauseous and dazed, like everything that is happening is not real. I go through the realm of feelings one might go through with a huge loss, anger, sadness, loneliness, as my world has been turned upside down.

I become very emotional during this time. From sad to angry, from guilt to despair, all causing me to become forgetful of details, loss of concentration and even confusion as to why some things are evening happening. At times it feels like I am the only one who cares, who feels anything. Things are said that make me cry or become volatile, while some things said confuses me.

Olivia makes a comment, "I guess you should watch what you pray for and what you say." The kids and I look at her wondering what she is talking about.

"Excuse me, what is that supposed to mean?"

She maintains her statement saying that we all wanted him home so bad that we got our wish. "I hope you are all happy now!"

Well now I am pissed off. I stand up, walk over to where she is sitting and standing in front of her shaking my finger at her I express my thoughts harshly.

"Listen here! If you think for one second this is what we wanted, you are dead wrong. You know I love him with all my heart and that he is the love of my life. We all wanted him home so we could grow old and be happy together alive, not dead!"

At this point, I notice that I am not just saying, this but am yelling it. "If you want someone to blame, look in the mirror. He took this job because you pushed him into it telling him it was all he was able to do. You made him believe he had no other skills or choice. You even told him you would pay for him to take the class to get the CDL's but if he was to do anything else he was on his own. How could he choose to do anything else? You gave him no choice!"

She just sits there looking hurt and shocked that I am saying anything. I didn't care. I continue unable to hold it in anymore.

"He would still be here with us alive if it weren't for you pushing him to do this. Even after you knew I was against it and didn't want him to do it. You even knew the reasons and risks because I made it all very clear." I storm out of the room and into my bedroom slamming the door behind me. I fall onto my bed crying.

My heart is racing. My head is pounding. My hands and legs are shaking. I can't believe she tried to blame me for his death. In reality, it is no one's fault. No matter where he would have been working, if it was his time to go he would have. Still, I don't need this. I have a funeral to plan even though I don't want to be doing this. It is not something I ever wanted to do.

After a few hours, I come out of my room. The kids ask me if I am okay giving me a hug. As I tell them I will be Olivia comes up to me, puts her arms around me and murmurs, "I am sorry Hun. I did not mean to blame you for his death. I am just very upset. Please forgive me?"

I tell her I accept her apology and then I apologize as well for saying some of the things I said. "It is no one's fault he died. It happened and we can't change that and now we need to deal with it."

I go into the kitchen, she says goodnight to the kids and leaves. The kids go to bed and I take two sleeping pills and head off to bed myself.

The next couple of weeks are a blur. People come and go, I am back and forth to the funeral home and many people are paying their respects and bringing lots of food for us so I don't have to cook. The funeral comes and goes and even though we bury him, it all seems like a distant dream or a movie I seen a long time ago. I remember bits and pieces but am numb all over. Olivia comes and takes Paige out for dinner or keeps her for a couple of days here and there. Chase and Razor also stop by periodically to make sure I am okay and even try to get me to go out even for an hour.

It doesn't work. All I do is nod and stare. It is like a dead moment that is never going to end. Moments when I feel like I can't squeeze a thought out or get any words off my tongue. I suppose everyone gets like that after the loss of a loved one. Like I am in a daze not able to think or even talk. These seconds were like bubbles, just like when you can't keep them from popping and you can't store them in your pocket either.

I can't function. I can't do anything. I can't even think straight. I really don't feel anything except emptiness. It's as if I am living a bad dream repeatedly and I just can't wake up from it. During this whole ordeal, even though I know it's happening, it seems very surreal.

I don't sleep much. I don't remember the last time I cooked dinner or even watched TV.

I hardly even notice Paige is here. I decide I need to start to get back into a routine, one without Josh, as he is never coming back.

It's all a haze and doesn't seem real but I force myself to do things as a mother should. I need to get somewhat of a life back, if for no other reason than Paige. She needs me, now more than ever and I am going to be there for her.

CHAPTER 15

TWO MONTHS HAVE gone by since we buried Josh and I only now begin to live outside the fog and haze. It is the beginning of May and spring time is here. The flowers are blooming, grass is turning green and the trees are budding. All are starting a new life, something we all need to do, including me.

During this time, Chase has made his intentions well known telling me how much he likes me and would like to date me when I am ready. I make it clear to him I don't want to be with anyone else except Josh, at least not now. Although he says he understands, he still tries.

It is a beautiful Friday afternoon and I have decided to take the kids to the fair this weekend, as it is in town and we love it there. We need to become a family again and start having some fun in our lives. I pick up Paige from school and wait for Ethan to get here so we can go for the evening.

Chase has shown up and tries to get Paige to convince me to let him come with us but it doesn't work. I only want the three of us to go and surely don't want another man in my life; at least not right now. As we get ready to leave the phone rings.

I walk to the table and looking at the phone, it is a number I do not recognize. We are still waiting on the insurance money to arrive, so I pick up the receiver. "Hello." I answer.

A woman's voice is on the other end. "Mrs. Joduin, this is Ashlynn Meyers with Brandon and Winslow Attorney's office. Please hold the line."

Wondering why a lawyer is calling me, and at this hour, I wait. It isn't long before a man comes on the line. "This is Mr. Sylvain Winslow and I am one of the attorneys here at our law office."

Mr. Winslow expresses his sympathies for our loss and then assertively begins to tell me how I have no right to the kids and they should not be here with me. I sit, bewildered and shocked. It turns out that their biological mother has filed for custody to have the kids returned to her in Ohio.

"What?" I shout. "This is ridiculous. Josh has full custody of the kids and she hasn't even exercised her rights to even visit with them these past four years. How can she do this?"

It doesn't matter what I say to him, he is adamant she has every right as their biological mother and I have none. I tell him to send me the papers she filed and I will get a lawyer of my own, "She's not getting them!" I tell him.

Now I am devastated, again! Even though Josh has full custody of his kids and they have been with us for four years, now the bitch is trying to take them away. I must have sounded like a ticking time bomb. My nerves felt like they were sparking, like I'm going to explode at any moment. I swallowed back the urge to scream and scream.

"Chloe, who was that?"

I just stand here, ready to bust like a ceramic bowl being dropped onto a cement floor. Finally, I take a deep breath, look at Chase, and realizing I am still clutching the telephone receiver, I hang it up. "That was Mr. Winslow. That bitch is taking me to court to get Paige back!"

"How can she do that?"

"He tells me that when Josh died, I lost all rights to her, she was his daughter not mine."

"I don't want to go back to mom or to Ohio. She can't make me can she?"

"I don't know sweetie. I will talk to your grandma tomorrow and we will get a lawyer to see that she doesn't do this to us. I promise I will do everything I can to keep you here with me."

Ethan tries to comfort her saying that he will be with us too and will do what he can to make sure she does not go back.

We all hug for a few minutes then decide to have some fun and head out. Chase comes with us to the fair. The entire time we are there I am livid. I can't believe that things are falling apart again. I try to have fun for the kids' sake but I can tell Chase knows I am faking it. They all try to help me pick my spirits up but it doesn't really work.

When we get back home, Ethan goes back to his apartment and Paige goes to bed. Chase and I have a few drinks and talk about the phone call for a few hours. I allow Chase to stay the night but on the couch. He seems genuinely worried about me and wants to be here if I need someone.

I don't get any sleep. I lay here in our bed crying most of the time. Chase has come to my door a couple of times but I pretend to be sleeping so he will leave me alone. I don't want anyone around me right now.

The next morning I call and tell Olivia about the phone call and she helps me to retain a lawyer. Just when I think my life is starting to get back on track, something else happens and brings me right back down. I sincerely don't know if I can handle any more of this. Something has to give somewhere, and I hope it is soon before I lose my mind.

IT TAKES THREE months of back and forth interrogations, accusations and retorts from both sides before it finally goes to court. Both sides have filed the required paperwork and we wait for a court date to be set. Now it is up to the judge.

Once it is in court, we will both have the opportunity to tell our sides but it will ultimately be up to the judge as to what happens. All I can do is hope for the best. I can't believe it. First, I lose the love of my life, and now I could lose the kids. It is like a bad joke is being played on me and I hate it; but, can't stop it. The court date has been set for next week and I can't wait.

My lawyer goes over some scenarios of what we can expect and some possible results, including the one should Paige have to live with her mom. It is not a fun time but I truly hope that Harlynn gets what is coming to her. She is heartless and clearly only cares for herself and not what is best for her kids.

The week goes by very fast and court is in the morning. I am worried and scared but have to find the strength to not show it and be strong, especially for Paige. I pray that she gets to stay with me.

Not wanting to get up I force myself to get out of bed and put on a smile. The kids, Olivia and I are now getting ready to go to the court house, praying the judge lets Paige stay. Ethan is on his own and of age so the ruling can only be for her. Chase comes with us saying he wants to be there for me and the kids.

The time is here and the case is now before a judge, a female one at that. We took the entire morning each pleading both sides before her. The judge breaks for lunch.

During lunch, their mom Harlynn comes up to us to talk to the kids. "Don't worry kids, it will be over soon and you will finally be with me where you belong and away from this bitch!"

Both kids are furious at their moms' callousness. Ethan calls her names and they both tell her I am not a bitch, that I have been a better mom than she ever has or ever will be. I try to keep them calm telling them she is jealous and scared of losing them again.

Lunch is now over and the judge calls the case back in session. She acknowledges the good life the kids has had with me and affirms that it would've been bad had they been with their mom. "However," she says, "the law is the law and I have to abide by it."

I have a very bad feeling about this. I don't like how she said that. The kids are now clinging to me shaking and scared that Paige may have to move again.

"Paige Allen is to be returned to her biological mother Harlynn to live. I will give you Mrs. Allen, thirty days to do what needs to be done. By then you will have the insurance money and Paige will be at her mom's in time to start school. As of September 5th she is to be with her mom. If not, you will be in contempt and can be charged with kidnapping. I am truly sorry but the law is the law." The gavel comes down and the ruling is final.

We are all devastated and I have a sense of great loss once again. It is official, I have absolutely lost everything. Everyone that meant the most to me will soon be gone and I can't do a damn thing about it.

It is now the end of August and I finally receive the insurance money. This past month has been extremely hard for us both and Paige has threatened to run away if she is made to move back with Harlynn. She does not want to live with her mom and swears that if she is made to go, she will leave. I talk with her several times trying to explain how it is not the solution to the situation. She finally agrees that the law is the law and she knows that no matter what she does, they will always make her go back there.

I tell Paige I will always be there for her no matter where we may live. "I am only as far away as the other end of the phone. You will always have my number and you know how to message me through faceplace."

She knows and agrees and I promise her that I will stay in touch with her by texting, faceplace, messaging and Skype. All the funeral costs are finally paid off, Josh's things have been sorted and divided among the kids and I have given them their share of the left over insurance money.

It is now September 4th and Olivia offers to take Paige to Ohio to spare me more hurt and pain. I say good-bye to Paige trying not to cry and be strong for her. Once they leave and I fall to the floor and cry uncontrollably. I feel dizzy and nauseated.

It takes me two weeks before I can somewhat function. I have decided that my life is not worth living anymore. The hole created in my heart and soul when my husband died just got a whole lot bigger. It is so big that I don't think anything or anyone can ever mend it. My life is over with nothing left. I feel like I have nothing left to live for. So I devise an exit plan and begin.

As I go through my things I come across an envelope that has my name on it. On the front of the envelope it says,

"Read this when you are sad."

On the back of the envelope it says,
"To Mom from Paige"

I sit down, open up the envelope and pull out the note. It reads,

Dear mom,

I love you and admire you will all the bones in my body. I call you mom because I trust you with all my secrets. I can talk to you about anything.

I admire you because you are smart, beautiful and you take care of me even though I am not your real daughter.

I know that no matter where we are in the world, you will always be there for me.

I love you very much.
Paige

I am extremely upset now. I sit here for an hour crying reading the note over and over. I decide to sell all of my belongings except for a few sentimental things, clothing and painting items, and then leave. I purchase a back pack, put what few belongings I do have in a storage locker at the local gym and head for the beach.

When I arrive, I load the backpack with rocks and sand weighing so much it is all I can do to lift it and put it on my back. Standing here at the waters' edge, thoughts of, *Do I Live or Do I Die,* keeps running through my head. The waves are three feet tall and crashing in at a constant pace. I walk in.

I am now waist deep and all at once, the waters calm. As I walk further out, it seems like it is getting shallower rather than deeper. I realize I have walked up on a sand bar. I keep walking knowing it will drop off at any second and it will be all over. Water is still calm. From out of nowhere, a gust of wind plummets me backwards to the beginning of the sand bar.

Not knowing what happened I struggle to remain standing. As I take a step forward another gust throws me backwards to shallower water. Shaking my head and wondering what is going on I walk backwards to the beach. Just staring out across the water, I can't see anything as my eyes shift from left to right, to see what could've done that. As I get to shore the waves once again come crashing in at over three feet tall. Feeling very strange, I take off the backpack, set it down at the waters' edge and walk back to my car.

I sit here for a long while trying to make sense of what has just happened. Not being able to, I decide to get my belongings. I head back to the gym, grab my things and head to Olivia's for a week then off to Razor's apartment only seeing Chase once for an hour before he was made to leave.

I take two weeks to say good-bye to the friends we have and his family who live near us and then I head to my mom's. Not sure what I am going to do I know that even though I feel like I have nothing to live for, taking my life is not an option. After some soul searching, I decide I need to move some place where I don't know anyone and no one knows me. Take time for myself, is what I think I need.

Maybe, just maybe, if I do this, I will be able to heal and move on. I would then be out of the place where I spent my last few years with the one man I always loved is now gone forever. I do know one thing, I can't stay where these memories are because if I do, they will imprison me forever and I won't last long.

I stay at my mom's until the Christmas holidays. She convinces me to stay here until after the holidays, before I make any decisions of whether or not to stay. Although I agree it is really only for her benefit. To me, I don't care if it is Christmas or not, I am not in a celebrating mood of any kind.

I just want to hibernate and cry as I miss Josh and the kids so much it hurts. Although it has been nine months since Josh's death and almost four months since Paige was forced to move away, it is like it just happened yesterday with the pain I still feel.

THE HOLIDAYS COME and go and it is the worse I have ever spent. Although there was the traditional egg nog, singing, family get together, and lots of food and gifts, I couldn't wait for it to be over. Everyone tries to get me to laugh and have fun; and, although I smile and force a laugh here and there, it is only for show. They see light at the end of my tunnel and have even remarked on how it is nice to see me having some fun. In reality, I am dying inside and don't want to be here.

With the holidays over with, it is now Jan 8th. I tell my mom that I have decided to leave. Not clear on what I want to do with my life, I decide to visit family I haven't seen since I was a child. "I just need a change of scenery and to be around people who don't know me all that well and won't be trying to 'fix' me at every turn." I tell her.

Although she hates it, she agrees. I call my aunt and uncle and make plans to stay with them for a while. Not knowing how long I will be staying, I buy an open ended plane ticket. Only a few people will know where I am going and they have all agreed to respect my wishes and not tell anyone where I am even if asked. "If I want anyone to know where I am, I will tell them."

A couple weeks later, I say good-bye to my mom and board the plane. I am now on my way to hopefully a place where I can heal and move on with some sense of direction. The entire time I wonder if it is the right move?

CHAPTER 16

IT IS A beautiful Sunday sunny day as the plane lands in Channing Texas. The six-hour flight seemed like days as most of the trip was spent me crying and upset. Although it has been almost a year since my husband's death, it still feels like it only happened yesterday. With the loss of our children as well, I feel empty inside and alone in the world.

I still don't sleep very much and when I do all I see and hear is him or the kids. I literally relive our life over in my dreams so I try not to sleep to avoid them. The last conversation we had and the dreaded phone call continue to play over and over like a bad movie. I am hoping that a new start in a new place will help me to move past this and move on with my life. If this place can't do this for me then I will move onto another place. For now, I will give Texas a chance.

As I exit the plane and pick up my luggage from the rack, I see my cousin Eric and his wife Jasmine standing at the gate waiting for me. They greet me with open arms as I begin to cry once again. This time for two reasons: One for the life I am leaving behind and know I will never have back and the other for the one I am about to begin and whatever it might bring.

Seeing I am still extremely upset and severely heartbroken they don't ask me anything about my loss or how I am feeling. They do ask about my mom, as she is their aunt, and then proceed to tell me about where they live and what they do. They explain and point out some of the activities and events that occur here as we pass by places and things, and describe some of my family members whom I have never met but will soon enough.

As we drive across town, they tell me stories of things that happened or what they did while growing up here. We then drive down a long dirt road towards my aunt's house in Amarillo, which is where I will be staying for the next little while. For how long though only time will tell, but for now I need to work on getting better, catch up with family and try to heal.

There is a quiet lull in the car as we drive along the dirt road. Making me jump Eric speaks up.

"Chloe, living a life that matters doesn't happen by accident. Every act of integrity, compassion and sacrifice that enriches, empowers and encourages those you touch is what matters."

"I know Eric. What does that have to do with anything?"

"Well," he replies, "everything. You are feeling depressed, alone, and wondering if life is even worth living."

"How did you know that? I know I didn't tell you any of this."

"I have been there; where you are at. Just remember what I said. It will help you to get through this and I will be around too if you need me."

Jasmine interjects here. "I know that your entire life, you have given your all and done everything for everyone else making them happy and putting them first before yourself. All only to get treated badly and have these things happen to you. Of all people these things should not have happened to you."

She continues saying they are all proud of me and admires me for my bravery, courage and strength to get through what I have. I thank both of them but am still unsure of what Eric meant by what he said. It's not long after when we arrive at my aunt's house.

My aunt and uncle meet us as we pull up the driveway. Eric takes my suitcase and carry-on bag out of the trunk as Jasmine and I go into the house. They don't stay long as they have children at home waiting on their return. After a while of catching up, I go to bed. It's been a long day and I have a feeling it's going to be a long night as well.

The first week is rather quiet. I have four cousins who have wives and kids or girlfriends and none of them live that far away from the house. They have all come by to visit and catch up the past few days but otherwise it has been pretty quiet.

The second week is when I meet some of my cousins' friends and even some people my uncle works with. The quiet time is good for me because it gives me time to catch up on some sleep with the help of my aunt, who gave me some of her sleeping pills. I usually don't take pills; however, I am desperate, as I can't remember the last time I have actually slept more than two hours in one night.

They have a quaint little house. It's a three-bedroom flat with old wood floors. When you first walk in you enter in the kitchen/dining area. The table is six feet long by three-foot-wide and is only a few feet from the door. To the right is a wood stove in the corner and along the east wall is their kitchen counter with stove and sink. The fridge is at the end of this.

Across from the sink is an island counter that also acts like a breakfast nook. To the right of the table is the west wall that houses a curio cabinet and couch table. In the north-west part of the space is their living room. A half wall divides the kitchen from this room and their couch rests against this wall.

At the end of the couch against the north wall is a rocker recliner. Beside this is a fireplace with firewood stacked up beside it in the corner. The far wall is where their TV sits on a simple stand. Between the TV and the couch table is the hallway that leads to the bathroom and bedrooms. The bathroom door is on the left about half way down and the master bedroom is at the end of the hallway. There are two doors on the right wall that lead into the other bedrooms; one of which will be mine for the next little while.

There is no ceiling throughout the house, only rafters that go up to the roof. The walls are painted over paneling and their furniture looks old as the hills but still have some elegance to them. The kitchen table, chairs, coffee table and end tables are all hand made by my uncle and my oldest cousin in their shop.

The house sits on a six-acre farmland that they use as their playground. There is a wooden platform in the middle of the mud field used for announcers and bands. They have two 6-foot long two and a half-foot deep trenches they fill with water to make lots of mud and one square ten by ten-foot by three-foot deep mud basin. They use these for their mud bogging, tractor pulls and races.

Closer to the house is a smaller platform where they put stereo and karaoke equipment with a twenty by thirty-foot size grassy area for dancing and picnics. Along the far side of the house is a very large, long building that is eighty-feet long by twenty-five feet wide by sixteen-feet high. It is their shop with lots of room for vehicles to be parked or stored. It is almost like a page out of the Little House on the Prairie series but with more mud, modern things and dirt tracks.

I have been here a few weeks now and it has gone by very fast. I spend most of my time on the couch or in bed crying and not really getting much sleep. I try to do stuff like go into town with my aunt a couple times a week or feed their horses and farm animals every day. It isn't much but at least I am out of the house a little bit getting some fresh air.

As the days go by my pain lessens but it is still there. I look at their pictures every morning and every night and there are times when someone says something or a TV show comes on that reminds me of Josh or the kids, and I start all over again.

'Time wasted is time lost, lost forever never able to get them back.' says this couple during a commercial on television. It makes me think. I thought about those words so hard that as I lay on the couch, I actually fall asleep. I wake up after a little bit sitting straight up as though a light bulb has just been turned on in my head.

I decide to snap out of it and take part to try to get somewhat of a life back and stop wasting time. I have been doing a lot of soul searching these past few weeks and after a lot of talking to my guides and aunt, I have come to realize that misery loves company, and I have been living proof of that so far. Looking to my past events and what has led me to this point in my life, what I have done and how I reacted to situations, I have decided to make some changes. I am going to begin with my attitude and behaviors.

During my spiritual training at church we were once told that every outcome you experience, the result is of how you responded to that event. When you respond to a negative event in a positive way, you are for more likely to guarantee a more positive outcome.

My decision is to do just that. With every situation presented to me, I am going to think of the positive side or edge to it, consider how different responses will give me what results then do the one that gives me the desired outcome I want.

It is now Thursday afternoon. I have been here three weeks and I don't seem to be much better, even though my family says they see a difference in the short time I have been here. My Uncle Arlo tells me about the events that will be taking place in the yard this weekend and strongly encourages me to attend some of the events saying, "I feel it might help you. It will help to take your mind off things and give you something to do other than just sit and think."

He knows I love this kind of stuff and that over the past few years I have not been able to enjoy any of these things. My Aunt Cheren agrees with him and says that I need to have some fun and what better way to do it than to be with family who loves me and doing some of the things that I really enjoy. They are right.

I go to bed thinking about what is going to happen this weekend. Realizing that whether I want to be a part of it or not I will be, simply because I am here. I decide to take part and attend it like they want me to do. Who knows, maybe I will actually have some fun. Something I have not done in over a year. If nothing else, it will take my mind off my sorrows even for a little bit and gets me out of the house into the sunshine. Thinking about this, I fall asleep.

It is now Friday morning. As I wake up, I realize that last night is the first night in a year that I fell asleep thinking about something other than Josh and the kids. Thinking that maybe moving here is just what I needed. I pry myself out of bed to a lot of commotion coming from the kitchen. As I enter the kitchen I am greeted by my aunt and uncle talking with three of my cousins about the day's events and what needs to get done for the weekend. I sit and listen tentatively while I drink my coffee, I actually find myself getting excited about all of it.

After a while, I tell them I want to be a part of it to help take my mind off the past year. "Can I help get everything ready for this weekend?"

Thrilled I actually want to do more than sit, sleep or cry, they all chime in unison as if they practiced it knowing I was going to ask. "Yes of course."

They rush me to get ready before I change my mind. I take a quick shower as my aunt makes breakfast. We take it on the go as she made bacon and egg sandwiches and head out the door.

CHAPTER 17

OUR MORNING IS spent pouring tons of water into the pits to make a whole lot of mud and set up the announcing equipment on the band stand. Having fun with my cousins horsing around, I grab the bucket of water. I poise it threateningly towards Dante.

He points his finger at me. "Don't you dare. You will regret it!"

"Oh what are you gonna do cuz?"

"Try it and see."

I am standing with my back at the edge of the mud hole now and he is two feet in front of me. As if not wanting to get wet he swerves from side to side. I move with him mimicking his every action. I grab the bottom of the bucket with my other hand and with a quick thrust I toss the bucket of water soaking him from head to toe.

He screams as the water is cold. I begin to run. "You witch. I'll get you for that!" He runs after me.

"Try if you can catch me."

As I run around the mud hole I begin to slip on the mud. He lunges at me and before I know it Dante has pushed me into the mud pit. It takes me a few tries to stand up. It is so thick it sucks you in. I am coated in mud from head to toe. Dante is standing there laughing at me.

I give him this look and put my hand up so he can help me out of the thick mud. He grabs my hand to pull me up. I pull him in falling myself back into the mud. Now we are both covered and trying to get out.

Bryce then comes over laughing at us. Dante and I look at each other and as if almost on cue we both throw mud balls at Bryce pelting him with mud. Uncle Arlo hollers at us telling us to stop horsing around. He approaches us and he and Bryce help us out of the mud hole. Eric is standing close by with a hose laughing as he rinses us off to get the worse of the mud, so we can get back to work.

"Well at least you know how much more mud you need in the pit." laughing as I say it.

Dante grabs the hose from Eric's hand and sprays him and Bryce with it. Now it is me that is laughing at them and I am enjoying this. It is the most fun I have had in a very long time and reminds me of times when we were younger at our grandma's house in New York.

Being ninety degrees outside, it doesn't take us long to dry off as we work. It is now time for lunch so we stop to eat. While we are eating Uncle Arlo gives us a ten-minute lecture on how much work needs to get done in a very short time.

"Please get serious and stop with the horse play. You are not kids anymore, you are all adults. Can you at least act like it?"

We all agree still smiling at the fun we did have.

After lunch, I decide not to go back out to the fields but rather to go into town with my Aunt Cheren to buy food and supplies for the weekend. Town is about a forty-five-minute drive down a very long, windy, narrow dirt road. At the end of this dirt road is pavement, which is where the town actually begins.

We jump into 'Old Blue' as they call it. It's an old beat up navy blue, 4x4 pick-up truck with extra-large tires and a homemade extra wide truck bed. A rack sits atop the cab of the truck and it's not long before I find out why they have it there.

Our first stop is the Tractor Supply store located at the edge of town. We pick up 5 large beer kegs, 10 pullies and 25 belts for tractors, 2 large drums for ice, and 2 new winches with harnesses for pulling stuck or dead vehicles. Our next stop is right down town at Rite Aid to pick up ace bandages, ointments, splints and slings, band-aids, peroxide, alcohol and 2 small tubs that they will use to soak hands and feet.

Our last stop is at Home Depot where we pick up 6 sheets of plywood, twelve 6 foot by 4 foot planks, ten 2-foot square cement pads and 12 cinder blocks. Needless to say, we are loaded down and with the plywood and planks atop the cab rooftop; we stay cool as it helps to keep the sun off us.

On our way back and as we reach the edge of town, we stop at this small mom and pop restaurant called Carmines to order food for dinner. While we are waiting, we grab a soda and sit on the bench outside the door. It isn't long before I notice a man sitting in his truck about three parking spaces down and all he seems to be doing is sitting there watching every move we make. Not having been there very long and not knowing anyone other than my family, I have no idea who this man is.

"Aunt Cheren, do you know who that man is that is watching us? He's sitting in the red and black pick-up three spots down to our right."

She glances over. To my surprise, she doesn't know who he is either. This shocks me as she has lived here for over twenty-five years and claims to know everyone.

Ten minutes later, the waitress comes out with our food. We take it and leave hoping that it is the last we see of the creepy guy who was watching us. As we head out of town and onto the dirt road, my aunt notices in her rearview mirror that the guy is now following us. I pick up my cell phone and call my uncle. He puts me on speaker so my cousins can hear me as I describe the truck and the man driving it.

"The truck is a red and black Ford F-150 with dual wheels on the back and a rack with three lights on the top of the cab. The driver is wearing a red baseball cap with the Rangers logo on it. He has dirty blonde hair, an oval face shape, and wears dark sunglasses that seem too small for his face. He seems strong because you can see the muscles in his arms. He is wearing a white t-shirt, wife beater style. That's all we can see."

My cousin Quentin says he might know who it is but won't know for sure until he sees him. They tell us to continue as we are and not let him know we see him following us, they are on their way. He and Bryce hop into a truck and head out our way to see who this guy is. It feels creepy having someone you don't know follow you for no apparent reason.

Before long, we see my cousins racing up the road headed right for us. As we pull off towards the side of the road the guy drives past us slowly making sure that we notice him. He looks into the cab of the truck smiling and to me seems like he looks right through my aunt and is staring at me. He is so fixated that if it weren't for my aunt yelling and my cousins honking their horn, he would have hit Bryce and Quentin head on and they would have careened right into us.

Thankfully, the accident is avoided by the narrowest of margins because my aunt slammed on the brakes and my cousins swerved off the road. We sit for a minute realizing that four of the cinder blocks have slammed so hard against the cab of the truck that it broke the back window. We have pieces of glass all over us and the seat, but we are okay and no cuts anywhere. The plywood that was tied to the roof rack has also come loose and shifted forward.

My cousins rush over to us making sure we were both safe and help us adjust the wood back on the rack before racing up the road to find out who this guy is. "I will pummel him into the ground." says Quentin as they rush off.

We secure the rest of the load once again, and we drive towards home. My aunt is visibly shaken and can't drive so I am now driving. We soon pass by my cousins who have stopped the truck. As we pass them, we notice they are all talking as if they know each other. We don't stop, wondering what they are talking about and who this guy is.

It isn't long after we get home before the boys return with the creepy guy in tow behind them. I am helping my Uncle Arlo and Cousin Eric unload the back of the truck when I notice them drive in. I tell my uncle that he is the guy that was following us from town. I stand behind my uncle as they get out of their trucks and walk up to us.

When they get to our truck Quentin and Bryce introduce their friend Craig to us. My uncle is first who asks him several questions, but Craig is evasive in answering them. Then Eric pretends to bother but just long enough for a handshake then he continues unloading the truck. Then it is my turn.

When he reaches out to shake my hand I just look at him. "Some friend you are. Do you always follow women around scaring them half to death? What the hell is wrong with you?" I turn and walk over to the platform without giving him a chance to respond. I start to rake the area where the cement pads are going to be laid.

The pad is seventy-five feet away from the truck but it isn't long before Bryce and Craig walk towards me. I look up at them so they know I see them, and give them a dirty look. They are less than ten-feet away when Craig stops in his tracks. I turn my back to them and continue to rake pretending like they aren't there.

When Bryce approaches me, he explains Craig's reason for doing what he did. "Craig knows who mom is because of the pictures on my Faceplace page, but she has never met him. That is why she didn't know who he was. He said he was staring at you when you and mom were waiting outside of Carmines because you were a beauty he hadn't seen in a very long time."

I stop working and stand there with my hands folded over the handle of the rake listening to what he has left to say.

"Craig knew we were getting the field ready today and was supposed to be here at eight this morning. He was leaving Carmines to come here when he seen the two of you. He followed you here simply because he was coming here anyway. He says that when he passed you he wondered if everything was okay and that's why he was starring as he passed by."

"Then why did he not get out of his truck and introduce himself to us at Carmines? Does he not realize that he could have went to jail and charged with stalking? That was really very stupid of him." I say as I look over at Craig shaking my head.

Bryce agrees with me. "I don't know what to tell you except maybe ask him. He realizes what he did was wrong and just wants to apologize."

I agree to let him come and apologize so I can hear for myself what an idiot he really is.

As Craig approaches, I realize that he is extremely nervous. His hands are shaking and he seems to be having a hard time holding himself up. He is sweating profusely and seems to be trembling. It is 96 degrees outside so he can't be cold.

As Bryce passes him, he says he explained to me why he did what he did. With that, he leaves and walks back towards the truck to help Eric and his dad unload the cement pads, blocks, planks and the plywood.

I watch Craig as he walks up to me. He has a sculpted body, very powerful and masculine. He has on a pair of jeans that seem a little tight but show off his butt well. He has long legs and long arms to go with his athletic body style. As he approaches me, I look away hoping he doesn't notice how I am watching him.

Still leaning against my rake, he proceeds to tell me that he did a dumb ass move by not getting out of the truck and introducing himself to us, especially when he knew who my aunt was. "I am so sorry I scared you."

"Why did you just stare at me non-stop to the point where you almost killed all of us with a head on collision?"

"I really don't know. All I know is that I was mesmerized and couldn't take my eyes off you, but why I don't know."

"Well, I accept your apology. Just don't do it again, you may not be so lucky next time."

"Okay, you're right. Is there anything I can do to help?"

"That, you will have to ask the guys over there." I smile, turn and start to rake again.

By this time, Bryce and Eric are bringing the first of the cement pads to where we are. After all the pads are brought over everyone works together to get them put into place. As we work, I notice that Craig, Bryce and Eric have stopped and are talking among themselves only a few feet away. They are whispering so I can't hear what they are saying but they keep looking at me every time one of them speaks or they laugh.

Finally, I stop and look straight at them. "What is it about me that has all your tongues wagging? Do I have something on me or do I look funny?"

Eric speaks up. "No, just the opposite. Craig said that " before he could say anything else Craig pummels him in the arm and gives him a stern look.

Bryce then hops about five feet away from them finishing Eric's statement. "Craig likes you. Says you are the most beautiful woman he's ever seen." He laughs and starts running as Craig chases him.

I look at myself with a puzzled look. "Ya right. I am sure that's what he said."

My hair is in a half ass ponytail and messy, coming out of its tie. I have on a pair of daisy duke jean shorts with a three-quarter sleeveless t-shirt, both looking like rags as they have holes in them, are covered in dirt from working all day and from the mud earlier. The edges are shredding and coming apart and I am wearing work boots and work gloves, I too am covered in dirt from head to toe.

As I put my arms out I ask, "How is this beautiful?"

Craig says without hesitation, "Trust me, it's hot!" As he looks at me, realizing that it was me he said that to, he blushes and turns away hoping that I don't see him blush.

I give him a bit of a smile, and shrug my shoulders. "Whatever." I say hoping that he doesn't notice how I liked hearing that.

Knowing that someone other than family acts like a school boy around me, makes me feel alive. I don't know why but I think to myself, coming here was a good idea as maybe I do have a purpose and can start over.

CHAPTER 18

THE REST OF the afternoon goes without incident. There is a look here and there and every time I look at or go in his direction, Craig looks or turns away. It feels creepy yet flattering at the same time because I know he is watching me. I can feel his eyes glaring at me as I work. I am not sure that I can trust these feelings because I am still not over the death of my husband or the loss of the kids; however, I flirt back knowing that I still got it.

After a while, Eric joins us at the pits telling me that his dad wants to see me. I leave the guys to finish the pits and lying the pads down and I go into the shed where my uncle is.

"There you are Chloe. The track around the yard is complete and I need someone to test it out. Do you still ride motor-cross?"

I am shocked. I didn't know he even knew I rode them. "It's been almost ten years since I have ridden. Why?"

"Well I know that you used to trick ride and did quite well in your competitions. Aunt Cheren and I followed you on the internet, all your competitions are there. I was hoping that you would give it a go on Bryce's old bike and test out our track for me."

"Can I see the bike first?"

"Of course you can. I wouldn't expect you to say yes without seeing it first." He takes off the cover that is behind him.

For an older bike it seems to be in great shape. It is a little dusty from sitting for the past two years so my concern is that the motor has ceased. His bike is a 450 SX-F 2013.5 edition dirt rider. It has a 450 exhaust and a WPA er48 fork with a 40cc stroke engine. Orange iodized in color with black trim, it brands a CNC machined triple clamps with rubber damping system. The handle bars are Nekens with ODI lock on grips. It's a featherweight bike weighing in at 220 pounds giving it a top speed of 90 miles per hour. It is a beauty and I can't wait to ride it.

"Do you have the leather suit and helmet to go with it?"

"Of course we do."

This is something I loved to do and at one time, I was very good at it. It would be nice to see if I still have it or if I lost my edge. Trick riding takes a lot of stamina, strength and edge but I am willing to give it a go.

He takes out the helmet. I put it on. It fit like a glove to a hand and it feels good. "If you go inside and ask your aunt, I am sure she knows where the suit is. They should fit you because Bryce was your size the last time he rode it."

I head for the house in a sprint as I am now really excited. "Aunt Cheren, Aunt Cheren." I yell as I approach the porch.

"Whoa, calm down. Take a breath."

I stop and catch my breath.

"Now, what's the matter child?"

"Uncle Arlo wants me to ride the bike around the track and says you have the suit for me to wear."

"Yes I do. Let's see if I remember where it is. I will be right back."

After a few minutes she comes out with the suit and hands it to me. As I put it on I can hear the bike, it has started and sounds good. It isn't long before I come out dressed in full leathers. I am surprised that it fits me as well as it does.

By now, Bryce is on his way across the field toward us because he knows it is his bike that he hears. I head back to the shed. It is like I have gone back in time and am thirty-four again getting ready for my last practice run before the competition begin. I feel alive as my heart starts to pound in my chest.

Knowing how to adjust motor cross bikes, I tune it up slightly as it is revving a bit high. I put on the helmet again, and before Bryce gets to us, I am off. No one knows that it is me riding the bike except my aunt and uncle. Bryce suspects but didn't see me to know for sure.

My first run around is simply to test the bike and make sure it runs well and so I can get used to how it handles. I also check the track and review the jumps to see if I can make them or not and if any tricks can be done.

As I go around the track, the boys stop what they are working on, and stand there watching as I drive around. You can tell they are trying to figure out who I am. I practice some easy maneuvers.

I stop back at the shop and have Uncle Arlo make a few more adjustments. By now, he has told Bryce that it is me on the bike and how I used to trick ride. "Are you able to test the track and jumps?"

"Yes I think so. As long as the bike holds out it should be no problem."

Bryce has promised not to say anything to the others. "Lets' surprise them when she is done." my uncle says.

Bryce agrees and goes back to stand with Eric, Dante, Quentin and Craig.

I tell Uncle Arlo that I am going to do one circle and take the small jumps first for practice before I attack the big one. He says okay and hops on his four-wheeler. "Just in case something happens during your jumps." he says as he starts his bike and takes off.

I sit here for a moment gathering my thoughts, then I take off barreling out of the shed and speed up quickly. I have to be going at least fifty miles per hour in order to make the jumps. I hit the ball rolling and make the first two jumps without issue. I take the third jump and do some small tricks but nothing big as I am still unsure how the bike will handle.

Everyone is watching wondering whom it is riding around on Bryce's old bike and exactly what I am doing or where I am.

After doing some tricks and having made all the small jumps with ease and precision I pull up beside my uncle and tell him I am going to run the track back to the front of the house and try to take the big jump.

"I need you to sit thirty feet in front of the jump. If I can hit eighty miles an hour when I reach you then I will do the jump. If I am anything less than that I will abort."

He agrees and moves into place as I drive around stopping at the front of the house.

Aunt Cheren has now joined the guys but does not say that it is me riding the bike. Uncle Arlo asks her to stand mid-way of the other ramp and when I land to tell me where I hit. She and Quentin head that way and Bryce, Dante and Craig stand beside Uncle Arlo.

By now Quentin has figured out it is me on the bike but Dante and Craig are still in the dark. Uncle Arlo tells the guys I am going to jump this big one and if I can make it across I will go a second time doing some flips as I am in the air.

I rev the engine, release the brakes and I am off. I give it all it has to get to its top speed as quick as I can. As I get to where my uncle and the boys are, I am at a speed of eighty-four miles per hour. I decide to go for it, but before I reach the bottom, something let's go and I lose power. I turn to the left of the ramp just catching the edge of it throwing me off and flipping the bike end for end three times before it comes to a complete stop.

Everyone comes running. As Aunt Cheren and Quentin approach me first, I take off my helmet. Uncle Arlo is now here on his bike with Bryce who jumps off the back. "Oh my God, are you alright?"

"Yes, I am fine."

He helps me up. Not only is everyone in shock that it is me riding the bike but they are also questioning me to make sure I am okay.

"I am fine." I keep telling them.

"What happened?" asks Aunt Cheren.

"When I got to Uncle Arlo, I was at eighty-four miles per hour. Before I reached the bottom of the ramp something gave way and I lost power."

Bryce takes the bike from me and we all walk back to the shop.

Craig and Eric are walking on either side of me giving me the third degree. Aunt Cheren steps in. "You can all leave her alone now. She knows what she is doing."

Craig gets his back up like a lion being challenged. "If she knows what she is doing then why did she fall like that?"

"She used to trick ride in competitions all the time and won many of them. She fell because the bike failed her, not because of something she did."

"And don't forget. It's been over ten years since I have done it too!" I added.

Aunt Cheren goes into the house and brings out her laptop. She then brings some of my competitions up on u-tube for them to see. They all seem impressed, and I have to admit, so am I a little.

I sit here thinking about what I have done, what could have happened, and how I am going to do it the next time. After twenty minutes, Bryce finds the problem and announces what happened.

"A sprocket broke in half. It seems like it cracked from sitting for so long and not getting greased or oiled."

I look over at Craig. "See, that's why I fell. A broken sprocket."

"Okay. I guess it wasn't you then."

"You got that right!" I say laughing.

He and Dante change the sprocket putting on a new one then adjusts and tightens everything else. Once it is done, I agree to give it a go again.

"I will go around once doing two small jumps just to make sure. The second time around I will hit the big jump. If I make it over, then I will do a third run with tricks as I am in the air."

They all agree and head back to where they were before. I sit here again for a minute saying a small prayer. I am praying that I am able to make it this time safely.

I put the helmet back on, rev the bike, release the brakes once again and punch the gas. Off I go. The first run is easy and goes without any complications or issue. I go around the track stopping in front of the house as I did before. They all look at me and Aunt Cheren and Uncle Arlo give me the thumbs up. I give it back to them saying I am ready and away I go.

As I approach Uncle Arlo I am at eighty-five mph and I can tell they are all holding their breaths. I give it all it has and up the ramp I go. I lift off the top of it and try the layback position as I fly through the air. As the bike starts to come down, I pull myself back onto the bike and land it coming down the other side. I drive up to Aunt Cheren and she tells me that I landed about half way down the ramp.

"Perfect. Okay then I am going to try a back flip this time, maybe two if all goes well."

My aunt raises her hand into the air and moves it in a circular motion to let my uncle and the others know I am going to do it again. They nod and I drive off.

I drive around the track again only this time I don't stop in front of the house. I give it all the bike has and continue. I approach Uncle Arlo at ninety miles per hour maxed out as I hit the top of the ramp. This is the speed I need to make the flip and land.

Up I go then lift off. As I come off the top of the ramp, I throw myself backwards tugging at the bike to follow. Around I go bike and all. It takes every bit of strength I have to do the one flip. I land the bike a quarter of the way down but I make it.

"I either don't have the strength to do two back flips or the speed." I say driving up to them.

However, the bike makes it through and I am asked if I would be willing to put on a show during the day between races this weekend. I agree and bring the bike back to the shed. I put the bike away and then join the rest of them to finish the pits of mud and get the bandstand together, before it gets dark out.

All afternoon there are looks and smiles along with gestures and sexy moves between Craig and I. I really like him and is seems as though he does me as well. I flirt to see if I still have it and to determine if I am ready to move on yet.

While I am behind the band stand plugging everything in, Craig walks up to me. "There's no use us pretending we don't know what's going on here."

I get up, take a step back, raise my left eyebrow and stand up straight, like one would do if they were standing at attention in the army. "What are you talking about? There's nothing happening here except me plugging in the equipment to make sure they work."

I turn from him and begin to walk away. As I do I look at him and hope that if I ignore it, he will leave it alone.

"You call that nothing? What was that then?"

I stop and spin around. My mouth opens like I am in shock. "What was what?"

"That look, that spin, and that smile. You don't do that if there's nothing. And the flirting all day long. What was that?"

"Nothing. It's how I always turn and look at people. As for the rest of it, maybe you think it happened when it didn't."

"I don't believe you. The sultry looks you've been giving me all afternoon."

"I haven't given you any sultry looks, it's you who have been giving them to me."

"Okay so we both have. See, you're doing it right now."

"You're seeing things. Go back to work."

I step away from him. He steps closer to me and grabs both my arms with his hands. He is now inches away from me as he looks at me dead in the eyes. We stand here for a moment.

"If it was nothing then maybe I will just kiss you. See if it is nothing then."

"No you won't."

"Yes, I think I will."

Before either one of us could do anything my uncle comes around the corner of the stand. "Okay you two, enough bickering and get back to work. There's a lot to do yet and not much time before the day light is gone!"

I smile and pull away from Craig. As they begin to walk away Craig looks back at me and I turn to finish what I was doing. He yells back to me, "I will kiss you Chloe. It's only a matter of time. Then we will see."

My uncle pulls him along as I shake my head even though I have a smile from ear to ear. *'It might be nice to be kissed by someone other than family'* I think to myself. It's been so long since I have been kissed, held or loved. I almost forget what it is like or how good it can feel.

It is now six p.m. and Aunt Cheren tells us dinner is ready. We stop and go to the picnic area just off the side of the porch to eat. My aunt has Craig sitting beside me at the table but Bryce, seeing how uncomfortable I am sits there in my place leaving me to sit between my aunt and Dante.

At first, I think it is better but as I sit down, I realize it is not. Rather than sitting beside Craig, I now have to eat my dinner with him directly in front of me. During dinner every time I take a bite or move there he is, watching me.

I eat as fast as I can without getting sick then excuse myself and go inside the house. As I enter the kitchen, I notice the calendar hanging on the wall. I see that it is Feb 12th, and then it hits me. One year ago today is when I got the call telling me my husband was killed. I begin to freak out.

I spent today having fun and enjoying myself and not giving him or the kids a second thought and here it is, the first anniversary date of his death. *How low can I get?* – I think to myself and begin to feel depressed and sad all over again.

Now I feel selfish and upset at myself for doing this. I slump to the floor with my back against the cupboards, put my head in my hands and begin to cry. Uncle Arlo comes in. "What's wrong Chloe?"

I point to the calendar. "See what today is?"

"Okay, what is today for you?"

"It is the one year anniversary date of the death of Josh. Of all days, how could I have fun and enjoy myself without even thinking about him?"

He stands me up and puts his arms around me. "You know, it is okay to have fun. Just because you didn't think about him doesn't mean you didn't love him or you don't miss him."

"I know but I feel guilty for having fun without him and not even think about him."

"You shouldn't feel guilty for having fun no matter what today is."

He hugs me.

"I know but I can't help it." I look up and realize that Aunt Cheren, Bryce and Craig are standing at the door. "If it's okay with you, the boys can help you pick up the tools and put the equipment away? I want to take a shower and head to bed."

"Of course it's okay. Are you going to be alright?"

"Ya I will be fine. I just need some time and rest. Thanks Uncle Arlo."

"You are quite welcome sweetie." He then turns and pushes everyone out the door.

The look on their faces says it all. They are worried about me and for some reason, it seems like Craig seems more worried than the rest of them. When they return to the table, my uncle tells them what is wrong and that I am going to take a shower and settle down for the night.

At first, I just sit at the kitchen counter trying to calm myself down and going over in my head the events of the day feeling guilty over the fact that I had fun. It feels like I am being dishonest or unfaithful to my husband. Even though I know this is not the case because he died a year ago, I still can't help but feel this way.

I can hear them talking outside. At one point Eric asks Craig if he is okay. "Ya I am fine. I hate seeing her upset like that and I know all too well how it feels. I wish I could do something for her."

"Why are you worried about her? You only just met her today. You don't even know her. It makes no sense!"

"Shut up Quentin and mind your own business." Craig replies.

"Okay. That's enough the both of you. We have enough going on around here without the two of you fighting over Chloe." my aunt yells.

As I am self-doubting and putting myself down, I can hear Craig asking them questions. They answer them vaguely but then my aunt tells him what has happened to me during my life.

I really hope she doesn't go into detail; I really don't want him to know everything. To my surprise they all do like it is nothing, so I sit and listen to what they tell him.

CHAPTER 19

AUNT CHEREN TELLS him the life I had with Josh, what I went through a year ago when he died and how I couldn't move on where I was. She tells him she didn't know how long I would be staying here for but it is up to me.

"I only hope that by being here, she can heal and get over her losses so she can move on with her life. Whether it means she lives here or somewhere else." She finishes.

Dante, who has been sitting quietly, not saying a word decided to pipe up. "I've been talking to her family and found out some things she has gone through prior to Josh. This past year was rough for her, we know this. But, her dad said she's been through hell for the past quite a few years. He said if she is having fun, it is the first time in a very long time she has had any kind and it is good to hear that she is."

"What exactly has she gone through that was so bad? I can't imagine anything being so bad that you can't have any fun." asks Craig.

They all nod their heads. Dante answers, "You wouldn't think so but it was for her. According to her dad, it's been at least 20 years."

Eric says he is worried about me and wants to spend the night. Quentin asks, "What are you worried about?"

"Chloe you dumbass! Are you forgetting that I went through something similar a few years back? If this is the first time she has enjoyed herself even a little bit and most of the time all we did was work, she is going to experience feelings of guilt, frustration and god knows what else. It's going to hit her hard and I don't think she should be by herself."

"Chloe won't be alone Eric! We are here."

"I know mom. But, of all of us here, Craig and I are the only ones who have experienced something similar and can relate. Only the two of us can help her get through this and after today, I don't think Craig is the one she will want to see when she wakes up screaming after the nightmares. I don't think she would be comfortable talking to him about what she is feeling."

"Although I do agree with you Eric, she may not want to talk to anyone about her feelings. She may not be ready to do that yet either."

"Yes dad, I know you are right but even if she isn't, just having someone there if she wakes up screaming that understands, will help. You know that's what got me through it."

Craig decides it's his turn to say something. "Do any of you realize there could be a bigger issue here?"

"And what is that?"

"Well Dante, the fact that Chloe realized today marked one year since her husband's death. That alone is devastating and with everything else, it could be bad, very bad!."

"Just how bad could it be Craig?"

"Trust me Dante, I have been there. I lost my wife and youngest son six years ago to a car crash. She was the love of my life and I truly believed there would never be anyone else for me. When she died, a big piece of me died too and if it weren't for my other two kids, I may have taken my own life just to be with her. So I know what can happen."

"Okay, Okay." says Uncle Arlo. "Calm down everyone. We haven't seen Chloe in over thirty years and of all our nieces and nephews, she is clearly our favorite."

"Ya we agree dad. She is our favorite cousin. She is always trying to help us and talk to us even though she wasn't here. None of her sisters or brother did that, for any of us." says Bryce.

"Chloe is a very strong, smart, witty woman, who got somewhere in life and only got to where she is at because of her two exes prior to Josh." adds aunt Cheren.

"Two?" Craig questions.

"Yes." says uncle Arlo. "Her first husband got it in his head when he married her that she became his property. He did things to her that no woman should ever have to go through. He beat her and raped her and when that wasn't enough had his friends do it to her too, while he watched. She got away somehow and almost died. This couple found her in a snow bank and took her to the hospital. The doctor said if she was there ten more minutes, she may not have made it. To this day no one really knows what she went through or exactly what happened for how long except her."

"And that was the second time she was left for dead. The first time was in high school from what her sister told me years back." adds Eric.

"What happened then?"

"I think that is something she needs to tell you when she is ready."

"Anyway, her second husband," uncle Arlo continues, "became an alcoholic a few years after their son was born and did absolutely nothing. Chloe worked, took care of the house, brought up their son, did everything with him and helped with after school activities like coach his bowling and volleyball teams, etc. While he stayed home and drank."

"And then he did things to her for many years." says Bryce. "And when he couldn't get anywhere with her anymore, he tried with their son. The lawyer said she suffered every type of abuse known to mankind – financial, spousal, adultery, physical, sexual, mental, battery. It was so bad, Chloe miscarried her daughter before having Dylan. Then having her only surviving child, try to commit suicide and having to put him into the hospital for two weeks because of him. That should've buried her then, but she got through it and moved on."

Craig is quiet. It's as though he is in shock. Quentin pipes in again.

"Her dad, our uncle Ken, told me that no one in Dylan's class knew his dad was alive until his grade eight graduation when Uncle Ken made him go. The kids all thought that Chloe had a boyfriend not realizing it was Dylan's dad."

"Two years prior to that," adds Aunt Cheren, "she lost her job of sixteen years. She was making almost $90,000 a year, had two vehicles one fully paid the other only had six months to go and they only had just over a year left on the house before it was theirs. After she lost her job she got a lawyer and after she won her case, she received almost $50,000."

Craig just sits there listening to everything just shaking his head in disbelief.

"To top it all off," Bryce says, "he blew it all on drugs and alcohol after telling her she shouldn't take a trip so they could pay bills. It was shortly after that, she found out it was because of her husband that she lost her job. Then the bit with her son took the cake and she left him. Two years later she found her late husband and, well you sort of know that story."

There's a quiet lull. Thinking they are done, I decide to take my shower. I've heard enough to know they are laying it all on the line and I am shocked they all know so much. As I am washing, I can hear muffles so I know they have started talking again but I can't understand what they are saying at this point.

Craig sits there for a minute. "Wow, and she's here. She survived all that and the only thing that is bothering her, or at least so it seems, is the loss of her recent husband. I don't get how she would even want to look at another man after all that. She must be a very strong woman!"

Dante decides to chime in now. "Although I was too young to remember her when we were younger; I have heard of these stories and often wondered if they were true. When I found out that they were, I decided that if she could survive all that, so could I."

"Chloe has been through more than most people." says Bryce. "I really don't know how she can be as happy as she is or is even able to look at any man. And how she was today, well, that's the Chloe I remember from when we were kids. Happy and fun to be around."

"When she was in grade ten, she was raped by four guys and left for dead. She would have died then if those people had not found her when they did!" remarks Quentin.

"There is no doubt she is strong. Most of us would have taken our own lives and none of us would ever trust another man again." Bryce adds.

"We don't know how she does it, but she pushes on and doesn't use her experiences against every man." says Uncle Arlo.

I have finished my shower and am in my room, when I hear them come in. Both Craig and Eric have decided to stay. Craig will take the couch and Eric will be in the spare room next to the one I am staying in. Bryce, Quentin and Dante all said good night and go home. Everyone else comes in and goes to bed for the night. Little do they all know, I am still awake and heard most of the discussion they all had.

All I can do is lie here quietly wondering why they would tell a stranger, at least a stranger to me, my life story. Most importantly, why is Craig so interested? Although I am still very upset and heart broke over my husband and the situation, I still feel guilty.

Today is the first day in a very long time that, even though it was only for a short time, I had fun. During this fun time, I actually forgot and didn't think about Josh, the kids or what happened. This makes me feel worse and the water works start again. After a while of lying here, holding the pictures of my late husband and the kids and crying, I fall asleep.

I wake up several times during the night. At one time I woke up, crying and sobbing. It must have been louder than I thought because before long, Eric comes in. "Are you okay?" He asks as he sits on the edge of my bed.

"Yes. I just had a bad dream, like I do every night." I say as I sit up giving him some room.

"Can I ask what it was about?"

"Usually I relive the last words we said, the phone call I got and how Paige was taken from me. Tonight was different. It was like he is taunting me for not thinking about him. At one point he even asked me how I could have fun without him. It was horrible."

He tries to comfort me by telling me some of the things he went through when his late wife passed away a few years ago. After a few minutes, Craig is standing in the door way listening so we motion him to come in and join us. He closes the door and he and Eric take turns telling me what they had gone through and how they coped and got through it. I knew Eric lost his wife to cancer a few years ago but I didn't know Craig lost his wife of ten years and youngest son to a car crash six years ago.

After a couple of hours pass, I thank them and ask them to leave so we can all try to get some sleep. "You both have a big day tomorrow and I don't want to be the reason you can't be a part of the day's events."

They both agree. Eric leaves and as Craig gets to the door her turns to me. "If you want me to stay in here with you I can."

"No, I will be fine. But thank you."

They both leave closing the door behind them and I finally fall back asleep.

My sleeping patterns are beginning to change since I have been here. I am falling asleep faster sometimes with no aids and am sleeping sounder and longer with the nightmares being less often. My appetite seems to be coming back and I actually have interest in spending time with others. I don't want to spend most of my time sleeping or crying and actually feel a little better.

Although I am happy about this, and it must show, I am still skeptical but hopeful that it is permanent and will only get better from here. I really hope it is not temporary and I end up back where I was, I am not sure I can handle that.

My life isn't perfect, and never has been, far from it. I have lost all that I loved. I certainly have been lacking love, sex and friendship but I don't want to go backwards. The road may be longer and harder than I had hoped for but I want something different. I need to be happy and I will do what it takes and keep working towards it.

CHAPTER 20

AFTER A VERY long night and not getting much sleep, I did sleep somewhat because I wake up the next morning to loud noises outside the house. I roll onto my back slowly opening my eyes to the new day. There was no need to check the clock to tell me the hour. I knew my aunt and uncle were getting up at 5 a.m. and the noises heard tells me it is around 7 a.m.

My hair is a mess and I am only wearing my green baby doll pajamas. The pajamas were really a short nightgown with spaghetti string straps and low cut in the back. As I sit on the edge of the bed I hear a knock at my door.

"Are you up?"

"Yes Aunt Cheren, I am up. I will be out in a second."

"Okay great, we will be outside."

"Okay, see you there."

Not even thinking about how I am dressed, I open the door and go into the kitchen to pour myself a cup of coffee. I step onto the front porch to see what all the noise is. It is just after 7 a.m. and I know that the mud bogging contest and tractor pulls aren't supposed to start until 12:30 that afternoon.

To my surprise there are quite a few people here already unloading their tractors and suiting up their trucks. Some are still driving in with their oversized pick-up trucks sporting really large, about three-quarter monster truck size, tires.

It is at this time that I realize what I am wearing. I turn and start towards the door of the house. As I open the door, I hear, "Good morning sunshine."

I turn my head to see it is Craig. He is getting out of one of the trucks that has just pulled in. I give him a smile and a nod and I walk into the house. As the door closes, I turn around and watch him as he leaps off the bottom step of his truck to the ground. Before I realize it, he is standing on the other side of the screen door looking at me and all I can do is watch him.

He smiles at me. "May I come in?" I open the door to let him in.

I walk to the counter and pour myself another cup of coffee. Before I can put the pot back on the hot plate I feel Craig as he brushes up next to me and grabs the pot touching my hand with his as he does this. Feeling myself blush, I turn my head and move to the other counter.

He pours himself a cup of coffee as I sit at the bar. He turns, leans against the counter and smiles. A couple of seconds pass, although it seems like an hour. "I am very sorry about yesterday. I didn't mean to scare you or put you and your aunt through that ordeal. I wasn't thinking and I hope you can forgive me."

"Yes, it's already forgotten."

"I am also sorry for what you have been through and are still going through. I know what it's like to lose someone so if you need anyone to talk to, I will be here all weekend."

"Thank you."

"Will you be joining us outside at the events this weekend?"

Not wanting him to know that I am because I want to watch him, I say, "I don't know yet but right now I am going to take a shower." I stand up and smile at him. He smiles back and I leave the kitchen to go into my bedroom.

I fall onto the bed to cool down. Every time I am around him, I get flushed, light headed and nervous. As I get up to get some clothes out, I hear him doing something in the kitchen. Although I am curious and want to look, I choose not to and I head into the bathroom. I turn the shower on to take my shower, a semi-cold one at that.

As I wet my hair, I am thinking of Craig and what he looked like yesterday digging the holes with Eric for the tractor pulls. With my eyes closed, I shampoo my hair and rinse it letting the shampoo run down my back pretending like it's his hand slowly caressing every inch of it. As I soap up my body and wash myself everywhere, I find myself still thinking about Craig.

How he looks in tight jeans and the way he moved when he got out of his truck. I stop, open my eyes, and say to myself *'get a grip woman; you're not supposed to be thinking of him, especially in that way.'* I finish my shower doing everything I can to not think about Craig, especially in that way.

I get out of the shower and now that I have dried off, I get dressed. Knowing that I love mud bogging, tractor pulls and racing of any kind, I decide to put on my cut off jean shorts with a thin cotton sleeveless top that has a bra built in. I love this shirt because I don't have to worry about my bra straps falling at every turn. I slide on the work boots my uncle gave me to wear while out there, so I don't ruin my running shoes and grab another coffee from the kitchen before heading out the door.

It is a beautiful sunny Saturday morning. Despite all the noises of the hustle and bustle from the people, vehicles and equipment, you can hear the birds singing and chirping, the cows mooing in the distance, a flock of geese flying overhead, and there is a slight breeze.

There were many smells in the air as well. Rotten eggs coming from the creek running behind the barn, fresh water smell mixing with the sand in the pits, fresh cut grass from the fields across the street, dust as it rises from the road when the trucks come rushing in, and the coffee being brewed on the porch. I stand here with my eyes closed for a moment to take it all in. It is so relaxing to me and I miss it. I open my eyes and venture off the porch to walk around, talk to who is here and see how things are coming along.

I stop and chat quick little tidbit stuff with family members and friends I have already met. Craig is nowhere to be seen. I feel relieved yet I wonder where he is; I even ask myself if he left because of me. As I cross the yard towards the stage where my uncle is setting up, Eric starts on a flying run towards me as fast as he can. I can see him out of the corner of my eye. As I turn my head to look at him, it seems like he is not going to slow down anytime soon. He is running way too fast, as he begins to slip and slide along the mud. He looks like one of those dolls on a string that can't stand without a tug here and there. It is quite comical.

As he gets closer, I don't have time to move out of the way so I brace myself for impact. He slows down a bit but not enough to stop. He slides across the mud patch in front of me and takes me out, wiping my feet right out from underneath me, laying me on my back.

With the wind knocked out of me and seeing white spots wherever I look, I can't tell if I am hurt or not. For what seems like an hour, I can't see or hear anyone and wonder what has happened. Everything is muffled and fuzzy. Then, from out of nowhere I feel hands on my arms and someone cradling my head.

All at once I hear voices, many all at the same time. Then my vision clears and I can now see Eric, Uncle Arlo, Aunt Cheren, a few other people standing around me. I ask them to speak one at a time so I can understand what they are saying. I hear Craig's voice but can't see him. As I start to tilt my head back to see if he is the person holding my head, he stops me and tells me not to move. I can't understand what all the fuss is about. I remember Eric sliding into me but didn't think anything came of it.

"What is your name?"

"Uncle Arlo, it's me Chloe. What's wrong with you?"

"Nothing is wrong with me.", he says. "I am making sure you are alright. You fell when Eric slid into you and hit your head pretty hard."

"Well, now I know why my head is pounding."

Craig then asks, "Does anything else hurt?"

Before I can answer, Eric starts apologizing left and right. "I am so sorry Chloe, I did not mean to hurt you."

"It's no big deal Eric. I am alright. Accidents happen." I look up at him then add, "my turn next time." and then smile.

Aunt Cheren asks me to move only what she tells me to move when she tells me to and if anything hurts or if I have a hard time to do it, say so. She starts with my toes and feet, then my legs. Then I move my fingers, hands, and arms. Craig lets go of my head and asks me to move it very slowly to the left. As I do, I feel a very strong sharp pain from the top of my head to the base of my neck. I stop and tell them this. Before I can do anything else, Craig holds my head and tells me not to move. That is when I hear the sirens, an Ambulance is here.

As the paramedics begin to check me out, I notice that Craig is walking away as if his job is done and he has other things to do. After a few minutes of them checking me out, they have me sit up very slowly. I can now move without the sharp shooting pain, only some stiffness.

"She doesn't show any signs of whiplash or concussion." the paramedic says, "but I would take her to the hospital for x-rays on her neck just to make sure there isn't a hairline fracture. If she is stubborn like the rest of you and doesn't want to go, then I suggest you put a neck brace on her and watch her for the next few hours. If she has no pain and shows no signs like slurred speech, loss of balance, sight or hearing problems, etc. then she should be fine." They then leave.

Bryce and Eric walk me over to the porch and help me sit in the couch swing. As Eric goes inside to get the neck brace, Craig walks over and sits down beside me and Bryce stands on the steps. Craig seems like he is about to cry. "Are you sure you are okay?" he keeps asking me.

"Yes, I am fine! Quite asking me that!"

"I am sorry. I just want to make sure you are okay. Jesus, I just want to kill Eric for hurting you like that."

"Don't do that. It's not as if he did it on purpose. Besides, it reminds me of our childhood years at our grandmother's house. Things like this happened all the time. In an hour I will be fine."

Just then Eric comes outside with the neck brace agreeing with me. "Craig, that it is true; we always did these things when we were younger. "Bream's are resilient."

I am adamant I am not putting that thing on because there was no need. My neck is only stiff now, and as long as I move slowly when I turn my head, I am fine. Craig is more adamant than me that I wear it.

"I will wear it but only for as long as it takes for me to drink my next two cups of coffee. Then it will come off and I will join y'all."

Craig agrees with this, as he puts the brace on my neck. Bryce is on the porch making sure that I am alright. Craig nods then asks Bryce to get me a large cup of coffee. When he comes back out, he makes Eric and Bryce promise that between the three of them they will check on me often over the next hour or so to make sure I have coffee and am okay. They all agree and then leave to get their trucks and tractors ready.

However, Craig does not do this lightly. He makes it quite clear that he is not happy leaving me here but I will not allow him to stay with me when he has things to do. He steps off the porch and heads to his truck looking back at me several times as he does.

CHAPTER 21

OVER THE NEXT hour I drink three cups of coffee and it is starting to take its' toll. Every time someone would come over to me, they would take my cup and warm it up with fresh coffee. It feels like I have been sitting here for almost two hours.

Aunt Cheren came to get some things for my uncle. She sits with me for a few minutes. "If you need to pee then go. I will stop them."

She lets me go to the bathroom. When I return she helps me take the brace off my neck. I am starting to sweat really bad and my neck is beginning to feel worse as it stiffens from not moving it.

"Promise me you will move slowly and stay here until one of the boys comes over to help you?"

"I promise. I won't do anything to make it worse."

"Okay. Well I have to take these to your uncle. Be good."

"Yes Aunt Cheren. I will."

I feel like an invalid or a child who can't do anything unless an adult is with me. I haven't been able to move or do anything without someone watching me. As I sit here, I am beginning to get annoyed. People who don't know me gawk as they walk by and those who do say hi as they pass. At least with the neck brace off I can rub my neck.

As I do, I slowly move my head. I do it so slowly that it seems to take forever just to move from one side to the other. After doing this a few times I try to stretch my neck – that hurt so I will not do that again for a while.

I am getting so that I can move my head without any pain or stiffness, so I stand up and stretch. As I do, Craig comes around the corner. "What the hell are you doing?"

I turn and look at him. "Moving around before I can't move at all."

"Oh my god! Please be careful!" He grabs me as if I am just learning how to walk.

"Let go of me, I am fine and I can do this all by myself. I am not a child!"

"I know you're not a child. Trust me I see it."

"Then stop treating me like one. And for your information I have already been inside twice going to the bathroom by myself; and I did just fine. I'm still here, alive and kicking!"

"Okay, okay. You win. Will you walk with me to the fence where the side-by-side mud bog races are going to take place? They are about to start soon and your uncle told me that you love them."

"Yes, that I will do."

I take his one hand and he carries a lawn chair over for me in his other hand. It's been a long time since I've held anyone's hand for any reason, and it feels good. It feels really good. I squeeze his hand as we walk. He squeezes back and looks at me with a smile. I smile back at him.

I find a spot at the center of the wood fence and lean against it putting my right foot on the first rung. He leaves and many of the women nearby surround me to watch as well, most of whom I have no clue who they are or whom they came here with.

There are a total of fourteen trucks entered into this race. The first heat is between Eric driving Blue Brute and Hunter in Black Stallion. Mud begins to fly as they make their way through the track and digging holes and ruts into the strip. After a few bumps and jumps and Hunter almost flipping on his side, they cross the finish line and Eric is declared the winner.

The next heat is Dante in Yellow Hornet racing against Red Lips driven by Zeke. They follow suit as Eric and Hunter did and Zeke is declared the winner. There are two more heats with Carmine in White Wonder racing against Flynn driving the Striped Zebra. Then it's Darby with Black Bandit against Bob in Grey Goose. Carmine and Darby win their respective races. One race after another only deepens the ruts and makes some good sized holes that the remaining drivers have to now conquer.

It is halfway through the competition and is now Craig's turn. Driving the Green Bomb, he is racing Jacob in the Bucking Bronco. As they get up to the third line to wait their turn, Craig hops out of his truck and runs to me. First, he makes sure that I am alright and when I tell him I am fine, he gives me his hat to wear and asks for a kiss, says it's for good luck. I kiss him on the cheek; he goes back to his truck and pulls up just in time to take his turn.

Mud is flying everywhere and by now, the mud hole is a huge mess. There were five heats before him and there are ruts all over. Some of the trucks have fallen onto their side and had to be pulled or dragged out. Others have gotten stuck and it made the mud hole even worse. However, even with all these obstacles, Craig wins his first heat.

All the single girls around me are cheering for him clapping, screaming his name and drooling over him. You would think they were teenagers at a pep rally rather than adult females in their 30's and 40's. As he drives his truck around the back side of us, as the others did, I notice these women turn as he drove watching his every move. Each one of them has a smile from ear to ear and is acting like teenage school girls competing against each other to get the same man to notice them. He jumps down out of his truck and they all melt. It is very comical to watch.

He walks towards us. I am standing behind these women but can't help myself; I catch myself chuckling at all of them. My aunt is now standing beside me. "Look at all of these women acting like girls drooling over the one man they will never have."

I look at her with a smile and we both chuckle.

As he walks through the crowd of women who has now gathered tightly between him and me hoping he will choose one of them, moaning, groaning, and prodding in anticipation, he pushes his way through. "Hello ladies." he says with a smile.

They moan in disbelief that he just walks past all of them rejecting them without a second thought. They are in even more turmoil when he walks up to me.

As he approaches, he reaches out and takes his hat off my head. "Thank you beautiful for keeping it safe for me." He then put his arms around me as I put mine around him. He leans in and gives me a peck on the lips. It is quick yet my heart pounds, my hands sweat and I begin to tremble. "Are you alright?" he asks as he looks towards me.

"Yes, I am fine. Just a little tired and have a slight headache but otherwise I feel good."

He turns around and we begin to walk back through the crowd towards the house with his arm around me.

About five feet away from the women, one of them yells, "Why her Craig? What's wrong with one of us?"

We stop. He looks at me. "Excuse me one moment please." He then turns to face them. "Look at her and look at you. She is beautiful, smart, and full of hopes and dreams. She has a strong will and can do what she wants without any man. Every one of you is only looking for a man who will care for you and give you everything you want without you so much as lifting a finger. Y'all want sugar daddies, something she does not need or want."

He turns back to me and puts his arm back around me. We start back towards the porch. I look back over my shoulder towards the women, smile, wink and then turn back with a smile on my face.

It actually felt good to be the 'one' for a change. Usually I am one of the women standing there wondering what she has that I don't. Now I am the one they are asking that question about and it feels really good.

As we are walking back we can hear the remaining trucks race against each other as Bryce in Orange Julius and Otto driving the Brown Beast are declared the winners of their race against Cortez and Hugh. As we get to the porch, he sits me on the swing and says he will be right back.

After a few minutes, he comes out with a sandwich, glass of milk and some aspirin. We sit and eat lunch before it is time for him to race again. We walk back to his truck so he can get ready to race again. "Do you feel good enough to ride with me for this next race?"

"Yes. I would love to."

We walk around the front of his truck and he opens the passenger door helping me into it. It's quite high and I have to pull myself up just to stand on the bottom step. The look on the women's faces when I get into his truck is priceless. All their smiles turn to jaw dropping awes. He walks around the front of the truck, puts his hand on his door, opens it and stands on the first step.

He stops, looks over to the other women, tips his hat and comments, "This is the all American woman that any man would love to have and one day I hope to call her mine." He winks at them, smiles and gets in the truck.

I look at him. "Why did you say that?"

"Well its true and look at them, they were jealous before. Imagine what this will do to them and how they will treat you from now on."

"Yeah, I guess so."

"Well then, let's go." With a chuckle and smile he starts his engine and off we go.

We drive into place in line which put us fourth pitted against Zeke as the others fall in behind. My heart is once again pounding really hard but this time for a completely different reason. It is the thrill, anticipation and anxiety of the action that is about to take place.

As I look over at Craig, he is looking at me with this bewildered look on his face. "What's wrong?" I ask.

"Nothing, just a little worried about you."

"Don't be, I am fine."

As we inch up to the next place in line putting us now second he says he is worried this will hurt me after what has happened this morning and I still have the motor cross show to do. "The doctor said you had to take it easy for a few hours and I'm afraid the bouncing and jerking will do more harm than good to you."

"I will be fine. Don't worry. If it hurts too bad after the bike show will wait until tomorrow." I look at him and smile. "Just do what you gotta do and win this race!"

It is now his turn and we are at the start line. He smiles and punches the gas just as the whistle blows. It is like nothing I have ever experienced before. Slipping and sliding from side to side as the truck bores down in the mud. Ruts as deep as the tires are high, drivers trying to avoid them to stay on top and keep from getting buried. We are being jostled about tossed all over the cab of the truck.

Looking out the windows all you can see is mud flying everywhere. As for the other truck, it is nowhere to be seen, at least not from where I am. Mud has coated the windows and the wipers are at full blast so Craig can see just enough to get through the maze. What seems like an hour only took two minutes to complete and next I know we are flying through the air. The last drive to the finish line brought us up an incline from the ruts. It threw us into the air at least six feet before we come crashing down, across the finish line.

CHAPTER 22

WHAT AN AMAZING experience, adrenaline rush to say the least and a ride like no other. It is very different from racing and flying through the air on a motor cross bike. Craig wins the second heat, which puts him in the running for the final race. There will be one more race before the final and if Craig wins that one, he will be in the finals against the other winner.

As he pulls around to get his truck rinsed off before the next heat, I look over and seen that there was another reason why I couldn't see the other truck we were racing against. What I thought was because of the amount of mud flying around was really because he rolled over into one of the ruts and couldn't get out.

We have some time before Craig's next race so he parks the truck and comes around to help me out. As I climb out, all the women who stood with me earlier cursing me because Craig came to me and not them, all gave me high fives and slaps on the back for winning the race. No matter what I said or how I told them it was Craig that raced not me and I was only there for the ride, didn't change anything.

All I know is that Craig was right and they are treating me differently. All because they think that I belong to Craig. As far as I am concerned I belong to no one, even if we were married I am still my own person; but these women don't think the same way I do so, I let it be.

Uncle Arlo comes up to us. "Are you ready to do the show? There is an hour before the next race begins so it is the perfect time."

"Yes. I guess I am as ready as I will ever be."

"Your cousins are grooming the track now."

"Okay great." I reply happy that it will be somewhat smooth after the trucks tore it all up.

"Is your neck too sore? Craig asks.

"No actually I think all the bumps and being tossed about in the truck helped to loosen it."

I have to admit, although I am not sore, I am feeling a little nervous, but I go inside the house and put on the suit as Craig does a once over on the bike to make sure everything is tight and working properly.

As I am getting ready, I hear Eric announce over the microphone. "We have a special treat for y'all today. If everyone can please find a spot in the grass somewhere and get ready for a spectacular show."

Well I don't think I am spectacular but I am going to do my best and give it my all to give them a good show. I decide that because of the accident this morning I won't push my luck so I won't be doing the big jump. Today I will stick to the small jumps doing tricks such as laybacks, twists, jumping over obstacles that Bryce and Dante have strategically placed here and there, acrobatic maneuvers, wheelies and burnouts. All things I know I won't get hurt doing, you know, the really easy stuff.

I head out to the shed to get the bike. I stand here for a moment and realize that I am thinking about Josh but not in the way I usually do. I actually ask him why we never did anything like this. We both loved this kind of stuff and I didn't understand why we never did this. Choosing to let it go, I get on the bike and kick start it. I rev the bike, let go of the brakes and come flying out of the shed.

As promised, I deliver what is the best show I have ever done. As I race up and down the track jumping tires and holes and climbing small hills jumping across others, everyone claps and you can hear the ooohs and aaahhs. When I am finished, everyone gives me a standing ovation. Not wanting anyone to know it is me yet, I ride the bike back into the shed and close the doors before getting out of my gear.

My heart is pounding, I am sweating and my legs and arms are shaking but I feel alive. I am exhilarated and hyped. It was a blast and I enjoyed doing it as much as everyone enjoyed watching it. I take my gear off as Craig walks in congratulating me on a show well done. "How are you feeling? Any pain?"

"No. I actually feel really good, alive."

"Good. I am happy to hear that!" He gives me a kiss. It is a longer kiss than before right on the lips. Even though it takes me by surprise, I welcome it and kiss him back.

"So?" he asks.

"So, what?"

"Is it still nothing?"

Forgetting about our conversation from yesterday, it took me a minute before I replied. "I guess we will have to see."

Craig smiles and walks with me to the house so I can help my aunt get dinner ready before he goes back to the barn to do last minute adjustments to his truck. After the last heat of mud bog racing it will be dinner time and after dinner, the first tractor pull competitions will begin. The day is more than half over and there are still lots of excitement to come. Throughout the afternoon everyone keeps asking each other who the bike rider was but no one is saying.

There are fifteen people in the kitchen, more people than the room can handle. I find my aunt by the stove so I walk up to her and tell her I will be outside getting the tables together, making more coffee and tea, filling up the punch bowls and making sure that the coolers are filled with beer and ice. I tell her to call me when things are ready to be put onto the tables and I will help to bring them out.

Usually I do this by myself but before I know it, several women who were in the kitchen with their children have come out. The kids go off playing in the sandbox just off the porch while the women help me get things ready.

As we are getting things together and on the table, the women start talking to me as though we have known each other for years. Because I only know Jasmine, I ask them for their names and whom they are with. It only takes a half an hour to get everything ready. Tables are set, food is out, drinks are filled and ready, and everyone is already walking across the field towards us.

Set up like a smorgasbord everyone simply grabs a plate and walks around the table grabbing what they want and sitting their children and families to eat. I go inside the house and make my plate from the food that is left in the kitchen. I sit down on the sofa to relax and enjoy my dinner in peace when the door opens.

It is Craig and Aunt Cheren. Both are concerned that I am hurting. "Everything okay sweetie?" my aunt asks

"Everything is fine. I just want some peace and quiet while I eat my dinner."

They both make their plates and sit with me. My cousins Eric and Bryce come in with their wives shortly thereafter and sit with us. Before I know it, the house is filled with people again all looking to get an answer to the one question that everyone wants to ask, *Were Craig and I an item*.

I don't really answer because only my family and Craig know what I am going through and they all know that I'm not ready for a relationship yet. Craig looks at me. "Is it okay to tell them?"

"No." I tell him. "I don't see a need for everyone to know and I sure as hell don't want everyone to feel sympathy or sorry for me just because."

"Okay baby, I won't say anything then."

Just then, Uncle Arlo walks in. "Will you all leave them alone and let them have some peace. Chloe is here to get through some things that have happened to her recently in her life. We are here to help her and Craig is a part of that. Right now it is all family and friends just trying to help someone get through a difficult time."

Bryce then speaks up. "We need to get this weekend back up and running so let's get to the racing. Dinner is over and what happens between Chloe and Craig or anyone else for that matter is their business and only theirs."

"Let's race!" Eric says.

Almost everyone leaves and goes back outside running and racing to their trucks and tractors. I stay behind to help Aunt Cheren, Jasmine and Selena clean up the mess from dinner. We decide to make it easy and put lids and foil over the food but keep it out in case someone gets hungry later. This way they can pick at it. The deserts that need to be kept cold are put back into the fridge but everything else is left on the tables. We restock all the drinks and coolers before heading to the stage area to see how everyone is doing in the races.

Jasmine and I stick together and we talk during the two hours we are putting stuff away. She asks me some personal questions about my life and what I have gone through before coming here. After a bit of a discussion, she then asks me a question that I really have to think about.

"If Josh and Craig were both standing right here in front of you and you were told you had to choose one, who would you pick?"

I am silent as I ponder her question. Looking at her with a blank stare she asks me again who I would choose. "I really don't know." I reply.

"I think you do. You said you have always matched everyone to the love you and Josh shared."

"Yes, that is true, I have."

"Well, how does Craig measure up to Josh?"

We are now walking slowly towards the fields. I am quiet, not sure what to say. She stops when we are about half way to the field, grabs my arm and steps in front of me so she is looking at me face to face. "Well? Does Craig measure up to Josh or not?"

"No. I think it is the other way around."

"Okay, what do you mean the other way around?"

"Well, I am not sure. When I was around Josh I got the butterflies in the stomach, sweaty palms, blank mind and the constant urge that I needed to be around him especially when he wasn't with me."

"Okay and is it the same way when you are around Craig?"

"Yes but no, with Craig it is different. I have those same feelings but stronger."

"Okay how? In what way are they stronger?"

"Well, I think about him all the time. I wonder what he is doing and how he is. If I know he is around somewhere, I try to find him just so I can see him. I also feel weak in the knees almost like I won't be able to stay standing and my stomach gets so tied up in knots sometimes that it feels like I am going to be sick. I want to be around him all the time, whether he is with me or not."

"Well, I agree. Those feeling are stronger."

"Then last night happened. Even though he was here on the couch, it tore me up."

"Why what happened?"

"Well you know Eric stayed and why?"

"Yes, he called and told me."

"Well, Craig stayed as well. Eric was in the spare room and Craig slept on the couch. During the night I woke up from one of my bad dreams again and both came in and sat with me for a while."

"Okay I knew that too. Eric told me this morning when I got here."

"Well, before leaving the room, Craig asked me if I wanted him to stay with me. I said no but I really wanted him to."

"So how did it make you feel to say no and have him leave when that wasn't what you really wanted?"

"Sad I guess. I wanted him to stay and be beside me. Even if it was just to lie there with me as we slept. I wanted to know what it would be like to be kissed and held by him. I wanted it really bad. It was so bad that I almost let it slip out."

"Did you feel anything like this with Josh?"

"No. Not really. I mean we were kids in the beginning and didn't know what sex was yet."

"True but you hadn't seen each other for years and then met back up. Surely if you said the feelings you had for him 30 years prior were still there, these feelings would have been too?"

"Now that you say that, you would think so but they weren't. I wanted to be with him and when he said he was moving to be with me, I was excited. But, if he hadn't of moved there, I would have probably just gone back to my motel and then back home ready to continue my life as it was. Things would have definately turned out different."

We begin to walk towards the pits again. "And if Craig was to turn and walk away from you and you thought it would be the last time you saw him, what would you do?"

"Probably stop him and at least tell him how I feel."

"I think you know your answer. You know what you want. You just have to admit it, tell Craig and let Josh go. I know it will be hard but I don't think it will be as hard as you think it will be."

We are now at the pits and I thank her for listening and talking to me about this. She hugs me and whispers in my ear, "You are welcome. We will talk more later." I thank her again and she heads off to sit with her family.

Craig and Denver are the two who will be racing in the semi-final mud bog race tomorrow afternoon. Two heats of tractor pulls have already been completed and the third and last one for the night is about to get under way.

It is dusk now and the sun is going down creating a beautiful sunset in the west sky. Beautiful array of red, orange and yellow as dark skies invaded the day. Over to the south of the field you can hear the roars of chain saws and the crackling of the wood as trees fall to the ground. Some of the men are cutting firewood for the bonfire while the children are running around with sparklers and women are holding onto bags of marshmallows for the campfire.

I excuse myself and head back to the house. I am starting to get a headache, most likely because my neck is feeling a bit stiff and it is having twinges. I want to take something for it so I can enjoy part of the night, as I love campfires.

Who could resist the crackling of the wood and the bright yellow, gold and white lights of the fire dancing against the dark sky. The smell of burning wood and roasting marshmallows. The songs of children singing their campfire songs learned in scouts or brownies. The stories told by some of the adults of their lives and ghost stories. Playing of musical instruments and singing of songs by everyone while enjoying their favorite drinks. That is the life.

As I get into the bathroom and reach the medicine cabinet to get some Advil. I take note of myself in the mirror. As I stand here looking at myself I begin to cry. All at once, it hits me. I have been all day enjoying myself once again and having fun and not once do I think of or even miss my late husband.

An intense feeling of guilt and remorse come over me like a wave crashing and engulfing me all at once. I can't breathe. It snuck up on me from out of nowhere. I didn't see it coming and didn't notice it was happening. All I can now think of is *'how could I have fun and enjoy myself without him?'* What I once thought could never happen, has. And it just proved me wrong. I have very mixed feelings over it.

Ivory comes running in saying she has to go pee really, really bad. She is only nine so I let her use the bathroom and I go into my bedroom. Within minutes, I hear her mom Jasmine come in to make sure she is okay. When Ivory comes out I hear her tell her mom that I was in the bathroom when she first came in and I was crying. Her mom asks her if she upset me and she said no I was already crying when she came in. Jasmine tells her that it is okay, I will be fine, and they left.

What am I going to do now?

CHAPTER 23

I LAY ON my stomach looking at the photo of my late husband and our kids crying. I have been feeling a bit emotional since the death of my husband and the loss of the kids. Wondering if I am ever going to get over it, I hear a knock on my door.

"Who is it?"

"It's Craig and Eric. Can we come in?"

"Yes, it's not locked."

They come in closing the door behind them. They want to know if I am alright noticing that I have been crying.

"I am okay I think. I mean, I am not hurt or anything. At least not physically."

Asking me what's wrong, I tell them how I am feeling guilty and why. Eric says he went through the same thing and totally understands how I am feeling. "It took me almost two years to get over those feelings but I don't think it will take you that long."

"Why not?"

"Because. You are already showing signs of being able to let go a lot sooner than I did. And that is a good thing. Trust me."

Just then, Uncle Arlo calls for Eric. He looks at me and says, "Craig can help you more, will you be okay?"

After I tell him I will be fine, he leaves.

I am propped up on my arms and have laid the picture upside down on the bed. Craig moves to sit beside me and picks up the picture. "You had a beautiful family." He says as sets it back on the side table.

I half smile at him but don't say a word. He faces me and as he does, he leans over me putting one arm on either side of me. Looking at me face to face, we are almost nose to nose. "I understand what you are going through and how you feel."

"No, I don't think you do." I say as I lay completely on my back turning my head to face the window.

He turns my head back so that I am looking at him. "Yes, I think I do. I told you last night a bit about my late wife and son. I have an idea how you are feeling. For me to help you I need to know what it is that you are feeling. Can you tell me?"

He wipes away the tears that have run down my face. "I don't know if I can."

"Please try. I know when I was going through my loss, I didn't get better until I started talking about it. Maybe it will do the same for you."

"Well, I guess I am confused. I am happy but sad. I also feel guilty and even though I know why, I know that it makes no sense and shouldn't be."

He sits up but still faces me. "Was it something I said or did that made you feel this way?"

"No. Not really. Well, maybe. I just don't know." Now I sit up, Indian style facing him.

"Okay, that needs explanation. It makes no sense what you just said."

"I will try but you have to promise not to get mad or upset. Some of this may come out the wrong way but, when I am done you will hopefully understand."

"Okay. I won't say anything and will listen to everything you say until you are done. I promise."

Even though I don't really know him, something tells me to trust him. He did show compassion and proved he cared about me today with what happened. And that is more than most men in my life up 'til now have shown me. I decide to tell him.

"Well as I said, yesterday was the first day in a year that I actually had fun and today was no different. I didn't even think about my late husband, our kids or that life. This is because of you mostly. This morning's accident and having to deal with that, was Eric's fault so to speak, but the rest was you."

He nods. "I know I said I wouldn't say anything but I have to ask, how was it me?"

At least I know he is listening which is a switch for me. All men I have been with never listened and Josh only pretended to listen to half of what I said.

"You were the one who was with me, stayed with me, cared for me, etc. You didn't give me time to think about anything else except the fun activities that were happening and keeping me going."

As I am talking I notice the expressions on his face. They go from happy to confused, to smirking to sad and then all over again. Yet he keeps his promise and doesn't say a word. So, I continue.

"This is not a bad thing, it is a good thing. It wasn't until I came in to get some aspirin for my headache and looked at myself in the mirror that I realized just how I was feeling. At that point, I was happy. Then it hit me like a ton of bricks, I hadn't thought about them all day long. Not once. Again, for the second day in a row, I got scared then felt guilty and sad."

I pause. Craig is looking at me; he hasn't taken his eyes off me the entire time. He takes my hands in his. "I know I said I wouldn't say anything until you were done but, why were you scared, guilty and sad all at once?"

This is a first for me, a man who not only listens but asks questions and is seemingly interested in what I have to say and how I am feeling.

"Well I am scared because, I didn't think I would ever be able to feel happiness again, especially this quick, yet here I was. That makes me feel guilty because I didn't think of them at all and I should have. Guilty because it's almost like I am cheating on him even though I haven't done anything. Just the fact that I had fun without him I guess did that."

"I know it's hard but that's a good thing. Don't you think?"

"I guess but it made me sad because I realized he wasn't here and will never be again. I am also sad and upset with myself because I am feeling this way."

I begin to cry again. I really didn't want him to see me cry but I can't hold them back. He puts his arms around me and pulls me close. "It's okay baby. Let it out. You need to let go of all of it so that you can move on. You are doing really well and I am proud of you for being able to have fun like you say you did. It means you are mending and healing."

I push away from him. I look at him face to face. "I'm not crying because I'm upset over what I just said or because I'm still feeling sad. I am crying because I am feeling guilty over what I am feeling."

He looks at me with a bewildered look cocking his head to one side. "Now I am confused again. Why are you feeling guilty over how you feel?"

Not sure how to say it I utter, "Well, I don't know if I can say it or if I should. I am not sure if what I am feeling right this minute is because of the situation or if it is truly real. It seems that on instinct you know what I need and you show me the love and support I need without hesitation."

It seems he knows what I am trying to say. He puts a smile on his face, and cups my face with his hands. "Let me be blunt if you will." he says.

"Sure why not. I always say honesty and being up front is best."

"When I said earlier to the other girls that one day I hope to call you mine I truly meant it. There is something I have wanted to say to you since yesterday but it seemed too soon. However, with the way you are talking right now, I feel like maybe it is time."

I pull away from him, remove my hands from his, and am now feeling somewhat scared and anxious. I have a feeling I know what he is going to say but am not sure if I'm ready for this.

I guess ready or not he was going to say it so I got a grip, sat up and braced myself.

CHAPTER 24

HE JUST SITS here for a minute holding my hands. I can tell he is nervous, his hands are shaking. He takes a breath and looks into my eyes.

"From the moment I first saw you there was something that drew me to you. I couldn't keep my eyes off you. It's as if you were mesmerizing, a beauty I have never seen before. You were different. At first I wasn't sure if it was infatuation simply because you were a new person in our small town or something else. Then I met you."

Now I am shaking and I really didn't know why. Am I shaking because I'm nervous? Excited? Worried? Choosing not to tell him how I feel, he continues.

"It was here as you know, when I came to you and apologized for scaring you and your aunt. I was so nervous I was shaking. I had only done that once before in my entire life and that was with my wife, whom you know I lost a few years ago as well."

I smile because at least I know that he understands what I was trying to say and where I was coming from; because, he is in the same boat.

This truly is different for me. I have never met a man that was so upfront and forthright about his feelings without having to be coaxed into it. Even my late husband, although talked about his feelings, did not do it so openly and freely, it had to be coaxed or warranted.

Now there is this man, sitting right here in front of me, talking to me, open about his feelings as if it is second nature and without a care in the world of what I might think or feel about it. It is different but definitely a good feeling.

"Anyway, just watching you yesterday and listening to you and everyone talk around the dinner table, made me realize just how I felt about you. Then when you went to take your shower and your family told me stories about you and what you had gone through in your life, it made me feel it all that much more."

Knowing most of what they had told him, I shrug my shoulders and lower my head looking down at my hands. He puts his fingers under my chin and lifts my head to look at him. My eyes have tears starting to fill them but he continues.

"You are a very strong woman who has survived a lot of turmoil, unhappiness and abuse in your life. I have never met a woman as strong as you. To go through all that and still have a good outlook on life, make things of yourself and not even hold a grudge against men. That's more than most men or women would or could do. Then today happened."

Bewildered I tried to think of the events that took place today and what could have possibly happened that did something to him, so I ask, "What happened today?"

"When you got hurt this morning I was really scared. My heart stopped pounding and all I could think about was you and losing you. Your Uncle Arlo said that when it happened I said aloud as we were running over to you, God please don't take her. You just brought her to me. Please let us have time to see where it can go. Now I don't remember saying that out loud but I do know I was thinking it. When the ambulance arrived and they checked you out and said you were going to be fine, I was happy. Remember when I left shortly after that and walked away?"

"Yes actually, I remember asking myself why you were walking away? I didn't know if it was because you didn't care other than the fact that I was alright and went back to finish what you were doing or if you were so mad at Eric that you walked away before hitting him."

"None of them was the reason. I walked away because I didn't want anyone to see me cry. I was so grateful that you were okay that I couldn't contain it and I didn't want anyone to see it. Little did I know that Eric and your aunt seen me but didn't say anything until later when I was by myself. They asked why I was crying and I told them it was because I was so happy you were alright that I just couldn't stop it."

I am to say the least shocked. I had no idea that he walked away because he felt like that.

He stops for a moment, let's go of my hands and takes a drink of water from the bottle he carried in with him. As he does, another knock is heard at my door.

"Who is it?" I ask.

"Bryce. I need to know if Craig is going to take part in the last tractor pull race, today?"

I look at Craig and tell him he should go. He replies. "No Bryce. I am in the middle of a story to Chloe trying to make her feel better so she will be able to enjoy the bonfire tonight with us."

"Okay, no problem. I will put that you lost the second race. It will still put in the first race tomorrow."

Craig thanks him and Bryce leaves. Craig turn back to me.

"Why didn't you go and race? I am okay and we could have continued this later."

"No, if I stop now I may not be able to say what I want to say or get up my nerve to tell you what I am leading up to tell you. I am sorry that it's taking so long to get there but please bear with me, I am almost done."

"It's okay. It's not like I don't have time. I am not going anywhere."

Leaning in, giving me a quick kiss, and very gently caressing the side of my face with his hand. He mutters, "I kept you busy and stayed with you all day long because I wanted to know for myself that you were going to be alright and safe, or not okay if that was the case. Thank god you were okay because if you weren't, well lets' just say I didn't want to think about that or depend on anyone else telling me. Anyway, there is a reason that I have done all of this. It's not just because I like you or care about you."

He stops, takes a deep breath, and looks deep into my eyes. "Okay. So what is the other reason?' I ask insistently.

"I am just going to say this."

He hesitates. As he does, I sit here on pins and needles. I am quite sure I know what he is going to say. I am not sure I am ready to hear it and don't know if it will make me cry or not. I am also not sure if he does say it, how he will react if I can't say it back. Not knowing exactly I sit here and wait.

All at once he blurts out, "I am in love with you and have been since the first moment I laid eyes on you."

He stops, lets' go of my hands and turns away from me. Okay so now he said it. I'm not sure what to say or feel. I am not sure how it makes me feel.

Before I can reply he says, "There I said it. I don't expect you to say it back or even feel the same thing for me but I feel that you need to know."

He stands up as though he is going to leave. I grab his hand and sit him back down. Looking at him in the eyes he looks back at me. The tears are starting to fill my eyes again and I can tell he is extremely nervous. "Where are you going?" I ask him.

"I figured I said what I had to say, so I thought I would leave and let you think about what I said. Besides, I don't want to say anything else that will embarrass me."

"I don't see why you are embarrassed. Being honest is always the way to be. At least that's how I am."

This time I lean in and kiss him as the tears roll down my face. "Why are you crying? Did I say something wrong or to upset you?" he asks.

"No. I am crying because I am happy. I have never had a man tell me that before and so quickly. It's always been me who says it first."

"So how do you feel about what I said? Really?"

"Well, I am not a hundred percent sure. I am glad you told me because I have been wanting to tell you all afternoon."

"So you're saying you are in love with me too?"

"Yes. At least I think so. Even though I feel it and want to say it, I don't think I can."

He lunges towards me and wraps his arms around me giving me a bear hug. It is so hard I have to push him away because I can't breathe he is hugging me so hard. "You don't have to say anything else."

"Yes I think I do." He is now looking at me with his arms around my waist and sitting so close you can't get a piece of paper between us.

"Okay so I guess it is your turn."

"Well maybe. You should know that I do feel the same way about you. I have to find out for myself if these feelings are real or if they are only because of the situation, like a rebound thing."

"Do you know how you are going to figure that out?"

"I think I already have with the help of Jasmine earlier tonight."

"Can I ask what was said or how she helped you?"

"Later. I think we have said a lot already and I need to process some of it and figure out what I am going to do from here. Besides everyone will be wondering where we are and if we don't go out there, they will be in here."

We sit here for a few minutes just holding each other not saying a word. Then he says, "It is good enough for me. I won't push it. You will say it when you are ready."

He excuses himself and goes into the bathroom. I pull myself together; change my clothes from the shorts and sleeveless t-shirt and sandals to jeans, a long sleeve shirt and running shoes. As I open my door to go into the kitchen and wait for Craig, he is already standing there waiting for me. He smiles.

"Are you ready my dear?"

"Yes I am." I say with a smile.

He puts his arm around me and we walk outside. He picks up a lounge lawn chair off the porch to take with us to the fire pit as we join the others. We find a spot to sit as Ivory, Jasmine, Eric, Bryce, Aunt Cheren and Uncle Arlo comes up to us asking if everything is okay.

"We are fine." Craig says.

Smiling I add, "I had a bit of a breakdown and needed to sort out some feelings I had about today. Craig helped me to do that."

We both apologized for taking so long. They tell us not to worry about it, as long as we are good, that's all that matters.

Craig sets up the lounge chair, sits down and has me sit in front of him between his legs, so to speak. The fire is high, hot and dancing around like a wild dance on stage. It is beautiful and relaxing. As the children roast marshmallows with the help of their parents, some of the others play their guitars and banjoes.

The stage isn't far from the fire pit and a few of the men start to gather on the stage. One of the guys plays the drums while a couple others are on their guitars. They begin to play country music, fitting for where we are. After a couple of songs Bryce walks up on the stage and picks up the microphone.

"Everyone listen up. Tonight we are all in luck. We have someone here with us tonight who was on American Idol. She made it through the first four stages and only missed being on TV by one person. Let's see if we can get her up here."

Well no one knew who he was talking about except for me, or so I thought. I am shocked, as I had no idea any of my family here knew I was on American idol let alone that I could sing. I sit up away from Craig a bit and shake my head no. Craig sits up and turns my head to face him. "Is he talking about you?"

I nod my head. "I don't feel like singing though. Not right now."

He tells me not to worry, gets up, and walks to the stage.

"Well, well. Either he's going to tell me she isn't going to come up and he will sing in her place or he is going to help me get her up here." Bryce remarks as he laughs.

Craig walks up onto the stage, takes the microphone from Bryce's hand and to my astonishment says, "Well I guess we all learn something new every day."

He pauses and looks at me with a smile. "Little did I know that the person I would fall in love with can sing. Chloe, you need to sing for us."

I sit here speechless. I thought he was going up there to tell them I wasn't in the right frame of mind or I didn't want to or something like that. I didn't know that he would be on Bryce's side and try to get me to go sing. I shake my head no and don't move.

Everyone claps and in unison chants my name. Bryce and Craig keep saying over the microphone, "Come on Chloe, let us hear you sing."

After a few times Craig says, "Baby it is really good therapy and we would love to hear you."

After a few minutes and with great reluctance I stand up. "Okay, only because everyone else here wants me to."

I walk up to the stage. When I take the microphone from Craig's hand, I make it clear to both of them that I'm not happy about this and tell them they will pay for this. Bryce hugs me, Craig gives me a kiss on the cheek and they both jump off the stage smiling from ear to ear as they walk back to their chairs.

"What would you like to hear?" I ask humbly. There are so many shouts at the same time that I can't make heads or tails of anything anyone is saying. Turning to the make shift band I ask them what they know how to play. Country music is best for them. After a few minutes of determining what to sing, we decide to play the songs that got me onto American Idol. They all know the songs and can play them well.

"Okay. This first song is the one I sang in my audition to American Idol which got me four yeses across the board to go onto the next stage."

The band begins to play – Man I Feel Like a Woman. I sing and dance across the stage moving like I did for the audition. The song is only two and half minutes long and when I am done everyone is clapping, whistling and screaming. I am now sweating and have noticed that the kids and a couple of the moms have gotten up dancing as I sing. Craig along with some of my family members who had no idea that I could sing, just sits there in awe, their jaws dropped to their chest.

"Are you ready for another one?" I ask. A resounding YES is yelled out by everyone. "This next song is the one that almost got me to the finals and on TV."

The band starts to play as I sing 'From This Moment'. I can see Craig, who seems captivated, as I sing it like it was sung for him. To be honest, it kind of is. As I sing, I am feeling the love and without even realizing it, Craig is who I look at mostly while I am singing the song.

Many couples are up dancing and those who are single or have their spouse up on stage with me, sit singing along with us. Some people including Craig actually have tears running down their faces. This song is a touching one for many people and it is evident here tonight. As I finish the song, I am wiping tears from my eyes too; however, they are tears of joy, love and happiness as it is for most people who cry at this song.

I then shout out, "One more for the night. This one is a very special song for me and I know that it is moving for many people for many different reasons. Its' power will grip you like no other and might even leave you reaching for your loved ones."

I look at the band and tell them to play Amazing Grace. They do saying they love this song as well as they begin to play. As I sing it, I cry, I always do. Whether it's me or anyone else singing it, I am always brought to tears. For me this song is always sung at funerals and even though it hasn't been all that many during my lifetime, the ones I have attended, were for those who were very close to me.

I wipe away the tears as I sing the song. I notice as well, that there is not a dry eye in the house either. The children are all asking their parents why they are crying only to be hushed. This song did as I said it would, it gripped and almost everyone held their loved ones in their arms. I finish the song, wipe my tears away, say thank you and then step down off the stage.

As I begin to walk back to Craig, I notice everyone is standing and even though they are all in tears, they are clapping. Jasmine comes up to me and hugs me really tight saying it was the best she has ever heard anyone sing that song. Others walk up to me doing the same thing. One after another they say it was the most beautiful thing they have ever heard.

As I approach Craig, he is standing there with arms open, and crying. I also notice that the band still hasn't begun to play any other songs. Before I can ask him if he is alright, he gives me the longest hardest hug I ever got in my life. After a few moments, I pull away.

I know I struck a nerve as it is an emotional song, but it is unintentional. After a few minutes, he calms down as do the others. "Are you okay?" I ask him.

"Yes. I am fine. I am in awe of the voice you have and how well you sing. I, like most here have never heard anyone sing like that unless they are a professional. I can see why you made it as far as you did on American idol."

"Thank you."

"Did you take any singing lessons as a kid?"

"No. My sister Rose and I were born with the talent to sing, neither of us ever took one lesson."

"I am very proud of you but I need to ask, am I is still going to pay for getting you up there?"

"Absolutely!" I reply laughing.

We sit back down on the lounge chair and I lay back into him as close as I can get putting my hands in his and wrapping his arms around me as tight as I can. I close my eyes and try to settle down, as I lay my head back into his shoulder so we are almost cheek to cheek. I always get hyped up on adrenaline when I sing and it takes a while to calm down.

As I sit here, Craig talks to everyone around us, holds me tight and even whispers in my ear here and there. I feel safe and at peace, something I have not felt in over two years.

As I take in the sounds of the night, crackling of the fire, children running and singing, musical instruments being played, people talking and even some singing and laughing, I feel someone sit on the end of our lounge chair. I open my eyes to see Bryce sitting here looking at me in dismay.

"Chloe, you said Amazing Grace is a very special song for you. Can I ask why it moves you like it does and how you sing it so well?"

"When I sing any song, it is from the heart. Before singing any song, I think of how it has or is impacting on my life. By putting a personal touch to it, I am able to sing it. As for why it moves me like it does, well," I hesitate for a moment and sit up.

I move closer to him, take his hands in mine. "That song always brings two people to mind for me and I remember how my life was when they were here and how I am empty since they have passed away."

"Who are they? Do I know them?"

Not sure how he will handle who they are I ask him a question first. "Do you think of anyone when you hear that song Bryce?"

He puts his head down and murmurs, "Yes!" and begins to cry.

I put my arms around him and whisper, "It's okay cuz. Grandma is one of them I think about with that song and I miss her a lot too."

We both sit holding onto each other for a few minutes crying. He then pulls away. "Who is the other person?"

"Linda, my dad's wife, her and I were really close. I thought of her as my mom for over 15

years. I was with her when she died."

"How do you get over it?"

"You don't. I still miss them every day. They helped me through so many things in my life that I most likely would not be where I am today without either of them."

I pause for a moment and Craig is now behind me with his chin on my shoulder and his arms around me.

"Bryce, you are going to think I am crazy but, having people around you, who love you, and understand the same type of loss as you, helps a lot."

He looks at me. "But you didn't have anyone around you to help or support you when it happened, either time."

"You're right I didn't. I had to be strong for everyone else. My dad, my brother, my son and her sister."

"How did you do it alone?"

"It wasn't easy and it took a while but I finally found something that allows me to talk to them when I miss them and if I need help with something, they are still here helping me."

"That's not possible is it?"

"Yes it is. The only way to explain it to you is to give you an example of how."

"Like what?"

"Well, yesterday, for example, I had a hard time dealing with some things around Josh's passing, the anniversary date, my feelings, etc. I laid on my bed and aloud I asked grandma to help me get through this. I told her the feelings I was having for Craig and how I beat myself up because of my feelings that I still have for Josh and how it all makes me feel. I asked her to help me with these feelings so I know if the ones for Craig are real like they were for Josh or if they are situational."

"Okay, so what did you ask her and how?"

"I asked her to bring me someone within 24 hours that would help me figure it out."

"Does that really work?"

"Yes but in order to get help and answers, you have to be willing to do some of the work yourself."

"Well, I have heard people do that all the time but I always think they are crazy because it seems like they are talking to themselves."

"Not always. They are usually asking for help with a problem or situation they have found themselves in and need help with. For it to work you have to ask for something specific so you know what the answer is.

For example, after asking grandma to bring me someone within 24 hours I said that if it didn't happen by tomorrow night then I would know that it is situational."

"And did it happen?"

"Yes. Earlier today, while Jasmine and I were doing the dishes she started asking me questions. They were somewhat personal but made me look deep within myself for answers. She then asked me something that made me realize just what my feelings for Craig are. So you see, I got my answer and in under the 24 hours."

"I am not sure if I believe that!"

"Well you don't have to. Not many people do. I don't know why or how it works exactly but it does. All I can say is try it. It can't hurt and the worst that will happen is nothing which means you are where you are now. What have you got to lose?"

"Okay so if I go home tonight and ask grandma or whoever to help me and give a specific time frame, it will happen?"

"It might. I can't say for sure but it won't hurt. If you don't want anyone to hear you then go into the bathroom or go outside and sit for a minute."

"Okay. I guess I can do that. I will try it tonight."

He gives me a hug thanking me and then returns to his girlfriend.

Craig and I sit back when he asks me what it was that Jasmine asked me.

"First she asked me how you stacked up to Josh then she asked if I had both you and Josh standing in front of me and I had to choose one of you, which one would I pick and why?"

"What were your answers?"

"You have to wait. I will tell you but not here, not now."

"Okay so when? How long do I have to wait?"

"Don't worry I want to tell you the entire conversation I had with her and what my responses were to everything she asked. But later though, okay?"

"Okay but please don't make me wait too long? I am curious and really want to know what you said."

"I won't. I want to tell you when we are alone and won't be interrupted."

He nods his head in agreement, sits back against the chair, pulls me into him and puts his arms around me. Feeling safe again, I lay back into him wrapped in his arms. I can now relax, or at least I hope.

CHAPTER 25

THE NEXT COUPLE of hours everyone sings campfire songs for the kids and tells ghost stories. I sit here in Craig's arms feeling warm, comfortable, safe and at peace. It is a feeling that I have not felt in a few years and it is a very nice feeling. I don't want it to end but I know it has too.

It is now almost midnight and I am getting very tired. I tell Craig I am going to bed and ask him to walk me to the house. I say goodnight to everyone and tell Bryce that I want to know what the result is if he tries what I suggested. We walk to the house.

"Would you like me to stay the night with you tonight?"

I am a little hesitant because I don't know what he is hoping will happen if he stays. "If you want to and if it is okay with Aunt Cheren and Uncle Arlo."

"Okay, once we are in the house I will ask them."

"If you do I will tell you the conversation I had with Jasmine earlier."

"Okay deal!"

"Before you ask them I have to make one thing clear though. If you do, there won't be any sex because I am not ready for that."

"Don't worry baby." he says, "I only want to stay to help you, support you and make sure you get some sleep. Sex is the furthest from my mind and not the reason I want to stay."

We are now inside the house. I go in to the bathroom while he gets on his phone. I'm not sure if he is calling someone at his home to tell them he won't be there tonight or if he's calling my uncle. I am a little nervous about him staying with me but I do feel at ease and comfortable when he is with me.

When I come out, he says that he talked to my uncle. "He said that Eric is staying in the spare room tonight. He also said it was alright for me to stay either on the couch or with you, whichever you wanted."

"Okay well then that's settled." I open my bedroom door and walk in. I notice he didn't follow me so I turn around. "Are you coming?"

"Yes. I wasn't sure if you wanted me in here or not."

"Of course I do. I already told you I would tell you my conversation with Jasmine. I can't do that if you're not in here with me now can I?"

"No I guess you can't. Your uncle also told me one other thing."

"What was that?"

"He said, if I hurt you in any way, he will personally hang me up by my heels and beat me with a whip in the barn."

I laugh. It sounded funny to me but I know what he meant. He excuses himself and goes into the bathroom. While he is in there, I pull down the covers. I get changed into my baby doll pj's. The same ones he saw me in this morning when I was on the porch.

It's not long before he comes back in. Closing the door behind him he says, "I will sleep on top of the blankets while you sleep under them if you want."

"It's okay, you can get in with me if you want. I trust you."

"Okay as long as you are sure."

I nod in agreement. He gets undressed keeping his underwear and undershirt on and climbs in. I snuggle up to him and he puts his arms around me.

After a few minutes of lying here, I rub my neck with my left hand. Realizing that it is stiff and a bit sore he asks me to lie on my stomach and he will massage it for a while. He lies on his side and begins to massage my neck, the upper part of my back and down my shoulders. We lay here for a bit talking. He does everything to make sure I am comfortable.

He then leans into my ear and whispers, "We are alone now. Let's stop dancing around the issue. I want to know about the conversation you had with Jasmine today. I need to know what you told her."

I smile at him. "Is it bugging you that much?"

"Yes."

Laughing I tell him I would. I roll onto my back so I am facing him then tell him what happened and what was said.

"At first Jasmine asked me a bunch of questions about myself like when I was younger and high school, etc. She then wanted me to tell her how Josh and I met. I told her the story of how we met in grade school and became the best of friends. Then, we became boyfriend and girlfriend until grade ten when he moved away. I told her how I measured every other man up to the love we shared and they all failed. That is when I settled for Dylan's dad."

"Okay what else? I know there's more." he says like a child in a candy store waiting for the clerk to bag up the candy he is buying.

I tell him in detail, the conversation she and I had after that and the questions she had asked me. I pause for a moment and roll onto my side. We are now facing each other on our sides and he is smiling.

"Okay I sort of remember the questions you said earlier. What were your answers?"

"Well, like I said earlier, first she asked me how you measured up to Josh."

"Right, so how do I measure up to Josh?"

"You don't. He measures up to you and that's what I said to Jasmine."

"Okay, I'm not sure what you mean by that."

"She didn't either but it's simple. It wasn't until things she pointed out and the questions she asked that made me realize it."

Craig is now smiling even more. "Really?"

"That is when she asked me the other question. If I had both you and Josh in front of me and had to choose only one of you, which one would I pick."

"Yes that I know. Quit keeping me in suspense will you."

"Okay, Okay. I told her what my feelings were, the same way I told you earlier. She then asked me the question again because I really didn't answer her at first, simply because I didn't know how to answer her."

He looks at me with a questionable look. I roll onto my side and he takes his right arm laying it across my waist so his hand is holding my lower back.

"Well?" he asks. "So what did you tell her after that?"

"Well, that is when I told her everything. I told her that the way I feel about you is nothing like I have ever felt with anyone else. Yes, when I was with Josh or watched him I got the butterflies in my stomach, sweating palms, weak at the knees kind of stuff but it's different with you. I told her that when I see you it is mesmerizing. I get lost in your aura. Watching you get out of your truck this morning and jumping off the last ladder to the ground made my heart stop."

"Okay so what did she say then?"

"She said that I knew my answer but didn't want to acknowledge it. She said that I didn't want to see it because I might not be ready for it. I then told her that all I wanted to do was run to you, tell you that I love you and never let go. With Josh, I felt like that but it took me a while to feel it and the feelings inside were not as strong. With you, it's as if my entire insides are on fire ready to crumble. It's like loving you is all I am here for, its' all I want to do."

He is just staring at me now. I stop talking wondering if I should continue or if I am scaring him off. I found myself running my hands up and down his arm and chest so I stop and pull my hand back. "Why did you stop?"

"I wasn't sure if you are upset or if I am scaring you off. You haven't really said anything."

"No not at all. I am a bit shocked but happy. Please continue."

"Okay, well, I then told Jasmine that I was scared and needed to know for sure that the feelings I have for you are real and if they are then how can I let go of Josh so that I can give 100% of myself to you, not 80%."

"I can understand that feeling. What did she tell you to do?"

"She told me that I know the feelings for you are real as I just said so. She also told me that I know how to let go of Josh but just didn't want to see it because I am afraid to. She told me that you would be there to catch me and help me, but I need to do it."

It was at this time that I moved the picture of Josh and the kids and showed him that I had taken off my wedding rings from Josh earlier this evening for the first time since he put them on and laid them here.

He looks into my eyes and without saying a word, he pulls me in close and kisses me. It is the most passionate, soft kiss I have ever felt. My body tingles. My heart pounds very fast like it's about to explode out of my chest. My hands start to sweat and shake and I can feel my whole body begin to tremble.

He stops, raises up and looks at me. Still not saying a word, he takes his right hand from my back and very gently runs it up the side of my body and up my arm feeling every curve. It gives me goose bumps all over. He gets to my face and caresses it pushing my hair away from my eyes. He leans in and kisses my forehead very gently. He moves to my left cheek then kisses my right one. With his right hand, he gently cups my chin and lifts up guiding my head back exposing my neck. I close my eyes and take a deep breath.

Before I know it, he is kissing me very softly on my neck working his way down. Even though I have on the baby doll pj's it is low cut so my chest is bare down to the top of my breasts. I am caressing him with my hands up and down his body and arms feeling his every muscle and curve.

As he gets close to the top of my baby dolls I stop him. I'm just not ready for it to go any further.

"It's okay baby. I wasn't going to do anything or go further. I know you're not ready and I will wait. If it takes a day, a month or a year, I will wait. You are worth it. I want you to feel safe and comfortable. I won't push for anything you don't want. It will happen when you are ready."

I have tears in my eyes because I am feeling badly that I let him get that far then stop him. It isn't fair, especially after I just told him that I was in love with him. He wipes the tears away from my cheeks. "We have the rest of our lives to make love to each other. Don't feel bad. I don't."

He kisses me once again on the lips for what seems like an hour. Then he lays back down beside me on his back pulling me in to him. I am now lying wrapped in his arms again. My feelings for Craig are very real and very strong. I lie here hoping that he really does understand and won't hold a grudge or hold it against me for stopping him.

I will know tomorrow. If he treats me the same as he has the past couple of days, then I know he has no regrets. If he treats me differently and pulls away, then I know he is at least hurt by it.

CHAPTER 26

I DON'T KNOW how long it took to fall asleep but when I wake up, it is morning, and we are still lying in each other's arms. I usually move around a lot when I sleep and this past year I have been awake more than I sleep. Last night I slept like a rock. Don't remember waking up at all and obviously, I didn't move because I was still in the same position I was when I fell asleep.

I lay here quietly for a few minutes keeping my eyes closed to gather my thoughts listening to the sounds emanating from the kitchen. It's not long before Craig is awake and lets me know it.

"So how did you sleep baby?" he says making me jump.

I open my eyes and look up at him. "Like a rock. I can't remember the last time I actually slept like that where I didn't move at all or wake up once."

"Good." he says, "Me too. It didn't take long for me to go to sleep and I only woke up twice just to make sure you were okay. I gave you a kiss on the forehead each time and went back to sleep."

"For me, I have never been so comfortable or felt so safe. Even as tired as I was, I have been more tired before and still didn't sleep. Even with the help of sleeping pills. Last night I took nothing and slept. It's because of you so thank you."

He gives me a kiss saying no thanks needed. "It felt good for me too and felt right. I hope we can do this again. For now, I hear someone in the kitchen so I am going to get up and get some coffee. Want some?"

As he gets dressed and opens the door, he asks me again if I want any coffee. Nodding my head yes, he leaves the room closing the door behind him.

I lay here for a few more minutes listening to the commotion out in the kitchen. As Craig passes by my bedroom door, I can hear Eric razzing him about staying the night with me in my room. Craig passes it off as being nothing telling him he slept in his jeans on top of the covers while I slept under them. Even though it is a lie, nothing did happen between us other than both of us actually getting some sleep, they will never believe it. I decide that if they say anything to me I will reiterate what Craig said to avoid a barrage of questions.

As I listen to everyone chattering about, I catch myself thinking about how it would feel if it was like this every day. Is it something I want again and this soon? Is it something I am ready for? I guess only time would give me the answers to these questions.

I roll over to the edge of the bed to get up and notice the picture of Josh and our kids on the nightstand. As I pick it up, I sit here looking at it and instead of crying like I have been doing, I smile. I feel sad they aren't here with me but it's not overwhelming like it's been. I kiss them as a few tears flow down my face.

Although I miss them very much, this is the first time in over a year I didn't have that lost feeling. I don't know if it is because Craig was here last night and filled that void or if because I am actually beginning to heal as Craig said last night. Is it possible and is that lost feeling finally leaving me?

Tomorrow I will know the answer to that as Craig will not be here tonight. For now, I put the picture back, wipe the tears away, and get dressed. I pull myself together and head for the washroom. By the time I get to the kitchen, the coffee is done. I put a smile on my face and no one knows the questions I have or how I am feeling and that's just the way I want it for now.

Today is the second day of the games and competitions, and I for one am actually looking forward to it. I glance at the calendar and realize that it is Valentine's Day today. Knowing that my husband, who was the love of my life, is not here with me, it is the second one I spend alone. The anticipation of what the day would bring and wondering if I will have the same type of day as I did yesterday, fun and happy thoughts is what I focus on.

As I drink my coffee at the counter Uncle Arlo, Eric and Craig discuss the daily events while sitting at the table and Aunt Cheren gets dressed. Just then, Bryce, Jasmine, Ivory, and Dinah (Eric's fiancée), come walking in. "So who's ready to lose today?" Bryce says laughing.

"I guess you are!" Craig laughs back.

They all sit around the table talking about strategy and times for each event to take place that day. Aunt Cheren, Dinah and I get more coffee made and fill the sugar bowl and creamer to put outside. Jasmine comes up to me, puts her arms around me and whispers in my ear, "Everything good? Last night go well I hope?"

I nod my head, she smiles then she and Ivory put the garbage cans back out around the yard.

When we are done, I begin to cook some scrambled eggs and ham asking if anyone else wants any. That was the wrong question to ask, of course everyone wants some. As if on cue and like his ears are tuned in to anything food related, Carmine comes walking in, "I do. And guess what today is?" he quizzes as he sits down at the table.

They all thought for a moment and then realize, today is Valentine's Day. He tells them he has a truck load of fireworks for the finale tonight and to celebrate the day. "With everyone here I figured we would all celebrate it together as a family tonight so no one is left out." explains Carmine.

The guys go out and help Carmine unload his truck and put the fireworks in a safe place. I cook the bacon and eggs, Dinah makes the toast and fries the brown beans and Aunt Cheren gets out the plates and silverware. Jasmine sets the table and watches the children. Once everyone has their food, I make mine and sit down at the counter beside Jasmine to eat.

Craig gets up from his place at the table and joins me at the counter. He gives me a peck on the cheek and thanks me for cooking breakfast. "Happy Valentine's Day, baby." he whispers in my ear then gives me a kiss.

I thank him as I choke back the tears. I'm not going to let anything ruin this day if I can help it.

He sits here with me as I eat making small talk. The rest of them are starting to head out to get their trucks and tractors ready. As I finish eating, I tell Craig I will be out once I am done with the dishes. He picks up a towel. "The truck and tractor can wait, I have time. Let me help you with them, there is a lot."

"It's okay Craig." says Aunt Cheren as she takes the towels from both of our hands. "There are six of us here. Chloe can go with you if she wants, we can handle it here."

"Are you sure?" I ask.

They all say yes so I grab another cup of coffee for both Craig and I and we head out the door.

Craig is happy I am going to be with him today. "I am going to stand at the side lines today." I tell him as we walk towards his truck.

He stops in his tracks, grabs my arm and looks at me as tenses up. "Please tell me it's not because of last night. I said it was okay. No remorse and no regrets."

"No baby, it has nothing to do with last night. It has to do with yesterday. Today I want to be at the finish line and run to you when you win rather than be beside you."

He smiles and relaxes. Then I add, "Besides, it would make everyone wonder about 'us' and will make the other girls even more jealous than they were yesterday. I kind of liked it yesterday when you did that to them."

He smiles back almost with a laugh. "Okay that works for me."

I help him tune up his truck. Although all I do is hold his coffee mug, the flash light and hand him the tools he needs when he asks me for them, he says I am helping him. He does all the work, as I stand here looking pretty, as he puts it.

Little does he realize, I want to learn a few things about car mechanics and this will help me. I had planned on asking my uncle teach me how to work on cars when this weekend is over.

CHAPTER 27

THE FIRST COMPETITION today is the finals from yesterdays' race to determine the winner of the side-by-side mud drag race. There are four trucks in the finals: Blue Brute driven by Eric; Black Bandit driven by Darby; White Wonder driven by Carmine; and, Green Bomb driven by Craig. The first heat is Blue Brute against White Wonder. On the gun shot the race is under way and within seconds the mud starts flying.

We are all standing along the wood fence watching and rooting for our drivers. Being biased, I of course want Blue Brute to win this race because Eric is my cousin. After a few minutes and both trucks almost getting stuck in the ruts from the previous day, Blue Brute wins the race but only by a hair. It is such a close race that they have to look at the video that is shot at the finish line to see who crossed it first.

The next heat is Black Bandit against Green Bomb. The gun sounds and they are under way. Half way down the pipe Black Bandit bounces off course and careens up into Green Bombs path. Green Bomb veers left bouncing all over like it he is about to lose control. I hold my breath; and, so did many others standing here. Next, we see Green Bomb careening up the largest rut sideways throwing him up and over Black Bandit as it goes down into a rut. Getting it under control as it hits the ground Green Bomb drives across the finish line leaving Black Bandit stuck in its ruts.

Thankfully, no one is hurt and Craig's truck isn't damaged so the final race to determine the winner is set to begin. As Black Bandit is dragged off the track, Craig and Eric sit at the starting line revving their trucks getting ready to gun it. I look at Eric who is in the truck closest to me. "Sorry Eric, I love you but…"

He smiles, nods as if to say he knows and then looks forward ready to pounce. The gun sounds and they are off. Half of us are rooting for the Green Bomb and the other half is rooting for Blue Brute.

Bouncing all over the place both trucks are trying their best to stay on top of the ruts so they don't get stuck. Mud is flying everywhere and Eric in Black Bandit covers us with mud as he flies through the muddy holes. It doesn't stop us though. We all run to the finish line alongside the race hoping to see who crosses over first. It is another photo finish as Eric crosses on the ground and Craig crosses while in the air.

We are all waiting with eager anticipation for the results. Both Eric and Craig have stopped their trucks and are now sitting on their windows' ledge waiting for the results as well. It is so quiet you can almost hear a pin drop. It is the quietest it has been in two days.

Craig looks over at me as I look up at him. He winks at me and some of the girls who are standing around me start to giggle thinking he is winking at them. I smile and laugh as does he. Then we hear Brianna on the microphone.

"Okay we now have the results." she announces. "After reviewing the video several times it is unanimous. The winner by a bumper is," she pauses. Looking over the crowd and smiling she finally says, "The winner is BLACK BANDIT."

We all clap and cheer for Eric as both drivers drive their trucks off the track and park them. Most of the people go up to Eric to congratulate him and I walk up to Craig. Although he wasn't the winner of the race this year, he still has the tractor pulls and track race yet and this one was close. He gave it his all and it was just the turn of the wheel that allowed Eric to win by a bumper.

"Winning this race or not means nothing." I say to him. "We both had fun and you are a winner in my books no matter what." I give him a kiss. We both congratulate Eric on the win and we all walk over to the tractors.

We stop part way there and Craig stands beside me. After a moment he turns to me and says, "You know, winning these races used to mean everything to me. That is until this year."

I don't have to ask what he means because I know. We walk to his truck as I say, "These races, whether you win or lose, brought you to me, so they will always be special no matter what."

He smiles at me, picks up some tools and starts to tinker with his tractor getting it ready for the upcoming race.

I leave him to do what he needs to do and I walk over to the porch to get a Gatorade. I am thirsty now and coffee just will not do. I walk to where the tractor pulls are going to be held. Half way over there Eric drives up to me in his tractor and pulls me up onto it. "So you and Craig are getting along well."

"Yes, but just as friends for right now. I told him yesterday I'm not ready for a relationship just yet."

As he drives to the other side of the property where the pulls are going to take place, he tells me that if Craig hurts me he will hurt him. "Thanks but everything will be okay. I trust him."

I get out of his tractor and help my cousins lay out the chains and spray more water into the mud hole.

"Here comes dad. Wonder what he wants?" Eric remarks.

"It must be serious. He's coming really fast." says Bryce.

Just then Uncle Arlo reaches us. "Chloe, there is at least an hour before the tractor pulls begin. Are you ready to put on another show like yesterday while everyone waits?"

"Yes, I would love to. I had fun yesterday and feel 100% better today."

"Great. Hop on and I will take you over to the house so you can get ready."

I jump onto the back of his four wheeler and we ride towards the house. As we do I tell my uncle what I am going to try to do today. "Uncle Arlo, I think today I am going to try the big jump just before jumping the pit as the finale."

We are now, back at the house. I jump off and as I climb the stairs he says, "Chloe, are sure you want to do that?"

I stop and turn to look at him. "Yes. As long as the bike is okay during all the other stunts with no problems I am going to do it. It was okay in practice the other day and I had no problems with the bike yesterday so it should be fine."

"Alright, I will go get the bike ready for you. Meet you in the shop."

"Okay I won't be too long."

Craig, noticing what I am about to do comes into the house. "Are you sure you are well enough to do this?"

"Yes, I did it yesterday and I am much better today."

"Okay just as long as you will be safe."

"I will be fine. My aunt and uncle are going to help me with the big jump like we did in practice."

"Oh. So you are going to do that today are you?"

"Yes. Why?"

"I was just asking." he says then turns and walks out of the house.

My aunt gets out the suit and helmet and helps me get changed. As I am getting ready, Bryce announces that we have another show for them today with something even more spectacular than yesterdays' show.

Everyone who was here yesterday knows what is coming so they all find spots and sit waiting with anticipation for the show. As he finishes, I hear a truck start. I look out the window to see that Craig is pulling out of the yard and headed into town. Shocked and concerned I wonder if he left because he is upset I am going to do this. I ask my aunt if she knows where he is going. When she says no, I ask Eric and Bryce who are now in the kitchen with us and they say no as well, but adds that Carmine went with him. Now I am baffled and hope that he isn't mad at me.

I make my way out to the shed. Still wondering about Craig, I ask my uncle if he knows why he left. Although he says he doesn't know, he has this look on his face that says different. I don't have time to question him so I leave it at that. I put the helmet on, hop on the bike and kick start it. I say a small prayer for guidance and protection to let me make it through today's events.

I rev the motor and let go of the brakes. Off I go just as I did during practice. I start by doing some wheelies and small acrobatic maneuvers along the straight away in front of the crowd. I then go around the track and begin to take a run for the smaller jumps.

As I begin the run I hear another bike as it comes up beside me fast from out of nowhere. It is the same bike as I have except blue and white in color. Confused and wondering who this is, I continue as if it is part of the show. One after the other we tackle the small jumps doing squids, acrobatic moves while in the air, burnouts when on the ground, etc. It is now time for me to attempt the big jump and I am a bit nervous.

We come around the track and I stop at the base of the big jump. The other bike stops beside me and nods at me as if to ask if I am ready. "Yes," I reply, "I was just sizing it up and hoping that my bike is fast enough for me to do the flips."

He gets off his bike, takes my handle bars in his hands and says, "Here take my bike."

"Craig?" I ask as the voice sounds like him.

He lifts his shield and smiles, revealing to me that it is him.

"But, how?" I ask baffled.

He tells me that his bike can go 115 mph and might give me the speed I need to make the jump. "Just go. I will explain later."

I nod, get off my bike and jump onto his. I take off around the track while he gets in place at the bottom of the other hill. If I land this jump, he and I will take off side by side and come around to jump the 125-foot pit through the hoop my cousins have put up, side by side. This has to be timed right and I pray we can do it.

I stop 150 feet away from the base of the jump. I sit for a minute saying a quick prayer, rev the bike and release the brake. It's now or never I think to myself and take off. As I reach the forty-foot mark, I am up to 90 mph. At the ten-foot mark, I am over 100 mph and decide to go for it. I hit the bottom of the ramp at 112 miles per hour. My heart is racing but I don't allow fear to enter in. As I lift off the top you can hear everyone gasp as they hold their breath. I throw my entire body backwards tugging at the bike to follow. I whip it so hard that doing two flips simultaneously is easily completed. My only concern now is that I don't over rotate.

As the bike uprights after the second flip, I look down. I steady the bike and land half way down the ramp. Thankful I made it I smile to myself and thank my protectors and god. As I get to the bottom Craig takes off and before long, we are side by side and everyone is standing and clapping. We round the far corner then take off getting up to 90 mph as we hit the forty-degree ramp.

Side by side, we lift off the top. As we fly through the air, we move into position. He leans back on his bike as if he is doing the limbo and I jump off my bike holding onto the back of the seat in a layout position as we go through the hoop. We clear it. He sits back up and I pull myself back onto the bike. Within seconds, we both hit the other ramp with a huge thud and race down the other side. We did it!

We turn at the end of the run, riding back to the top of the small jump where we landed. We stand beside our bikes and take off our helmets as everyone cheers. We get standing ovations and can hear lots of whistles and yelling. We are a big hit. We hug each other and drive our own bikes back to the shed.

When we shut them off, I turn to him still in shock. "You didn't tell me you could ride. Why didn't you tell me you could so we could practice together?"

With a smile he says, "I wanted it to be a surprise. Your uncle and Bryce knew I was doing it. I was just worried that I wouldn't make it back in time."

"That explains my uncles' comment and look when I asked him if he knew why you left."

He walks up to me and puts his arms around me. "Are you upset with me for not telling you?"

"No just the opposite, it was fun."

He kisses me and we get undressed out of our leather outfits.

Within a half hour, the tractor pulls are under way. It is a competition of strength, one tractor against the other. They back towards each other at the edge of the mud hole and a heavy chain is clipped onto the rear of each of the tractors. At the sound of the gun, they go forward as fast as they can and the one who pulls the other into the mud wins. Some of the tractors have their chassis pulled off. Other tractors are pulled into the mud hole so bad that the drivers have to jump out before being sucked in. Other pulls are so hard that the chain breaks and everyone in the crowd ducks so we aren't hit by the flying chains. It is a great time.

During these races, some of us leave and go back to the house to put out some food and refill the drinks and coolers. For the first time in several years, I grab an ice-cold beer. Shortly after we finish, some of the people have started to fix plates for their kids and themselves. Then the men and other drivers join us.

Craig comes over to me and hands me a plate full of food. I thought he wanted me to hang on to it for him so he can grab something to drink. Instead, he says, "Here, this is for you. You need to eat something."

"I have been eating and munching as we put the food out."

"I didn't see you eat. Come and eat with me. Please?"

I take the plate, pick up my beer I have open and sit beside him at the picnic table. Although I am not hungry, I eat a little bit to keep him happy.

After lunch, those who are still in the tractor races go back to the far side of the property while the rest of us go to the back side of the barn. Uncle Arlo, Eric, and Bryce have made a small mud lane so the kids can join in the fun and have their own mud races. Craig goes with us to help with the kids' races, as he is out of the tractor race.

We have six motorized 'big truck' kid size for them to race in. Quinn and I are at the start line helping the kids into the trucks and lining them up. Aunt Cheren and Jasmine are at the finish line to help them stop and say who the winner is. Craig stands off to the side lines with Corinne, Liana, and Selena acting as their cheering section. It is a fun time and every once in a while I notice Craig watching.

CHAPTER 28

IT IS NOW 2:45 p.m. and the track race is set to begin at 3:30. The tractor pull races are finishing up and we hear them announce the winner. We declare a boy and girl winner of their races and we all go and find a place around the track to safely watch the race.

It is something this race track. My uncle and cousins spent three days setting it up. The track goes around the outside of their entire property. There are mud holes, sand hills, dunes, loose sand, hard packed ground, rocks, small bushes and a cement wall for them to maneuver around and through. It is the same track where I performed my bike show on. The track measures just over a mile and is quite impressive.

Everyone who has a truck still running from the races enter into this one. It is a winner takes all. There is a trophy with name labels for the past four years on it with six empty spaces. Past winners on the trophy are Darby, Johnny and Gregory. The winner today will also get a $100 gift certificate from the local tractor supply store and $250 in cash.

I choose to sit on a branch up in a tree located in the center of the east side of the property. It is perfectly situated. From this view, I will be able to see most of the race. The branch extends out over the track yet it is high enough up that should one of the trucks be launched into the air, it will not reach me.

Uncle Arlo, Bryce and Eric are walking the track as a last minute check before the race begins. As I sit here waiting, I notice that they have stopped below me. They don't know I am up here. I overhear them talking. Bryce's business is going under and he doesn't know what to do. Eric and Uncle Arlo tell him that they will do what they can to help but aren't sure if it will be enough. Bryce says that if he can't get the cars he has in the shop now out within the next two weeks and paid, he won't be able to pay his rent and will have to close up. They begin to walk the track again and I can't hear what else is said.

That was heart wrenching for me. I know Bryce has put everything he has and all his energy and efforts over the past three years into his shop. I wonder if I can help him as I have gotten businesses out of large debt before in short periods of time. I need to think about this, to see what I can come up with. For now, I will focus on the day's events and then sleep on it.

The start/finish line is at the entrance of the driveway, which is only 12 feet away from the house. Many people have lined up on the porch so they can see how everyone starts and who finishes first. The drivers will have to go around the track five complete laps and cross the finish line first before being declared the winner.

It is now almost 3:30 and engines start to come alive as they roar when revved. Ten of the original fourteen trucks approach the start line; Craig, Bryce, Eric and Carmine are among them. They are now all lined up waiting for the gun to sound.

It does and they are off to a roaring start. As the trucks drive the track, their back ends slide around at different angles as they drive through the corners.

On the short straight ways, the trucks speed up bouncing back and forth as they hit ruts, rocks and small mounds. On the larger, longer straight ways, they race up larger hills jumping to into the air as they clear the top of them. A few have rammed into the cement wall, others have toppled over into the mud holes as the rest swerve trying to avoid the wrecks.

The first two laps, Bryen and Eric are neck and neck for the lead. On the third lap, Carmine sneaks between them as they go up the largest jump and Bryen topples over onto his side, as he lands. As they land, Carmine takes over the lead with Craig and Bryce close behind. It's a great race. Lots of jumps, twists and turns, and like a professional race, this one does not disappoint. There are roll over's, crashes and first place is not dominant to one driver.

It is now the last lap and there are only five trucks left in the race; Bryce, Dante, Craig, Eric and Carmine. Around turn one Dante is in first place with Eric and Craig volleying for second, and Carmine and Bryce doing the same for third. By turn three, Carmine is in first place, Eric and Craig still side by side for second, Bryce is close behind for third and Dante has crashed into the wall between turns two and three.

The last straight way before turn four and crossing the finish line, Eric takes over the lead with Bryce and Carmine close for second and third.

Craig has rolled over into the far mud pit taking him out of the race. As they complete turn four, Eric has spun out, allowing Carmine and Bryce to pass him. Giving it all they have, they are neck and neck to the finish line. A small mound in the track throws Bryce to the right and Carmine crosses the finish line first, winning the race.

As the race finishes and Carmine is given his money and gift certificates, the guys go around the track with tractors to get the broken down and stuck trucks. While some of the women get dinner ready, others take care of the kids. I run over to where Craig has rolled over to make sure he is okay.

Relieved that he is, I give him a bear hug and a kiss. "I am so glad you are okay. I was worried."

"I'm okay baby believe me. My truck on the other hand, well, I'm not so sure about it."

Laughing I reply, "Okay. I will let you get back to your truck and try to get it out. I'm going to help get dinner ready."

"Okay baby, have fun."

We kiss each other a quick one on the lips and I head back to the house while he hooks up the tractor to the truck.

It takes almost two hours for everyone to be ready to eat. It is now almost seven p.m., dinner is over with and cleaned up, and all the trucks are back to the front of the house. Some will be towed home, those still running will be driven home and the rest will remain here for the next few days until their owners can retrieve them.

It is dusk and the fireworks are being set up as we all gather to sit around the bonfire and wait for them to begin. It's not long before we hear a loud bang and they begin. We are all in awe of their glory. Many colors braise the sky. There are some that sport the red white and blue with one coming together to form the American Flag. There are many red, pink and white colored sparklers as well.

There are enough fireworks to last almost an hour. The finale was one of magnificent beauty. A Large Red heart that grows from small too large followed by many smaller white and pink hearts ends the spectacular display.

As it quiets down, I start singing, 'I Do It For you'; a song by Bryan Adams. Before long those who know the song join in with me. After this, I begin to sing my all-time favorite love song and being that it is Valentine's Day I feel it is most appropriate. The song is, 'Don't Know

Much' originally sung by Linda Ronstadt and Aaron Neville. It is not long before I get another shock of my life, Craig can sing. I start with the chorus to get everyone's attention and to see who knows the song,

"I don't know much, But I know I love you, And that may be all I need to know."

As I sing this Craig stands up off the chair, holds out his hand for me to stand with him and he starts to sing.

"Look at this face, I know the years are showing. Look at this life, I still don't know where it's going."

We walk up to the stage. By now the band is beginning to play, we both grab the microphones and chime in together.

"I don't know much, But I know I love you, And that may be all I need to know."

We take out turns singing the rest of the song looking at each other; me singing Linda's part and Craig singing Aarons part and both singing the chorus together.

We got a standing ovation and lots of whistles as we finish the song with a romantic kiss. Some gasp and we even here ooh's and aah's. The next hour is spent with everyone singing and telling stories of how couples met.

Shortly thereafter, I head off to bed. Craig tells me he won't be staying tonight but I will hear from him tomorrow. We give each other our cell phone number so we can stay in touch, kiss good night and he leaves.

I am exhausted and for once I don't feel sad or guilty for having fun. It is a good feeling. I do look at their picture, give them a kiss and then set the picture back down on the table. I lay here for a minute in my bed thinking about the weekend, Craig, and how I am feeling. It is something I thought would never happen again; and if it did, not for a very long time.

I wonder what tomorrow will bring for me? I think to myself as I fall asleep.

CHAPTER 29

IT DOESN'T TAKE long before I fall asleep.

It is now Monday morning and I lay here with my eyes closed already missing Craig, wondering how he slept last night, and what he will be doing today. The sun is peaking in the window through the curtains and I smell a hint of roses. Wondering what my aunt is cooking that smells like roses I open my eyes and sit up slowly.

I sit in amazement and in shock. All around me on the bed are what looks like thousands of orange and yellow rose petals. Not wanting to move, I pick up a handful of the petals and bring them up to my nose. I am lost in its' fragrance. The smells of beauty, sweetness and warmth is like a bright spring day. I look around the room. On the table beside my bed is an envelope that says,

"OPEN ME FIRST"

Curious I reach over and pick it up. Inside is the most beautiful card I have ever read.

The front of the card is red with different shades of red and pink hearts all over in white wash style. A white teddy bear holding a red heart covers the center. In the heart, it says Happy Valentine's Day in fancy Brush Script lettering. I sit for a moment and think, valentine's day was yesterday, why am I getting this today? Now even more curious I open the card. There is a preprinted verse on the right side surrounded by hearts on sticks with a different word on each: kiss, love, happy, romance, heart, and forever. There is also a long, handwritten note on the left. I read the preprinted first,

"You are so beautiful; you are so fine.
I wish so dearly that you would be mine.
Today and always you are in my heart.
Please make me happy and be my valentine.
Forever and always, we will never be apart."

My eyes tear up but they are happy tears. I don't even have to read the signature because there is only one man in this world that would give this to me, Craig! I take a minute then read what he personally wrote on the left. It reads:

My Dearest Love

I see you in my thoughts and dreams, no matter how far away you are. Even though you aren't here with me now, soon I hope you will be.

No one truly knows or understands just how you have my heart in your hands.

My love and devotion is what you truly own, I can't wait until you are mine.

Inside your heart you are doing your time, not being here with me truly is a crime.

You light up my life every time I see you, you are my stars and my moon.

So when you sleep, take this to heart, no one and nothing will take me away from your heart.

Chloe, I love you with all my heart and soul.

All my love, Craig.

So now I am crying and it must be louder than I thought. Aunt Cheren comes running to my door, knocks and as she opens the door, and asks if I am okay. I tell her yes and have her come in. She walks through the door and looks around in amazement. Her eyes light up as she asks, "Who and how?"

"Craig," I reply, "but I don't know how. Had to be sometime after I went to sleep last night, none of this was here when I came to bed."

Just then Eric walks in with a grin like a cat that just ate a mouse leaning against the door frame.

"What do you know about this?" my aunt asks him.

He shakes his head and with a smirk on his face. "Absolutely nothing."

Knowing better than that, my aunt keeps on him to get him to tell her.

I look at the card again and notice that at the bottom it has a 'p.s. Look on your dresser and in the top drawer.' I look at Eric and Aunt Cheren with a puzzled look.

"What's wrong?" she asks.

"Nothing." I reply telling them what it says at the bottom of the card.

Now Eric is having a hard time to contain himself. His mom is trying to get him to tell her what it is he is excited about. All he says is, "Wait one minute and you will see."

From my bed I can't see the dresser because it sits behind a four-foot half wall. I get up and walk over to it. On the top sitting center stage is a vase filled with twelve white roses, each with red and blue tips on their petals. They are the most beautiful roses I have ever seen. Some are opened fully; some are still in bud form while the rest are opened ever so slightly. Their aroma is intoxicating as it fills my senses with delight.

Now I know where the rose smell was coming from. I take out two roses and tip them to my nose as I open the top drawer. Sitting inside are two boxes; one small and one medium in size. I take them both out, grab a couple more roses and sit on the bed to open the boxes.

Eric tells me to open the medium one first like he already knows what is inside them. My aunt is relentless questioning him on what he knows about all of this. As they banter back and forth, I open the bigger of the two first.

It is octagon shaped and wrapped in the most beautiful pink and red foil paper. It is a box of chocolates; but, not just any chocolates. It is filled with my favorite kind. A mixture of white chocolates from solid to covered peanuts to coconut and vanilla. I eat a couple and offer some to Eric and my aunt who decline. I can't help it, I just have to eat white chocolate when it's in front of me no matter what time of day it is.

I then open the smaller box. It is wrapped in textured red foil paper tied with a beautiful light pink bow. I open it. Inside is the most beautiful necklace. It is a red ruby pendant surrounded by a 10k gold open encasement showing its' beautiful red hues at every turn. Where the encasement comes together at the top, there are three small diamonds placed around it. It is all hanging from an elegant yet fragile gold chain. I can't help it, I cry again.

I look up at Eric. "So how did you and Craig pull this off?"

Eric looks back at me with that grin. "I think that is something he should answer."

"Well he's not here now is he? Talk!"

Aunt Cheren takes the necklace out of the box so she can put it on around my neck. Just then a figure is in the door way. It's Craig. He was standing in the hall way the entire time listening.

"Here, let me do that." he says as he takes the necklace from my aunts' hands.

He sits on the bed beside me in my aunts' place and puts the necklace around my neck. I turn around and kiss him then hug him not wanting to let go. "You have no idea what this means to me."

"Yeah, I think I do."

"How did you do this without waking me up?"

"Very carefully. Eric and I planned this whole thing for Saturday night so you would wake up yesterday like this."

"That was spoiled when he ended up staying in here with you that night and fell asleep. I tried to wake him up but didn't want to press it because I didn't want to wake you up. You looked so peaceful and I know you haven't been sleeping much."

"That's when we decided to do it last night. Better to do it a day late than never at all." Craig says with a smile.

I didn't expect anything, as we have just met. However, he did this and it is like nothing I would have ever dreamed of happening.

"Well?" Craig questions me.

"Well what?"

"What's my answer?"

"Yes." I reply, "Of course I will."

With curious looks and mouths open, my aunt and Eric both look at us. "And just what is she saying yes to?" my aunt asks.

Laughing I reply, "It's not what you think. He didn't ask me to marry him or anything like that."

"I asked her to be my valentine in the card." Craig tells them.

A little relieved she smiles, pats Craig on the back and says, "Good job dear."

She leaves the room. Eric excuses himself as well giving Craig and I a minute.

I tell him how happy I am. "Craig, I am beyond words. No one has ever done anything like this for me in my entire life. It is more than I have ever hoped for from anyone and much more than I ever expected from you."

Seeming kind of put off by what I said he asks, "What do you mean more than expected from me?"

"Sorry baby that came out wrong. I didn't expect anything from you because we have only known each other for a few days is all I meant. I didn't mean to upset you. I am extremely happy that you did this and would not change it for anything."

Relieved he kisses me and tells me he has to leave. "I have things that I have to do so I won't be around for a couple of days. I will call you every chance I get."

"It's okay. I totally understand. Don't worry about me, I will be fine and you know where I am."

Hesitantly, he kisses me again and leaves.

I look at the gorgeous necklace for a moment, get up, get dressed and go into the kitchen to help my aunt clean up and put things away from the weekends' festivities. We spend the morning talking about Craig and what he did last night as we clean.

It is lunch time now and I tell my aunt that I will bring out Uncle Arlo's. "I have something I would like to ask him."

She makes him a plate and I take it to him out in the shop. While he eats I ask him if he will teach me how to work on cars. "It's something I have always been interested in and wanted to do. However, dad said it wasn't a girls' place and never showed me."

For a woman I do know how to change a tire, spark plugs, hoses, belts, check/change/fill fluids, and change head/tail lights because my step-dad showed me.

"I would love to teach you. I think it would be fun. We can get to know each other again and it would be a great pass time for you."

I hug him and thank him and work with him the rest of the afternoon learning how to change head gaskets and brake pads.

While we are doing this, Dante walks in and with a shocked look on his face. "What is she doing in here?"

Not sure how I should take that and before I can respond, Uncle Arlo replies, "Teaching her what I taught all you boys. Your Uncle Ken never showed her anything because she is a girl and she wants to learn."

"Oh, I thought women weren't allowed in a car shop."

After a short discussion between the two of them, Dante goes to his truck. Uncle Arlo looks at me, shrugs his shoulders and we get back to replacing the gaskets. Within minutes Dante is back with his hands full.

"I got all the things you need to fix that bug dad."

Elated, my uncle helps him put them on the work bench. "I will be back tomorrow to help you work on it."

"Okay great. Thank you Dante."

Dante gives me a look of disgust and leaves.

It is now 3:30 in the afternoon and we have finished putting new head gaskets on the motor for his pick-up truck. "I want you to help me drain the oil and other fluids out of the Volkswagen."

"Okay great. Thanks for teaching me Uncle Arlo. I am having fun and learning a lot."

"You're welcome sweetie. I am glad to do it."

We stop what we were doing and get to work on the bug.

We push it onto the lift so he can raise it in the air. "It's much easier to drain the fluids when you can reach them." he tells me. That was common sense but I let him tell me what he feels he needs to.

It takes us over an hour to drain everything and take out the pump. "Dinner will be ready soon. We had better start cleaning up so we won't have to do it after dinner."

It takes us an hour to wipe down and put away the tools, sweep and wash the floor to clean up the spills, and put the parts from both vehicles away on their trays. Just as we finish, we hear my aunt hollering at us that dinner is ready.

Turning off the lights and closing the doors, we head to the house.

That evening after dinner, Uncle Arlo sits in his chair as usual while Aunt Cheren sits at the kitchen table playing her computer games. Me, I lay on the couch watching TV relaxing and thinking of this morning's events. I then think about what I overheard Bryce, Uncle Arlo and Eric discuss about his business the other day.

"Uncle Arlo." I say wondering if I should ask him about Bryce's business concerns or not. "I overheard you, Eric and Bryce talking about his business and how he is looking at closing it."

Uncle Arlo sits up in his chair and is now more interested in what I have to say rather than what is on TV, he turns it down. "Okay, what about his business?"

"I was wondering; do you think that Bryce would allow me to help him?"

"And how do you propose on doing that?"

I explain to him how I got the non-profit organization out of $60,000 in less than three months and a for-profit business out of debt over $186,000 in less than six months. I also remind him of what I did for my dad and his sporting goods business eight years ago. As I am telling him this stuff, my aunt is bringing up all the reports on these. More stuff about me on the world wide web that I did not know was there. Now I am wondering what else is on there about me that I don't know about.

"If Bryce is willing to listen and leave it to me, I can do the same for him in six months or so."

"I am going over to his garage in the morning. If you want to go with me, you are more than welcome to go with me and pitch your idea to him if you want."

I smile. "Okay that will work. Do you think he will go for it?"

"Well, all we can do is ask and see what he says."

I agree with him.

It is now 10 p.m. and I am tired so I say good night and head to bed.

It takes me almost two hours to get to sleep. All I can think about is helping Bryce and what will need to be done. As I lay here, thinking about Bryce's problems, my thoughts start to drift and I notice that I'm holding onto and feeling my necklace, thinking about Craig and what he did for me this morning. The things we did this past weekend, what was said between us and wondering how long it will be before I see him again, or at least hear from him.

He did give me his phone number and I gave him mine but I didn't want to be the first one to call or text. I don't want him to think I am desperate or needy or clingy.

But should I?

CHAPTER 30

BEFORE I KNOW it, I wake up and it is already the next morning.

Uncle Arlo is already gone to town leaving me a note to clean the pads and shoes before he gets back. On the bottom of the note it reads:

'p.s. we will be going to Bryce's garage after lunch'.

I grab some coffee and make myself a couple pieces of toast with peanut butter and head to the shop. I put on some music and clean all the brake pads and shoes dancing around and singing with the music as I go about my work. It is fun and I can't remember the last time I actually sang and danced around to music simply because I was happy.

When I am done I go back to the house, talk with Aunt Cheren for a few minutes and grab another coffee. I head to the barn, get a bucket of carrots and feed for the horses and walk over to their coral. They are outside prancing and bucking. They have beautiful horses.

The mare is an exquisite beauty. All four legs, her head and tail are midnight black. She has a snow white mane that flows like a waterfall breaking its' crest. Her body is that of an oversized Dalmatian. Pearl white body with midnight black spots, she prances around like the perfect show horse. Her legs are strong and she is very agile. She is a gentle giant and very inquisitive. She sees me coming and with her foal beside her, heads in my direction.

The foal is a mix of browns, white and black. With long skinny solid pearl white legs, she gallops like a doll on strings. Her brown head is long and narrow sporting a white spot around her left eye like she is wearing an eye patch. Her mane and tail are scraggly looking and all over the place like a woman's on a bad hair day. Her body looks too big for her legs. It is muscular like her dads with a mix of brown, white and black patches throughout. Being only a few weeks old she is young and clumsy yet very energetic.

The stallion is in the distance grazing on some grass fully aware I am there and he lets me know it. He lifts his head and lets out a few grunts. Midnight black is the only color on this magnificent beauty. His thick neck, powerful legs and muscular physique resonates an equestrian presence. He is head strong yet majestic with his mane cascading down his neck and back like a beautiful curtain.

I am petting the foal as she shows her good nature. I feed it some carrots along with the mare as I play with them. I can tell she is in a good mood so I decide to tease her a bit like I have been doing all week. I sit on top of the fence after giving the foal a carrot and tease the mare with another. She nudges me then takes the carrot out of my hand.

As she does this, I catch myself before I slide off the top of the fence and readjust myself. As she eats the carrots, it seems like she is looking past me then she starts to snort and neigh. She comes up to me and nudges me with her nose over and over again until I can't hold her off anymore, and she pushes me off.

I close my eyes and brace myself waiting to hit the ground expecting to hit it hard landing on my back. After a few seconds and no thump, I open my eyes slowly not knowing what has happened. That's when I see him. Craig stands here and has once again caught me before I hit the ground. I don't know how or why he is even there but, there he is, when I need him most he is there catching me again.

He stands me up. I look over at the mare who seems to be laughing at me. I don't understand what just happened, it's like she did it on purpose. We walk back to the house.

"Why are you here and how did you know to be there at that exact moment?" I ask him.

"I didn't. It was simply by chance."

"I thought I wouldn't see you for a few days? Don't get me wrong I am very happy to see you." I look back and shake my head. "Quite glad actually, but am surprised just the same."

He tells me that my uncle left him a message on his phone last night asking if he could come here today by noon. Said he has something to discuss with him, so here he is.

We are now inside the house. As he talks with my aunt at the kitchen table, I lay on the couch and close my eyes trying to figure out what happened, and how. After about half hour Craig comes over and sits beside me. As I start to sit up he stops me.

"No. Stay there. I want to look at you lying there as you are, beautiful and at peace."

I lay back down with a smile and he leans in. He kisses me then whispers, "Don't ever do that again. You scared the crap out of me. What would have you done if I wasn't there and caught you?"

"Fell hard."

"So are the shoes ready young lady?" asks my uncle as he walks in the door.

"Yes they are and I fed the horses too. I was just relaxing a moment while waiting for you to return."

We get up off the couch and the three of us head to the shop. While they are checking them out, my uncle talks to Craig. "I am glad to see you got my message. Are you able to join us this afternoon?"

"Yes, that's why I am here."

"Good. I am glad, there's something I want you to hear this afternoon. I think it will be worth your while."

"Okay. Can I ask what it is pertaining to?"

My uncle looks over at me and smiles. "No, I think it is something you need to hear from her when she tells it."

Looking at me Craig is now really wondering what is going on. I had no idea that my uncle wanted him to hear the idea I am going to pitch to Bryce. Now I am wondering why myself.

For the next hour my uncle and Craig re-bore and re-groove the brake pads and shoes then measure them to see if they are still legal. As they do this I watch so I can learn how it is done. After they are done, Uncle Arlo says only one is still within legal limits so he will buy a new set while he is in town this afternoon. "I don't want there to be any second guessing. Better be safe than sorry, especially where brakes are concerned. I don't want to take any chances."

"Lunch is ready." yells Aunt Cheren.

We head into the house and eat. When we are finished, we head outside. "I will take my truck." says my uncle. "Craig, if you wouldn't mind taking Chloe with you? I want to pick up the new brakes first and then will meet the two of you at Bryce's garage."

"Yes of course. I would love to take Chloe with me."

"Good. Chloe wants to talk to Bryce anyway so it will give her a chance to do that."

"It will also give her and I chance to talk. There is something I have been wanting to say to her anyway and now I have the chance."

Uncle Arlo smiles and gets into his truck. He drives off towards town.

We get into Craig's truck and leave behind him. As we drive off I am curious as to what Craig wants to talk to me about. "What is it you wanted to tell me?"

He smiles like a cat that just ate a rat.

CHAPTER 31

CRAIG STARTS GENERAL chit chat like he is nervous having me in the truck with him. Quickly, I change the conversation to a more serious one. "Craig, if you don't mind, I would like to ask you something before you tell me what it is you want to say?"

"Sure, what is it baby?"

"Well, you know quite a bit about me. These last couple of days while you were away I did a lot of thinking and realized that I don't know much about you."

He looks at me. "Alright, what would you like to know?"

"Well, your job, if you even have one. A family like sisters or brothers, and any kids you may have, where you live, etc. I only know bits and pieces but not much."

"Slow down." he says laughing.

"I'm sorry for asking so much at once. You don't have to answer them all now. I just want you to know some of the things about you that you already know about me."

"Well, I have two wonderful kids, both married and have given me three grandchildren so far." He tells me they don't live here and where they are and how often he gets to see them. "My dad died over 10 years ago in a mining accident where he worked. My mom lives here in Texas only a few miles from my place and I get to see her almost every day."

"I am sorry about your dad. I didn't know."

"It's okay. It was many years ago. As for my job, well I do have one so to speak. That is one reason why you didn't hear from me yesterday and why it was almost noon before I got to your place today. Your uncle called me last night asking me to come by around eight this morning but I had to finish a few things first."

"Okay that answers them then."

"I know that you probably aren't ready to hear this but I have to tell you something."

I look at him with a bewildered look as I have no idea what he is going to say. "Okay, what is it?"

"Even though it has been two days since we last seen each other or even spoke, all I could do was think about you. I really missed you and it made me realize something."

By this time, we are coming into town and are on paved roads. Bryce's shop is across town. Knowing there is still time I get inquisitive.

"I missed you too, what was it that you realized?"

"Well," he stops for a minute and looks over at me. I guess he thought I would leave it at that because like he said 'I may not be ready to hear it'. Without even thinking on my part and kind of curious, I asked because I really want to know what things he realized.

"Well, I know it's only been about a week since we have known each other. In that short time, we have spent a lot of time together. Hell we even spent the night together, granted not like what most people think but we did all the same."

"Yes that is true."

"Well I really didn't want to leave you Sunday night but I knew I had to. Now I know Eric and I set up your room while you were sleeping and even though I did spend the night, it was on the couch. It wasn't the same because you weren't beside me."

"Okay, I did not realize that you slept on the couch."

"I did. Anyway, when I woke up this morning I felt empty. You weren't there with me and I thought I wouldn't be seeing you again today. I was actually sad about it. I haven't felt that way in over six years about anyone. When I picked up my phone to call and tell you I miss you, that's when I got the message from your uncle. I was very happy knowing I would see you today so I decided not to call as I wanted to surprise you. That is when I realized it."

"Realized what?"

"Well," he pauses, "I know I said it Saturday night when we were talking. However, I only realized just how true it really was this morning."

Now I am anxious, because it seems like he is avoiding my question. "Out with it already."

"Before I tell you what I realized you should know that I had picked up the phone several times yesterday to call you but kept hanging up. Every time the phone would start to ring my hands would sweat and my stomach would tie up in knots so I hung up."

"Why did you do that?"

"Because I was really nervous. Would you not answer because you didn't want to hear from me or if you did answer, what would I say?"

"I waited for you to call. I wanted to call you too but you said you would call when you had a chance. That's why I never called you. I didn't want to bother you if you were busy."

"Anyway, I realized then and there that," he pauses again, looks at me as he watches the road then says, "I am in love with you and really hated to be away from you. Just the thought that you would not be in my life, made me sad."

I sit here for a minute. Looking at him as it sinks in what he just said before I reply.

"Craig, I can say that I know exactly how you feel. I was going to call you several times yesterday but didn't want to seem eager and wasn't sure myself if you wanted to hear from me either."

"Let me ask you. Does it matter to you what I do for a living or how much I make?"

"No. I never asked about your job so I could know how much you make. I wasn't sure if you even had one because you were here for three straight days. How much you make does not affect how I feel about you. I love you for who you are not for what you do or how much you make. If you were poor, rich or somewhere in between, I love you for you either way."

He looks over at me with a look I had not seen in many years. It was the same distraught look my dad had when my step mother passed away seven years ago. Without saying a word, he just keeps looking between me and the road as though he was really worried something. Maybe I said something that upset him or reminded him of something.

Not knowing why he is acting like this, I begin to get worried. "What's wrong?"

He just shakes his head. Next thing I know he whips the truck into a parking lot and throws it into park.

"Are you alright?" I ask.

He takes off his seat belt and turns towards me. "I am fine. Do you realize what you just said to me?" He puts my hands in his.

Raging Desire

Bewildered and confused I say in a shaky voice, "Yes, I said that I love you for you and not for what you do for a living or how much you make or don't make. Was that the wrong thing to say?"

"No, but, I don't think you realize what you said. Repeat the first part again."

"I love you for you and not for what your job is or what you do."

"The first part of that!"

"What about it?"

"Say it again, please."

"What that I love you for you?" I say again getting a little bit annoyed that he keeps asking me to say the same thing over and over again.

"Yes, that!"

Then it hit me. Without realizing it or even thinking about it, I told Craig that I love him, and more than once. I take my hands out of his, pull away from him moving to the other side of the seat and sit here looking at him with my back against the door.

"Are you okay?" he asks me nervously.

I look at him in shock. A few minutes go by before I tell him, "I told you that I love you."

"Yes, you did."

Tears are welling up in my eyes and he is shaking. I am not sure if he is upset or happy or something else. That is until he said what he did next.

"You said you didn't think you would ever be ready to say that to another man for a very long time. I think I am in shock. I asked you to repeat it so many times because at first I wasn't sure I heard you right. Then you said it again and again."

"I'm sorry. I didn't realize I had said that out loud. I am sorry if I upset you." I turn away to look out the window, almost as shocked as he is.

After a few seconds he turns me to face him. "Don't be sorry, you didn't upset me at all. I am very happy you said it but shocked all the same. How are you feeling about it?"

"I don't know. Conflicted I guess and shocked as well. I guess I don't really know how I feel about it. I do know that I didn't have to think about it and I said it like it was second nature. I am not sorry I said it either."

He put his hand along my face, and then puts his arms around me. "It's okay baby. I understand." He kisses me then holds me for a few minutes. I pull away as he says we should get going because my uncle and Bryce will be waiting for us wondering what happened.

As he drives, I look at him. "It's not okay you know."

"What's not okay?"

"I told you I love you because I do. You shouldn't have to hear me say it then wonder if or when I will say it again."

Not sure what else to say or do, he holds my hand tightly not letting go as he drives on. We barely say another word the rest of the drive there. All I can do is stare out the window and fight back the tears. I really don't know why I feel like crying.

CHAPTER 32

I JUST SIT here not sure what to say or do. Just before we get to Bryce's shop, I wipe away some tears that are running down my face, look over at Craig and give him a smile. He smiles back. "Are you alright?"

I nod my head. "I am not sure what I am feeling. All I do know for sure is that I do love you and I don't regret saying it."

We pull into Bryce's yard and up to the garage. We get out. I tell Craig I need a few minutes to gather my thoughts that I will be in soon. He walks around the front of the truck an up to me. He puts his arms around me and while hugging me asks if I am sure I am okay.

I look at him, give him a kiss and tell him I am fine I just need a minute to process. He goes inside and I walk over to the front of the cars Bryce has on the other side of the parking lot. I sit with my back against a car facing the three-foot cement wall he has fencing the edge of the yard.

While sitting here I close my eyes and talk to Josh. 'I know you are here with me as you always are. I need your help. If you are fine with me and Craig, then give me a sign, something that tells me how to let you go. If you are not okay with it, I need you to tell me and tell me now.'

After a few minutes, I get a vision in my head. I am shown the two pictures I have on my nightstand with him and the kids and the wedding bands I placed there a few nights ago. The pictures placed down and the rings are gone. That is my answer. He is alright with me and Craig. In order for me to move on, I need to put the pictures and rings away. Out of sight, out of mind and that is what I am going to do.

Now that I know Josh is okay with it and know what he is telling me, I feel a little better. I tell him that I love him and always will and nothing will ever change that. I want to be happy again and knowing that I do have room in my heart for two great loves, I need to do this; if for nothing else, my own sanity.

Well there you have it. The love bug has bitten once again in my life. How many people get a second chance at true love? Not many, yet here I am. I can't let it go by and do nothing. I decide that I need to let Josh go. I realize then that love has forced my hand and I now need to take action.

Just as I decide what I am going to do, I hear someone coming up between the cars. I wipe my eyes and try to act like I haven't been crying. I look up and it is Bryce. "Are you okay cuz?"

I hold my hand out for him to help me up and then hug him. "Yes I am fine. Something happened between Craig and I on the way here and I wasn't sure how I felt about it or how I would deal with it."

He informs me that Craig has already told him what was said. I explain how I needed some time to pull it together and then ask him if I can use his phone to make a quick call. "Yes, of course you can. It is in my office."

I look over and notice that Craig and Uncle Arlo are standing by his truck looking at us. Bryce and I walk back to them. They ask me if I am okay and I nod my head. "I know Craig told you what happened, I needed time to figure out exactly what I was feeling and how I am going to deal with it. I have my answers and know what I need to do."

I look at Craig. He has a worried look on his face. I smile, hug him and whisper in his ear, "No worries, I do love you."

I look over at Bryce. "Okay where is your phone?"

We all walk into the garage and he shows me where the phone is in the office. I go in and close the door. I pick up the receiver and dial the number as I sit in the desk chair. "Hello."

"Hi Aunt Cheren."

"Hi Chloe. Is everything alright dear?"

I say yes and tell her what happened between me and Craig on the way over here.

"Oh my, are you okay?"

"I wasn't sure at first, but when we got here I took a few minutes to gather my thoughts about it." I then tell her what I did when I got here and explained what happened with my vision. "That's why I am calling you."

"What do you need me to do?"

"Well I need you to take the two pictures and my rings from the night stand and put them away. They need to be someplace where I won't find them. If you have to give them to someone outside the home, then do so."

"No problem. I will do anything you need to help you."

I tell her that it needs to be for two weeks. No matter how much I ask or cry or get mad, she can't give in. If I can go for two weeks without looking at them, I will be able to move on with my life.

"I will do it now when we hang up so that it is done before you get back home."

"Thank you Aunt Cheren. I love you."

"I love you too. Is there anything else you need me to do?"

"No that is it, at least for now."

She says okay, we both say goodbye and hung up the phone.

As I sit here with my head in my hands trying not to cry, I hear a tap on the door. I look over and there stands the three of them looking at me through the doors' window. I wave them in. "Can I speak to Craig alone for a few minutes? I promise I will tell you what is going on but the decision I made affects Craig more than anyone else."

"Sure sweetie." Uncle Arlo says as he and Bryce leave the office closing the door behind them.

I look at Craig, smile and take him by the hand leading him to the love seat. I sit him down on the couch and then sit on the edge of the coffee table in front of him. I want to be face to face when I explain things to him and with him being taller than I am, this will put us almost eye level. I take his hands.

"I want to explain to you first what I decided, who I just called and why."

"Okay but," I stop him telling him I just need him to listen right now. He agrees sitting back holding my hands tightly.

"You know I felt conflicted with my feelings when you made me realize that I told you I love you out loud."

"Yes."

"Well, I asked Josh about us because I needed to know that he was okay with me loving someone else. Within seconds I got my answer."

"What was that?'

"What I am going to say next will answer all of your questions, I hope."

"Okay."

"When I came in here I called my aunt right away before I changed my mind. I told her that I needed her to put the pictures of Josh and the kids along with the rings away where I can't find them. Right now as we speak she is doing that for me. I instructed her not to tell me where they are no matter what for at least two weeks. If I can get through the next two weeks without looking at the pictures or rings, I will be able to move on and give you 100% of myself."

"That's a good thing, isn't it?"

"Yes it is but, I need you to be patient with me for the next two weeks to give me time to do this."

"Okay. You know I will do anything I can but what do you mean by be patient? Do you not want me around for the next two weeks while you deal with this?"

"No, that's not what I am saying at all. I have never been through this before and really don't know what to expect or what I am going to go through. When I say give me time, I didn't mean I don't want to see you. In fact, it is just the opposite."

"Okay I feel better. What is it you need me to do?"

I explain to him that I will need him more than I have ever needed anyone in my life. I tell him that I want him to be with me as much as possible throughout this.

"I don't know what will happen or when. I might fall apart. I might yell and pull away. I might want to be held or need a shoulder to cry on. I might need nothing. I want you to be this person for me but only if you can or want to."

After a few seconds, he lets go of my hands, leans forward, and puts his arms around my waist. "Baby, I will do whatever it takes to help you and I will wait for you as long as I need to."

I can't help but smile because I wasn't sure if he would do this. Saying you love someone, and wanting to be there for them every way possible, and actually doing that are two different things; and, other than Josh, I have never had that. Usually when someone tells me they will be there for me, when the time comes and I need them, they are gone.

He kisses me then looking into my eyes he says, "If it takes two days, two weeks, two months or even two years, I will still be here waiting and helping you, no matter what. I love you and am in love with you. When I said this earlier to you I meant it. Now let me prove it to you."

I hug him really hard trying not to cry telling him that I love him too and thank him for doing this. We then go into the garage and stand with Bryce and my uncle.

I thank Bryce for letting me use the phone and apologize to the both of them for leaving them out of the conversation. After being told that Craig has told them what happened, I briefly tell them I have decided to let go of Josh, explaining what needs to be done and thank them for their patience as well. They both say they will be there to support me and help me through this in any way they can. I thank them all again and then look at Bryce.

"There is a reason why I am here. It is more than just wanting to get out of the house and see the sights of this town. I have a proposition for you Bryce and I believe it is one you won't be able to turn down."

"She's right! And as your father, if there is ever a time you listen to me, this must be that time. She told me her idea last night and you need to listen to her."

Bryce pulls up a stool and sits as do I in front of him. "Okay, so what is so important that even my dad is telling me to listen?"

Uncle Arlo and Craig stand beside each other off to my left leaning against the tool bench. Before I start, Uncle Arlo whispers to Craig, "That is one smart woman. If you were half as smart as she is, you won't let her go! You need to listen. This is why I wanted you here today."

They both look at us and smile. Realizing we heard what was said, Craig starts to blush, even though he is still smiling in agreement.

"Anyway, I overheard you talking this weekend about your business to your dad and brother about where it is at and how you are looking at having to declare bankruptcy if something isn't done quickly."

"Yes and what does that have to do with you?"

"Well, a lot actually. You see, I can help you not only get out of debt but become profitable in a short period of time."

Craig walks over and stands beside Bryce.

"And just how do you propose to do that?"

"Ya, I'm kinda wondering that myself." Craig says with his arms folded.

"Pull up a stool and listen and I will tell you."

Craig gets a stool and sits beside Bryce.

I explain to them what I have done in the past, just as I told it to my aunt and uncle last night. It's like I was telling the best love story ever, they were so intent. Listening to what I am saying, neither of them has noticed my uncle go outside for a smoke. No one knows that he is still smoking. I walked in on him at home a few nights ago and promised I would not tell anyone.

You see, Uncle Arlo had a heart attack last year and the doctor told him he had to quit smoking and change his diet or he would die very soon. He told me that changing his eating habits and not drinking was hard enough but smoking he just could not give that up too. So he cut way back, from almost three packs a day to just six cigarettes a day.

Anyway, I don't miss a beat as I continue to tell them what I have done and how. You can see the wheels turning in their heads and their eyes twinkle. Almost like it is Christmas and even though they know what's coming, they get excited and can't wait to open up their presents.

I explain in detail what I did for other businesses; in the non-profit sector including the ministry of health, in the profit sector and to my dad's businesses. I then hand Bryce a piece of paper.

"Your mom wrote these down for me last night. When I told your dad what I just told you, she said it was on the internet so I asked her to write down the website addresses. These are the websites where you can see that what I just told you is true and what others have to say about my work. I want you to go and read for yourself what I can do. When you are done, come back and I will answer any questions you may have. Then I will tell you my idea."

Intrigued they both go into the office at a fast pace as though they can't wait to see proof. As they are in there, I turn to my uncle who has since come back in and ask, "So how do you think that went?"

"Well you have them thinking and wondering."

Nodding in agreement we talk back and forth for about fifteen minutes discussing whether he thinks Bryce will agree to do this or not. "It depends on what is it you are going to tell him you can do."

Just then they come back out. As they walk across the garage towards us, Bryce seems to be in shock. "Wow, you are good." he says as he sits back down.

"She is downright amazing." Craig says as he moves his stool beside me, sits down, and puts his arm around me.

"I heard what you said but actually seeing the results and feedback especially the recommendation letters from the government, well, I am impressed and blown away."

Agreeing with them Uncle Arlo decides to grab a stool and join us. "This part I haven't heard. I am anxious and curious to hear what Chloe has planned for you."

"First, do you have any questions?" I ask the boys.

"Just one."

"Okay, Bryce. What is it?"

"What is it that you think you can do for me?"

"Well, I am glad you asked me that. Here is what I'm proposing."

"I can't wait to hear this." says Craig.

"Me either." says my uncle.

"In order to do the same thing for you, I will need your 100% full cooperation."

"No problem there."

"Well, wait." I express quickly. "I need to tell you first what that will entail because if you can't or won't do it, then all I can do is promise that what you help me with is all that will happen."

"Okay, still no problem."

I explain to all three of them that they need to listen completely before saying anything. They agree so I begin and assertively I tell them my ideas.

"To give me 100% cooperation means to put your total faith, trust and control of your entire business into my hands. You will have absolutely no control over anything. This means you won't even be able to spend $1 without my permission first. It also means that you give me everything I ask for and when I tell you to make a change or to do or not do something, you do. You need to act like it is my business and you work for me."

The look on their faces is priceless. You can tell it is not what they were expecting me to say. I am saying it with determination and full eye contact. I need them to know that I mean business, and I know what I am doing. I have to make them understand that it will work ONLY IF they do their part.

"During this process you will be kept apprised of everything. You will know what I am doing, why I am doing it, and where I am at every step of the way. You will get reports and I will be asking a lot of questions. Not just of you but from Craig, your dad, brothers, suppliers, contractors and even some of your customers. When I am done I will know what, when and how long."

All three of them sit with their eyes wide open and scared looks on their faces. It is like they are watching a scary movie where they are excited and scared of at the same time.

"Today is Tuesday already but, if I start this afternoon, I can guarantee that by this Friday, your eviction notice will be cancelled, creditors will stop calling and your suppliers will give you what you need to finish the jobs you have here now."

"Are you sure that is even possible?"

"Yes and within a week, I can have two to three people here every day helping you with this work. Now I don't know yet if it will be all day every day, just mornings or afternoons; but, you will have the help you need without having to pay a dime and with very little training."

Now they really can't believe what I am telling him. "How can all this be done so quickly like you say it will?"

"It is very simple. I will call your landlord in the morning along with your creditors and suppliers explaining that you are undergoing an audit with complete restructuring. You will tell them that I am the person in charge during this process and anything that needs to be handled, dealt with or discussed goes through me. I will negotiate terms with them for repayment letting them know that once this process is complete, they will be paid in full as per our new agreement. They will leave you alone."

"And why would they do that?"

"Well Uncle Arlo, it tells them that Bryce recognizes there is a problem and is trying to do something about it. Otherwise he would have closed his doors, declared bankruptcy and left them out in the cold writing off another bad debt. By telling them he is trying says he is not trying to get out of paying them, he is in fact doing what he can to pay them. It looks really good in their eyes and will help him greatly down the road."

They all nod accepting that maybe it is possible.

"As for the help every day, this too is easy. All we have to do is get workers from the local trade schools you have around here. The students have to put in a number of hours in real world job experience before they can graduate and you are not allowed to pay them for it. All I have to do is make a phone call and set up an appointment for us to meet with them next week. You will then choose the two or three you want to work for you and they start the next day."

They all seem excited now. "I would have never known that." Bryce says.

Impressed Craig holds me tighter and gives me a kiss on the cheek. I pause for a moment letting this all sink in. "Do any of you have any questions so far?"

They all shake their heads. "So far it is self-explanatory."

"Okay, as for the rest I can't give exact time frames yet as I need to go through all your paperwork, files, receipts, reports, financials, contracts, work, etc. that you have had for the past year or so. Once I have gone through it all, it will allow me to give you more definite answers to time frames with exact debt reductions."

"And what does that do?"

"The time varies and is determined by many things. For example: How much you are in debt and the paperwork you have that tracked it. How much time it will take for me to find out why and where you got in debt in the first place then figure out what changes need to be made so they don't happen again. How long it will take me to get and go through all your paper work and what if any, figuring out I will need to do from the accountant. How well we work together and how well you follow instructions."

"That doesn't sound too bad. I can answer most of that now."

"Wait, I am not done. Other things that affect the end result is how long it will take to implement the necessary changes. All of these determine the results and time frames." To them it seems like a lot but if all goes well, I know I can do all of this in two weeks or less and give him definitive answers. I then throw a curve ball at him.

"From what I have heard and been told, I estimate that you are in debt somewhere between $50,000 and $75,000. Right?"

"Wow, you are good. My accountant told me that it's almost $63,000 as of December 31st."

"Based on that and given that it is a true amount, I can tell you this for sure. If you agree to do this and I begin today, by September 30th you will be out of debt and by Christmas you will be making a profit. Now how profitable depends on many variables; however, you will be making money and not losing it like you are now!"

After a few moments of silence and bewildered looks on their faces, I am still not sure if Bryce will agree to this.

"So, do you think you can really do this? Do you actually think you can get me out of debt in six months? From what you just told us you would have to do, it seems like it would take a lot longer."

"There is no doubt in my mind. It is very possible that it could happen in less than six months."

"How can you be so certain?"

"It usually only takes me a week or two to go through all the paperwork but, I gave you the outset because of the decision I made earlier and in case I hit a snag and extra work needs to be done. Keep in mind that I haven't seen any of your paper work yet."

With bewildered looks on their faces, my uncle is the first to begin smiling as he is starting to understand what I just said to them.

"I understand it is a lot to think about and not something you expected. Think about it, discuss it and talk it over with whoever you need to discuss it with and let me know what you decide. Just keep in mind that the longer you take to decide, it's that much longer it will take for me to do what needs to be done."

Standing up I tell the three of them I am going outside for a bit to clear my head and let them process everything I just said. I tell them to come and get me if they have any questions, I give Craig a kiss on his cheek and go outside.

CHAPTER 33

SITTING HERE IN the back of Craig's truck I take a deep breath and close my eyes, letting the sun's rays' dance across my face. As I wonder what the result is going to be, I hear chatter inside. Although I can't understand what is being said or who is saying what, I do know they are talking and this is a good sign.

As I smile, I am thinking about what I said and wondering if I missed anything that might sway him to say yes. Soon, I catch myself thinking about Craig and what was said in the car on the way over here along with the decision I made to let go of Josh.

Putting those thoughts and fears out of my head so I can concentrate on the task at hand, I open my eyes and sit up to see that my uncle is standing at the door waving me over. As I walk into the garage, I am greeted with smiles from ear to ear on all three of them. I took this as a good sign.

I put a smile on my face and ask, "Is everything okay?"

"Everything is great! You are very smart and confident. Not something we see around this town very often."

"Thank you Uncle Arlo."

As we approach Craig and Bryce I ask them, "Do you have any questions?"

"Yes actually, I do." Bryce replies.

"Okay shoot."

"You never said what you wanted in return for helping me. Do you know what it is?"

With a smile, I sit back down. "I didn't because it is not much. If you agree to do this here is what I want in return. My cell phone paid every month at $60; a way to and from here every day so I can do this; and I want to learn how to fix vehicles."

Lifting an eyebrow with a surprised looked, he takes off his hat and scratches his head. "Fix vehicles?"

I tell him how I want to rebuild from bottom up including the paint job a 1969 Shelby GT convertible. "I learn very quickly, you can ask your dad. He's been teaching me some things over the past few days."

He looks at his dad. "Yes it is true. I have been and she picks it up almost as quickly as all you boys did."

"Okay. Well then let me see if I have this right. I turn everything over to you giving you complete control. I do nothing unless you tell me too and," Bryce stops for a moment. Wondering what he is doing, he stands there like he's counting on his fingers before continuing. "By Christmas you will have me out of debt the full $63,000."

"No! You will be out of debt by the end of September, and making a profit by Christmas."

I sit back on my stool and then ask the one question I need an answer to. "How much time do you need to make your decision?"

"None, we all discussed it and we all agree that whatever you need it's yours. One last question though. When can you start and what do I need to do?"

I smile and hug him. "Right now, if you are willing to give me a ride home by five for dinner."

"No problem. I can do that. One of us will make sure you get back home for dinner."

"Great."

Uncle Arlo asks if there is anything I need him to do before he leaves. "No, I think we are good." I reply.

"Well then Bryce, I will leave you in Chloe's capable hands and talk to y'all later."

He gives me a hug whispering 'good job', says his goodbyes and leaves.

Craig asks if I want him to stay or leave. "That is up to you. I don't know if you still have other work that needs to get done."

"No. I finished it before arriving at your place this morning."

"Well then it is up to Bryce. If he is okay with you being in on the discussions and knowing things about his business, then I am okay with you staying."

"I am okay with it. Craig knows almost everything now. He was with me when I started this business and has helped me many times."

"It is settled then. Both of you will stay and help me get started."

AS BRYCE IS showing me where he keeps all his paper work, he asks, "Do you mind if I ask you what your decision was today?"

"Oh my God Bryce I am so sorry. I had every intention of telling both you and your dad. With everything else I totally forgot."

"It's okay. Will you tell me now?"

"Yes. First, what is it that Craig told you?"

He tells me exactly what did happen. At least I now know that Craig does not embellish or make things more than they are to better himself, he tells it like it is or has happened. This is a good thing, at least in my book.

I then tell him about my vision and that I called his mom to help me and what I asked her to do.

"If there is anything I can do to help please let me know."

"Thank you, and yes, I will. I have another question for you but it's not about your business."

"Okay what?"

"Did you ask grandma to help with the problem you asked me about on Sunday?"

"Yes I did and you are my answer."

"What do you mean I am your answer?"

"I asked her that same night to give me a sign if my business was going to close or not. I told her that if it wasn't then I need someone to come forward who can help me by Wednesday. If no one did by Wednesday, then I would give my notice and start the closing procedures. You came to me today with my answer." he said in tears and smiling.

"See. It works, you just have to ask." I then gave him a hug and we pull out papers.

Bryce is now out in the garage with Craig working on one of the cars as I sift through the paperwork. After about an hour, I go out with the phone in one hand and a note pad in the other. I walk up to Bryce and tell him he needs to call his accountant.

"This is what you need to do. You need to tell her NOT ask her, that you will be there tomorrow morning at 10 a.m. to pick up all your files, paperwork and financials from the past two years."

"Why?"

"I need these things to do my audit. I also need a breakdown of what she charges you for, including price for each. Tell her you also need a printout of the ledger, journal entries and tax returns for the past two years as well."

"I'm never going to remember all of that."

So I think for a minute of an alternative. Then it hits me.

"Okay, then call her and put her on speaker phone. Tell her you are going through a business

audit and restructuring and you need a few things from her. Then you tell her you have me here. Give her my name and tell her that I am the one in charge and I will be the one telling her what I need."

He agrees. "That I can do." he says dialing her number.

While on the phone Bryce is talking to her like they are acquaintances not like he is her boss. I am looking at him with disgust. Craig notices this and mouths to me, are you okay? I shake my head no but mouth back, I will be. Once he introduces me, I tell her she is on speaker so Bryce can hear everything being said between us.

I then say very assertively, "Ms. Baker. Time is very critical here. This is what I need from you. All financials, reports, charge statements, ledgers, journal entries, tax returns, paper work and all files Bryce has brought you for the past two years. I will also need a break down of what you charge him every year and for what, they need to be separated in the report."

"I can get it together but I will need more time. There is no way I can get all that together by 10 a.m. tomorrow morning."

Kind of put off by this I reply very sternly. "I am not playing games Ms. Baker. Bryce is your boss not the other way around and he has asked for these things. Everything I have asked for should already be printed off and filed in your file boxes and very clearly labeled. Not my problem if they aren't. It should take you only ten minutes to print off the ledger and journal entries and a breakdown of the charges."

"Yes but," I stop her there.

"No buts. Simply put, bring up Bryce's file on the computer and send these things to print. Go into the file room, pull out all of Bryce's file boxes for the past two years and have them brought to your office. Make sure his name is on them. Once the files from the computer are printed, initial each page and sign the letter with the breakdown of charges. Put them all into a folder and stick them in one of the boxes. It is that simple. No excuses. We will see you tomorrow morning at 10." I hang up the phone and look over at the boys.

Bryce is shocked. "Why do you need all these things from her when I have most of them here already?"

"I need them from her because I need to do a comparison. I am an accountant but because it was in Canada I can't practice here. That does not mean I don't know what takes place or how long it takes to do things. Most of these people who work in corporate offices like that, pilfer money from clients and line their pockets. I want to make sure this hasn't happened to you first and foremost."

Craig is just standing there like a lost puppy not saying a word. I look at him, "Are you going to be okay?"

He nods. "I have never seen anything like that."

"Well when I said I know what I am doing, I meant it."

"Yes and you weren't kidding." he says with a smile.

"Bryce, this is the attitude you need to have with these people. They work for you not the other way around and you need to let them know that. You are not their friend either. Being pleasant is one thing but friendly is unacceptable. Sometimes they need to be reminded of that or they will take advantage."

"I know you are right but I have never had to be that way."

"Well, if my suspicions are accurate, you could not be more wrong. Let's just hope I am wrong. However, if she thinks that because she has pulled the wool over your eyes these past few years, that she can do it to me, she can't be more wrong."

"We can see that." says Craig still smiling.

"Well, if that is what she's thinking, she will be in for a rude awakening because that won't happen."

They laugh and go back to work on the car while I go back into the office to go through some more of the papers he has here.

I get everything in order and into boxes. I print out everything he has including financials in his computer and put them into a file. I get together all his contracts, work orders, invoices, etc. and put them into a file. I ask the guys bring all of these out to the truck so I can take it home and sort through it some more before going to bed tonight.

When they are done, we close up the garage and get ready to leave. As we are walking out to the trucks, Craig tells me that he and Bryce put the stuff into his truck because he is taking me home. "I have something I would like to discuss with you."

"Okay."

So I say good night to Bryce telling him I will be here around 8:30 in the morning.

He leaves and so do we.

CHAPTER 34

ON OUR WAY to my aunt's house, Craig informs me that he already told my uncle what I've decided and what I had asked him to do. "Good, now I don't have to say it again when I get home. What did he say about it?"

Before he could answer his cell phone rings. "Hello." he answers.

I have no idea who it is and the conversation I hear gives me no clues; at least not right away.

"Sounds good to me." he says pausing to listen to what the caller has to say. After a few minutes he says, "Ya I think she will be okay with that." Then there's another pause. He smiles looking at me then asks, "Do you want me to say anything?" After another pause he answers, "Ten minutes."

Now I now know he is talking to my aunt or uncle because we are only ten minutes from their place. "See you then." he says then hung up.

Wondering what that was all about I ask. "So what did my aunt or uncle have to say?"

"You will see here in about five to ten minutes."

Curiosity killed the cat and that's how I am beginning to feel. I am really curious to what's going on. I know they are planning something about me but he won't tell me anything. He is getting fidgety, almost like a cork on a champagne bottle ready to pop.

"What is it you wanted to discuss with me?"

"It can wait, what is going to be said here soon takes precedence."

"You know I don't like it when others makes plans for me without my input. Especially when it affects me directly. Planning a trip or a surprise is one thing but I have a suspicion from your conversation that it is not that type of plan."

"It will be okay baby. It is nothing bad. You will see, I promise."

I am little worried. We arrive at the house. Once inside I notice the table is already set for dinner as it is ready and waiting. Uncle Arlo and Craig bring in the boxes from the truck and place them beside the fireplace in the living room. As they bring the last of them in, Quentin walks in behind them. Aunt Cheren asks him to join us for dinner and he does.

During dinner my aunt tells me she did as I asked earlier. I thank her and begin to tell her what I asked Craig to help me with she stops me. "I already know. In fact we all do and we respect your decision."

"Okay that's good. Thank you."

"Chloe, we have been talking since all this happened this afternoon."

"Who is we, Uncle Arlo?"

"Well, we are me, your aunt, Craig, Bryce and Eric." I look around at all of them sitting around the table. He continues, "We all love you very much and are honored you chose us to help get your life back together. We also want to help you any way we can."

"We have come up with a plan of our own." adds my aunt.

"I gathered that from the phone discussion you and Craig had when we were on our way home. He won't tell me anything."

"This plan will help you get through this and we are all here to run it by you to make sure you are okay with it." she says.

"Is this going to make me cry? I've been doing a lot of that lately and really don't want to do anymore of it."

Just then, Quentin stops eating. "What's going on? Did I miss something here?"

Craig pulls him aside and quickly summarizes the events of today between him and I. As he is telling Quentin what happened, Aunt Cheren starts talking again.

"Well, none of us are sure what toll this will take on you, but we all do agree that helping Bryce with his business is going to help you in so many ways."

Nodding in agreement Craig comes back to the table with Quentin and they sit back down. Craig then says, "This plan came together once everyone knew what happened and how your aunt and I are helping you."

"Wait a minute." I say. "Please tell me that Bryce did not agree to my proposal only to help me with this!"

Everyone shakes their head. "No no baby. That happened before any of this. When you were in the office and Bryce and I were in the garage, we called your aunt and uncle and told them. They then told Eric and we went from there."

"Okay good."

"I'm going to help your aunt with you, if you ask for the pictures. I'm also going to help keep you busy when you are here out in the shop with me just like we planned earlier."

"Okay, that works for me."

"We all figured if we kept you occupied and your mind busy, it is less time you will have to think about the things that brought you here and you will heal quicker."

"I understand Uncle Arlo, but you aren't telling me anything I didn't already know."

"It works!" states Eric as he walks in the door. "Sorry I am late everyone." He takes a seat at the table. "We have you covered from the time you get up in the morning until you go to bed at night. Our only concern is during the night."

I look at him with a raised eyebrow. "What do you mean you are concerned for the night time?"

"Well, like I told you before, I have been through something similar a few years back. When I did, all kinds of things happened to me that I did not expect. My family and Craig all planned something similar for me and it worked. Today we decided that maybe it was time to do the same thing for you so you can move on with your life and be happy again. Just like me."

Quentin is sitting across from me and he and I are looking from one person to another as they take their turns telling me their plan to help me. I am still a bit confused. "So far, I already know most of what you have told me. Is there anything with this plan that I don't know yet?"

Quentin then blurts out as he stops eating. "Can we get on with this please? I don't have all night and I really need to talk to dad!"

My uncle pulls Quentin outside and we can hear him yelling at him about how insensitive he is being.

Eric speaks up. "Now, we know what you asked Craig to do but we took it one step further. I can be here the odd time in the spare room or on the couch but it's not the best if you need someone and no one is right there. That is when we talked to Craig and asked him just how far he would go and what he was willing to do to help you."

"And what did you say?" I ask looking at Craig.

"I said anything, as far and as long as it takes. I told them what I told you earlier when you asked me the same question."

My aunt says that Eric and Craig came up with the idea and they feel it is the best for everyone. "We believe that you will be okay with it. At least we hope you are."

"It seems okay so far but you still haven't told me what that part of the plan is."

"Remember, we all agree it is best for you and seeing the way you have been, we believe it whole heartedly." chimes my uncle as he and Quentin walk back in.

"Okay, so what is it?"

"Baby, I will be the one spending the nights with you. It will be either here or at my place."

I am perfectly fine with that plan and they know this from the smile on my face.

"I will be in and out, here and at Bryce's shop to help. And you have my phone number to call if you ever need me or want to talk, anytime."

"Yes Eric, I do."

I am now just sitting here. I'm in awe and a bit in shock of what they just told me. All I can do is look around the table at everyone sitting here. I can't believe what they are all doing not to me but for me.

Quentin looks over at me as he stuffs more food in his mouth. "Are you alright, Chloe?"

Nodding my head Craig puts his arm around me, "Are you sure?"

I nod again with tears in my eyes. "I can't believe that y'all are doing this for me. It is much more than my own family would do."

Surprised at what I said my uncle asks, "What do you mean more than your own family? We are your family."

"No I mean my immediate family, mom, dad and siblings."

"Okay so explain that one please."

"I don't know how you and dad have the same jean pool. You are so much like Grandma was and dad is very much like Grandpa was. You help your family first then everyone else after. Dad, well, he helps everyone except family and then when something happens, he wonders why no one is there to help him."

"Wow. I would not expect that from my brother. I always thought he was better than me at raising a family. All you girls turned out different than my boys did."

"Well, that's because we had different environments and I was the one who raised my sisters after dad left us." I then explain how my mom and siblings don't bother with me unless they want something but when I need the help they won't even answer their phone or messages.

"Wow, we didn't know any of that."

"I feel very warm and loved here, more than I ever did there, if that makes any sense." I say. "No one has ever cared enough about me to help me, especially to this extent like y'all have. I just don't think that saying thank you is enough."

They all tell me not to worry about it. I am here now and not there and I am family. If I get better that is all that matters and it's all the thanks they need.

Tears are now running down my cheeks. "Thank you. I don't know how I can ever thank you enough."

"No thanks needed sweetie. We love you and are here for you." says my uncle.

They all get up. My uncle gives me a hug and he and Quentin go into the living room. Eric helps his mom clear the table and Craig sits here with me a moment with his arms around me.

"Are you sure are okay baby?"

"Yes, I will be fine. It's a lot to take in and I still can't believe all of you are doing this for me."

He gives me a kiss before saying, "Baby, I have to go home and get a few things but I will be back very soon."

"It's okay I will be fine. Everyone is here and I have to go through these papers anyway. I will be here when you get back." I say as I am now smiling.

He brings me the boxes, gives me a kiss and leaves. I ask my aunt if she needs help with the dishes. She says no Eric is helping her, so I open the first box and begin going through Bryce's paperwork.

Twenty minutes go by and I am surprised at how much I have been able to get through so far. Uncle Arlo then calls me to go in to the living room, so I stop and join him and Quentin. Quentin sits up on the couch and slaps the seat beside him for me to sit. I do wondering what is going to come next.

"Chloe, I was just telling Quentin here what you are doing for Bryce."

"Why?"

"Well, Quentin was telling me how he is having money problems with his business so I mentioned he might want to talk to you."

Quentin is looking at me with a weird look. It's like he is smiling but very nervously. I look back at him but do not smile back. "Why would you want me to help you when you've had a grudge against me since the day I got here? Why the sudden change of heart?"

"I don't have a grudge against you. Where did you ever get that idea from?"

So I tell him where I got it from explaining his attitudes and behaviors towards me since the day I got here. "I don't like being used. I won't help someone who only pretends to like me or work with me because I can do something for them and when it's over they no longer talk to me. I get enough of that from my own family and I moved here to get away from that!"

Quentin just sits there looking at me like I am from outer space, like he can't believe I said that to him.

Looking at my uncle and pointing to Quentin, I say, "If he can treat me with respect and not just because I can help him, then I might think about it."

"Okay that can be done. If you did, how soon could you help him?"

"It won't be for a couple of weeks, maybe a bit longer. I just started working on Bryce's stuff and depending on what I come across and how much work needs to be done will depend on how soon I can work on his. It's easier one at a time so I don't get them mixed up. Plus not knowing how my decision will affect me, I don't want to make any promises I can't keep."

"Okay, let me talk to Quentin about this. I will make him understand what you are doing with his brother and we will get back to you."

I say okay, get up and go back to the table to continue on Bryce's paperwork.

About a half hour goes by when Craig comes walking in. He says hi, gives me a kiss on the cheek and puts his stuff in my bedroom. When he comes out he is asked to join Quentin and my uncle in the living room. Before he sits down he looks over at me, winks and blows me a kiss smiling. I smile and wink back then blow him a kiss before getting back to the paperwork.

By now Eric and Aunt Cheren have joined me at the table and start to tell me about Quentin. I don't know him like I do the others because he wasn't even born when they moved to Texas. Neither was Dante but I've been talking to him since he was in high school where Quentin, never bothered.

They tell me how Quentin is different and although may seem normal, he is a bit slow. He thinks differently than the rest of us. They paint Quentin to be a spoiled brat who got everything he wanted as a child and now has attitudes about certain things. He takes temper tantrums when things don't go his way even though he is now 34. They tell me that's why he has no girlfriend or wife.

"Why are you telling me this stuff about him?"

"I think that if you can, you should help him with his business." Eric says. "It might help to bring the two of you closer together as well."

"Ya or push us further apart!"

"At least think about it, please?"

"Okay I will but because you asked me too, not because he wants me to."

Eric then says good night and leaves. The next thing I know my uncle, Quentin and Craig are at the table with us. *Am I ever going to get any work done* I think to myself.

Sitting here as they all look at me, I try to continue on Bryce's papers. After a few minutes I lay my pen down and look up at them. "Okay, look. I said I would think about it and I will. But, if y'all keep trying to push me, all it will get you is me pissed off and helping no one!"

"We understand that Chloe, but I told you I would talk with Quentin and let you know what he decides. He is ready to talk."

I look at Quentin. "Okay, so what do you want to tell me?"

"Dad pointed out a few things to me and I want to say I am sorry. I didn't realize I was being like that towards you. I am willing to work with you if you are willing to help me."

"If I do this your attitude needs to change. I won't work with or help you if all you are going to do is argue and question every little thing I do. I can't do a good job if I have to spend most of the time breaking down walls rather than doing what needs to be done."

"I get that. I promise to try not to do that."

"You should know that I am very good at what I do and your attitude of what women should be doing versus what a man should be doing is unacceptable to me."

As I am saying this I am only getting more upset. He seems to get it but does not seem sincere. He is talking like he is only doing this because he knows I can help him and not for any other reason.

Seeing this, Craig reaches over and puts his hand on my left arm and gives it a little squeeze. I put my right hand on his and smile at him. I then look back at Quentin and calmly say, "If you can get over that and realize that woman or not, I might know more about business than you do, then I can work with you. Otherwise it won't work out."

He just sits there like he is mulling over what I am saying. Not saying a word in reply I tell him my suggestion. "If you really want me to help you, then you have one month. During this month, you talk to Bryce and see what I am doing for him and get his opinion and thoughts. Come around more. Get to know me. See how I involve everyone and how we work together. Get over the fact that I don't belong in a garage simply because I am a woman or it won't work. If you can do this, we will talk."

I sit here for a minute and look around to see what the rest are thinking. My uncle gets up smiling. "Quentin, you should listen to Chloe. She can help you." He leaves and goes to his shop to shut things down and lock it up for the night.

Craig looks at me with raised eye brows. I look at him. "I am okay." I say to him.

Aunt Cheren goes back to playing her game on her laptop, smiling as she does.

Quentin takes a minute then moves to the chair closest to me. He looks at Craig then me. "I am sorry if I made you feel inferior. I really don't have any issues with you, like I said earlier. I actually have a lot of respect for you and at times am scared of you. I guess I suck at showing these things. I am willing to try."

He puts his hand out to shake mine. I take it and smile. "I hope you are serious about this because if you aren't."

"I am, trust me. Let me prove it to you."

I nod half smiling. Quentin gets up, says good night to everyone and goes out the door.

I put my glasses down and look at Craig. "I will be right back."

I follow Quentin outside catching up to him just as he opens the door to his truck. "Look Quentin. I am sorry if I was hard on you but you left me no choice. I don't take these things lightly and we are family."

"It's okay Chloe. I understand and I promise to try to work on changing the way I say things."

"Can I ask why you are scared of me?"

"You have the confidence and smarts I wish I had."

I give him a hug and he gets into his truck and leaves.

I come back in with my uncle who has now made his way back. I start picking up the papers and put them back in the boxes. It's almost eleven and I am getting tired. Tomorrow is going to be a long day.

As Craig and I move the boxes out of the way I tell my aunt and uncle about the meeting in the morning with Bryce's accountant and how it all came about. I then say good night and head to the bathroom.

When I am done, I open the door to go into my bedroom and notice the rest of the house is dark. I go into my bedroom, Craig is already in there waiting for me. "Your aunt and uncle have already gone to bed."

"That was quick."

"Yeah, I guess it was. They said they are usually in bed by 9 and it's almost 11 so I guess they were tired."

"Maybe."

"I will be right back."

"Okay, I will be right here." I reply back with a smile.

Craig goes into the bathroom and I get out of my clothes. Tonight I am only wearing a long t-shirt to sleep in. Craig comes in as I am climbing into bed. He closes the door, gets undressed to his underwear and slides between the sheets with me.

CHAPTER 35

AS I GET home and walk through the door, I see the note on the table. It reads,

*'We have him. Meet us at the K spot in
Garndland in twenty minutes.'*

Oh My God I scream out, he's gone. Not knowing how long it has already been, I run out the door and do as the letter said. As I get to the K statue in the park. There he lays, I can't wake him up. I check him, he's not breathing. CPR does not work. He's gone. I cry uncontrollably.

Next thing I know, I am sitting up in bed sobbing.

The dream seemed so real, like it really happened, tears are running down my face and it takes me a minute to realize where I really am. I look around the room then beside me. There he lays, still. Craig is in my bed. I watch him. His bare chest rises and falls as he breathes in and out. I bring my legs up, put my arms around them and rest my head on my knees trying to calm down.

"Babe, are you okay?" Craig asks as he sits up with me.

I lift my head off my knees. "Yes. I just had a bad dream."

He rubs my back for a bit. "Come. Lay down with me, and tell me about it."

I lay back down beside him. Putting my left arm across his waist and my leg across his, he pulls the covers over us then puts his arms around me. A few minutes later I move laying my head on his chest still keeping my arm and leg where they were. He keeps his left arm around me and strokes my head with his other hand.

For some reason this relaxes me. It reminds me of when I was a young girl. My grandfather used to stroke and brush my hair for hours as we talked and it always made me feel good.

"Are you sure you are okay baby?"

"Yes I am fine. I want you to make me a promise but it's one you can't keep. No one can so I won't ask."

"I promise to do anything you ask me to."

"I am a strong believer that you only make promises you can keep and this one you can't."

"Look at me for a minute please."

I lay on my back with my head on my pillow and face him. He sees I have tears in my

eyes so he leans up on his elbow. "Please tell me what it is?"

He now has one arm over me with his hand caressing the side of my face. "Don't ever leave me."

"Why would you say that? I'm not going anywhere."

"I dreamt you were gone."

"Chloe, I promise to always love you, take care of you and be there for you. I am not going anywhere without you."

"Every man in my life so far has left me in one way or another. Either moving, leaving, divorce, death, stop talking, remove me from his life, etc. I keep having these dreams, for the past three days now, that you are taken away from me."

He tries to calm me down. "It was only a dream. Try not to worry about it. I am not going anywhere. I am right here with you. Besides, I am not like any other man you have known or been with. I promise and I will prove that to you."

He then kisses me, passionately. His hands are running up and down my body as I bring my knee up and rub my leg up and down his. My hands are all over his body and through his hair. He lifts my shirt but only to touch for a few minutes. He stops.

"Sorry. I don't want to take advantage of the situation or you and I know you're not ready yet. If we are going to be intimate with each other it will be when you are 100% ready." he says.

Agreeing with him that I am not there yet, we lay back down holding each other until we fall asleep.

IT IS SEVEN a.m. now and everyone is up except me. As I get up I take out the black knit dress I am going to wear for this meeting at ten today. I walk into the kitchen and grab a cup of coffee and notice no one is around.

I go onto the porch where my aunt is sitting in her rocking chair. "Where is everyone?" She points to the shop.

I sit here with her for a few minutes drinking my coffee then ask her a question. "Aunt Cheren, does uncle Arlo still have his guard uniform?"

"Yes he does, it's hanging in our closet. Why do you ask?"

"Do you think it would fit Craig?"

"Yes, it might. Why?"

I tell her about my idea for the meeting with Bryce's accountant. "Wow what a great idea." She gets up and goes into her room to find it.

I follow her in and put on a pair of shorts to go to the shop and get the guys. I figured I should tell them what my idea is and hope Craig will play along with it. As I pull them up over my hips, I hear them come in. I go out to the kitchen looking at the both of them with a grin on my face. "Great you are both here."

"Good you are finally up."

"Very funny Craig."

"Okay, what's wrong?"

"Nothing is wrong Uncle Arlo. But, I do have a question for the both of you."

"What's up?" asks Craig with an inquisitive look.

I explain to them how I want Craig to wear the uniform and why, that is if it is okay with my uncle. They both think it's a great idea. Just then, my aunt comes in with the uniform in hand.

"Yes, of course it's okay. I'm not sure it will fit you thought." he says looking at Craig as though he is sizing him up.

"Only one way to find out." he says as he heads to the bedroom to try it on.

I go into the bathroom to finish with my hair then it hits me, Eric used to be a security officer at the local jail. I rush out to the kitchen.

"Uncle Arlo? Can you give Eric a call and ask him to dress in his security uniform and meet us at Bryce's by nine?"

"Sure but he is going to ask me why?"

"That's okay, tell him what I am planning and that I will explain in detail when we all get there."

"Okay, I will do that."

Thanking him I turn. Craig is coming out dressed in the guard uniform. The uniform fits him really well and he looks really sexy in it too. I melt inside but try to hold it together on the outside. It is hard and

I know why. I smile at him then go into my bedroom closing the door behind me and fall onto the bed.

My aunt follows me in. "Are you alright?"

Nodding my head, I get up and pick up my dress with belt from the chair and bring it to the bed. "It's just he looks so handsome and sexy in that uniform. I didn't know if I could hold it in so I came in here to get dressed and calm down."

She laughs, "Okay honey, I'll leave you to it." she says as she walks out the door closing it behind her.

As I pull the knit dress over my head, I wonder if I will be able to contain myself today with him being in that uniform. I adjust my boobs and pull the dress down past my hips then below my butt. It stops half way down my thighs. It is a tight form fitting dress and the top is low cut showing some cleavage. I put on the two-inch-wide red with black rivet belt around my waist. I slide on my red and black pumps, put the red heart necklace I got for Valentine's day around my neck and grab my earrings. I walk out into the kitchen as I put my earrings in my ears.

My uncle is standing at the island facing me and Craig has his back to me pouring a cup of coffee. My uncle mouths 'WOW' as he stares at me. As I get close I ask, "So how do I look?"

My uncle says out loud this time, "Wow!" and can't seem to get any other words out.

Craig then turns, stirring his coffee. He looks at me and falls back against the counter. His eyes get big, his mouth drops open and he stops stirring his coffee as he drops the spoon on the floor.

My aunt laughs. "Chloe looks good, doesn't she?"

Craig stands there with both hands on his coffee cup and tries to stop from shaking. I look at him for a minute. "Are you okay?" I ask with a smirk.

He gathers himself together and shakes his head as if to say get a grip man. He then manages to say, "Yes. I just," he pauses, sets his cup down, walks to me and takes my hands in his. "I have never seen anyone more beautiful."

He spends the next several minutes staring at me. My aunt then asks, "Isn't it about that time you leave?"

I nod and ask Craig if he is ready. He nods, let's go of my hands and turns away saying, "Wow!" again.

"Uncle Arlo, did you get a hold of Eric for me?"

"Yes I did. I told him what you need and why and he said he would do it. He will meet you at Bryce's by nine."

"Thank you." As we walk to the door I look at Craig asking him if we are still one for dinner tonight. Saying yes I tell my aunt and uncle we won't be here for dinner. We then say goodbye and drive off.

Heading into town Craig doesn't stop smiling and is having a hard time focusing on the road. I try to take his mind off me so he can drive. "Tell me more about your mom and kids."

It only takes a few minutes as he gives me short answers. Knowing how Craig feels because I find myself doing the same thing with him, I turn my head smiling and pick up my cell phone and dial

"Hello."

"Good morning Eric. Craig and I are one our way and will be stopping to get some coffee. Would you like us to pick you up one?"

"No thanks. I just pulled out of there and I bought one for all of us. So you don't have to stop."

"Ok great, thank you. We are only fifteen minutes away, see you soon." I hang up.

I tell Craig there is no need to stop at Dunkin because Eric already has. He just nods, and smiles as he tries to keep the truck on our side of the road. I then call Bryce to give him a heads up that Eric is on his way and how he is dressed saying we won't be long. "I will explain everything when we get there."

"Okay, see you then."

Once we arrive at the garage, I gather everything Bryce has printed off for me earlier. I then have the three of them sit as I tell them my plan of how this will go.

"Eric and Craig are only for effect. Other than looking authoritative, they will help carry out the boxes but they have no other role."

I take a drink of my coffee. "It's the intimidation factor and can be very effective in situations like this."

"I love it." says Eric with Craig and Bryce agreeing with him.

"Do I need to change?" Bryce asks.

"Are you usually dressed like you are now when you see her or do you wear something different?"

"Like I am now."

"Then no. You need to be as you usually are when you talk to her."

"Then why are you dressed so nicely then?"

"Being in the position I am in, I need to look professional and better than her to get what I want."

I then explain to them how it works and how we will walk in, what will be said and done and by whom when we get there.

"First either Eric or Craig will walk in, which one first, does not matter. Then Bryce you will be second and I will follow. Then the other 'guard' will fall in behind me. Bryce, you need to be the one to ask for Ms. Baker. The three of us will move off to the side."

"Okay, then what do I do when she comes out?"

"Introduce her to me but only me. If she asks about Eric and Craig, I will answer her. You are then to ask her for the papers we asked for. If she gives you any answer other than, they are right here, I will speak."

"Can't I just let you do it all?"

"No Bryce, she works for you not me. You need to do it. Don't worry, it will be fine. I will be right there beside you. I know what I am doing, trust me."

After a few minutes of explaining some of the scenarios that could happen and what to do for each, we grab our coffee and jump into Eric's SUV. I am in the back with Craig. On our way to the office, I prep myself mentally as I drink my coffee.

"By the way Chloe."

"Yes Eric."

"You look really good in that dress."

"Thank you."

Craig and Bryce nod in agreement as we get out of the truck and go in the door.

The boys and I go right and stand at the edge of the waiting room as Bryce goes up to the desk, there is one person ahead of him. I scan the entire entrance and both waiting rooms, as there is one on either side of the entrance door. Straight ahead as you walk in sits the reception desk. To the right of the desk there are six boxes with Bryce's name on it. There are four people sitting in the left waiting area and three in the right.

Bryce steps up to the desk and asks to see Ms. Baker. After a few seconds I hear the secretary tell Bryce that she is in a meeting and can't be disturbed. I step up beside Bryce and say, "Excuse me!"

She asks who I am and Bryce tells her I am with him. She then says sorry but she won't be able to see us today. Now I am pissed off. "Sorry is not good enough! Get her back on the phone now!"

She picks the phone back up and buzzes her extension. She tells her that we won't take no for an answer. While she has her on the phone I say very loudly, "We are not playing games here. She knew we were coming and what we want. You tell her that if she is not out here in five minutes, I will go back there, find her and bring her out here myself!"

Before she could hang up the phone, she walked through the door. She walks up to Bryce and starts idle chit chat with him. I stop her quickly. "We are here for business, NOT a social call. Where are the files and papers we asked for?"

She looks over to Craig and Eric then back to Bryce asking who they are. Before he can reply I answer, "That is none of your concern. They are here with us and that's all you need to know."

She then points to the six boxes I had seen with Bryce's name on them. "That's all of it. They have been there since yesterday afternoon waiting to be picked up."

I look at her. "WHAT! More than two years of paperwork, files, receipts, letters, financials, tax returns, etc. and it's all in six boxes?"

"Yes."

"I don't believe you. And what about confidentiality? Do you not work according to those protocols?"

Looking at me with a questionable look, actually everyone in the room including the two who just walked in are now doing the same. "What?" she asks nervously.

"All of his information is just sitting here, out in the open for anyone to peruse through. No one is monitoring it! It's not hidden! It's just there, not secured or sealed. Anyone could have gotten any information on Bryce both personal and business."

Everyone in the office has a shocked look on their faces as others come out from their offices to see what is going on. "Well, umm, you said put them out front."

"No! You are not putting this on me. I told you to bring them to your office with his name on them. Besides, you should know what your job is and what it entails without me having to tell you. All of his information has just been sitting there since yesterday. That is a confidentiality breach if I ever seen it and I will have your job for that!"

I turn around and ask everyone sitting here, "Do you trust a company that allows their employees to put your information out for anyone to look at and get?" Most of the people sitting in the waiting rooms are shaking their heads in shock.

I then motion for the guys to bring the boxes out.

As they do I turn to Ms. Baker. "If any information is missing; if you are withholding any information from us; or if confidentiality in fact has been breached, you and this entire company will pay!" I follow Eric out the door.

We all get into the SUV, this time I am in the front. I tell Eric to start the engine but not to drive away yet.

"Why not?" he asks.

I tell him how I put the fear of god into her. "She is watching us right now and in a few minutes will run out with files in her hand apologizing. She will give me some excuse as to why they weren't in the boxes. She might even tell us there are more boxes she forgot about."

They all look at me in disbelief shaking their heads. "Do you really believe that?"

"Yes I do. Watch and learn Patawan."

After five minutes I tell him to back out but very slowly. We don't move four feet when I see her walking swiftly towards us with files in her hand. I tell Eric to stop and I roll down my window. She comes up to me and as if on cue hands me files. "I forgot I still had these on my desk. There are two more boxes of files inside too. They were put in a different spot so they got missed."

I tell Eric to back up to the door. As Craig and Bryce go and get the boxes, Eric opens the trucks' back gate. I keep my window down as they load the boxes.

"What I said before still stands. I will be in touch!" I roll up my window, Eric puts the truck in drive and we take off.

As we head back to the garage the guys ask me how I knew she would do that. I tell them again, that I have not only done this many times before but I have been on both sides of the fence.

"I know what words to use and the attitude that goes with them to make a point. I knew she was holding things back so I made her aware that I knew this."

They all laugh and we finish our coffee as Eric drives us back to Bryce's shop. After we unload the truck, Eric thanks me for a fun morning. "I haven't had that much fun since I quit being a security guard." We hug and he leaves.

Craig gets ready to go back to the house to change so I ask him to bring me back a change of clothes. "Sure. Anything in particular you want to wear?"

"One of the dresses hanging in my closet will do just fine. I will also need my sandals, they are more comfortable than these heels."

He agrees, gives me a kiss on the cheek and heads back to the house.

I spend the rest of the morning making phone calls to Bryce's landlord, creditors, debtors, and some of his customers. I go out and have him show me the jobs he has that still needs to be done before I call his suppliers. He tells me what he needs to get them done and who he would usually order them from so I know what to say to who when I call.

As I am making these calls, Craig returns and walks in with a box in his hands. I look at him puzzled while on hold, I ask him if he brought me back some clothes to change into. "Yes kind of." he answers me.

Looking at him questionably as I finish the call I was on, I ask, "What do you mean kind of?"

"Here, sit down on the couch for a minute and I will show you what I mean by that."

As I sit he walks over to me, sits on the table in front of me and hands me the box. "I know you wanted me to bring back a dress from your closet and I hope you don't get mad but I bought you one instead."

"Why would you buy me one?"

"I saw it in a window as I drove by and thought of you. I figured you would look great in it so I bought it."

I open the box. He tells me how he got my size from the dresses in my closet so he knows it will fit. I unfold the paper that wraps it up to unveil the most beautiful, summer dress I have ever seen. "Oh My God, I love it. And it is my favorite color too." I say as I pull it out.

The entire dress is emerald green. The top is tied at the shoulders with white ties. It is mid body cut with white edging and a white tie goes around the waist. The dress flares out in four different layers. It is beautiful.

I give him a kiss and go into the bathroom to put it on. He is right, it fits to a tee. I walk out but still have on the red and black dress shoes because that is all I have here.

"Wait. I almost forgot." he says as he hands me sandals to match. They are white, open toe, half inch, cork wedge sandals. They are beautiful as well and I put them on. Again they are a perfect fit.

"So are you mad at me?" he asks.

"No, why would I be mad at you?"

"You told me you wanted a dress from your closet. I thought maybe you had your heart set on wearing that one."

"I only asked for one of them because it was all I had clean. I haven't had a chance to do laundry in the past few days and they are comfortable."

"Okay good. I was worried you would be mad but I really thought you would look great in this dress and I was right." he says with a smile.

I let him know how happy I am and how much I love it. I give him a kiss and then leave him in the garage with Bryce and go back into the office to finish making my calls.

After forty-five minutes I come out and give Bryce the low down of what has taken place. "Okay Bryce." I begin.

Before I can say anything, he looks at me with his mouth dropped to his chest. "Wow Chloe, you look great. That's a good color for you."

"Thank you." I reply then tell him I have something to tell him. Stopping what he was doing, he stands there and I tell him what I have done so far.

"I have called your landlord and he will stop the eviction process for six weeks. He is giving me two weeks to come up with a payment plan and once it has been paid in full we will renegotiate your lease."

With a smile on his face, he gives Craig a high five. "Cool. I was worried. He can be a bear sometimes."

"Well, there is more; that is only the beginning."

"Okay, I can't wait to hear it."

"I have also called all your debtors and creditors and they too have agreed to stop sending the hate mail and you won't get any more phone calls either. In two weeks, I will be meeting with all of them to approve of a payment plan. When they are all paid, we will renegotiate the payment terms because I feel they are charging way too much in interest fees. In fact, I am going to come up with a settlement option for them which will be less than what they claim you owe right now."

Now he is ecstatic and can't stand still. He is smiling from ear to ear like he just won the lottery. "You are fantastic. You have just made my day. Thank you."

"Wait there is more." I tell him with a smile.

"Okay wait a minute. I have to sit down. I don't know if I can handle any more good news. I am not used to this."

As he sits on a stool Craig leans against the work bench waiting for me tell them what else there is. I pause for effect, put on a smile then continue with the rest.

"I called all of your suppliers too. Each one has agreed to the same deal I made with your creditors. Also, with what you need to finish the jobs you have here so you can get paid, I also got Johnson's Battery Plant and J. J.'s Distribution to agree to send you what you need. All you have to do is fax them your order before the day is out and they will guarantee delivery by UPS within 48 hours."

Well now he really can't believe it. He not only doesn't have to pay anything for about a month, but he gets the rest of the stuff he needs to finish his work. He stands up and hugs me.

"Thanks for the hug but I am not done."

He sits back on the stool. "What else can there be? You already saved me $30,000 or more with the accountant, stopped the eviction, got me the supplies I need and got all of them off my back for at least two weeks, maybe more."

"Well like the others, your contract with your suppliers will be renegotiated so your interest charges are less and you and I have to be at Thomson's Auto Tech trade school Monday at 1:30."

"What's there?"

"We are meeting with them to get the two to three students you need to help out around here in the shop for the next month or so. There are ten of them that need eighty to one hundred hours of on-the-job training. You pay them nothing but you will need to complete questionnaires for their school and sign a paper once a week to say they were here."

He sits there on his stool for a few minutes and then gets up with tears in his eyes. He is not a man to cry or show much affection at all. He then tries to summarize what he has just heard me tell him.

"Let's see if I have this right. In less than five hours you have managed to, save me a lot of money, stop the eviction, hold off people I owe, get me the supplies and staff I need without costing me a cent and possibly save me even more money when this is all done, with contracts?"

"Yes, and there is one more thing."

"There can't possibly be anything else. You haven't been in there long enough."

"Well, there is and I promise, this is it."

"Okay, lay it on me."

"I called five of your customers that owe you the most money. I explained who I was and reminded them that they have debts owed to you. I told them they were past their due date and if we didn't see payment by Tuesday we will be imposing high interest rates and begin with credit notices."

"Who did you call and what did they say?"

I tell him who I spoke with and then say, "Two said we will get paid by Friday and the others said by next Monday at the latest."

If any of them thought I was only blowing smoke up their ass when I first came to them with my proposal, they now know I meant what I said and I know what I am doing.

"Wow, I can't believe this. You said you could do this but I didn't expect all this this quick."

"Well, I hate to say it but, I told you so." I say with a smirk.

"Yes. Yes you did."

It is now four o'clock in the afternoon and not having eaten since breakfast I tell them I am getting hungry so I am going to get my stuff and am out of here for the night.

As I gather my stuff, Craig and Bryce sit on the stools, not moving almost like they are in disbelief, or in shock. Their eyes are wide, mouths dropped and Bryce looks like he is shaking.

As I come out, Bryce hugs me hard thanking me for everything I have done. I tell him it was nothing and Craig and I leave for our dinner date.

Personally I can't wait. It may not have taken me long to do what I did but it has taken a lot out of me and my brain is on overload right now. I need the break and I am starved.

CHAPTER 36

WE ARE AT a small yet charming restaurant having dinner by candlelight. It is very romantic. Soft music is playing in the background, lighting is dim, and tables are spread apart for a more intimate atmosphere. The tables are covered in burgundy linen table clothes accented with black and burgundy linen napkins, black bud vases with white, yellow and red roses in them and white candles are lit.

Knowing I am allergic to red roses Craig asks the waitress to change the red roses for yellow or white ones as he explains my allergies. She takes them with a smile and brings back some yellow ones in their place.

Leaving everything to him, he orders for the both of us. We start off with triple berry sangria drinks as we wait for the entrees to arrive. While we wait, we hold hands and gaze into each other's eyes sipping our drinks. It's not long before the waitress brings us the first course of our dinner, the entrees. We share platters of garlic shrimp scampi, crab stuffed mushroom caps and mozzarella sticks.

After we try each of them he stands up, holds out one hand and asks me to dance. I take his hand. Not letting go he brings me in close, and puts his other arm around me as I do him. We slowly move around to the music when he says, "Chloe, you are so beautiful. I love you very much. You are the love of my life and I don't know how I ever survived without you in it." He leans down, as he is six foot four and I am only five foot six, and kisses me.

When we stop kissing, I look at him saying, "I love you too. I've never met a man like you and I am beside myself that someone like you wants to be with me. Sometimes I pinch myself or stare at you just so I know it is real."

He kisses me again but not for as long this time because the waitress tells us our food will be here soon. She sets another drink down on the table for us as we take our seats again.

The main course is impeccable. He orders a bottle of their finest red wine as she brings us our food. The meal is one that rich people eat. Wood grilled lobster with lots of brown garlic butter served with baby gold potatoes. It is extremely delicious, I've never tasted anything so good, and the meat melts in your mouth as it drips with butter. It is extremely delicious.

Eating a meal together in a public place can be romantic, so I decide to have fun and enhance the already sexual tension between us. I want him to know how I am feeling and what I want without having to say a word.

I look at Craig with a gleam in my eye and a smirk on my face. I grab the body of the lobster in one hand and the tail in the other and twist in opposite directions breaking the tail free of its' body. I set the body back down on my plate and then roll the tail onto its' side on the table and push with both hands until the shell cracks underneath the pressure.

Picking up the tail I insert my thumb into the flipper end of the tail and push the meat out slowly through the other end. I pick up the piece of meat and dip it into the hot melted butter dish laid between our plates. Once covered, I lift the meat into the air sticking my tongue out to catch the dripping butter. I lay the meat onto my tongue and slowly bring it into my mouth enjoying every flavor it brings.

I pick up a claw and crack it at the knuckle snapping them with my hands. I remove the meat using the tips of my fingers. One by one I remove the flippers from the tail extracting the meat in the same fashion. After each piece of meat is removed I dip it with my fingers into the warm melted butter and slide each one onto my tongue bringing each piece into my mouth slowly; only to lick my lips after each swallow.

Then come the legs. One by one I yank them off. Holding a leg between my thumb and forefinger, I look across the table into his eyes. I smile then open my mouth as I bring the leg up to it. I slide my tongue down the center of it and place my lips gently around the outside of the leg. Still looking at him and smiling I suck on the leg until all of its delicious white meat has come loose and slithers onto my tongue.

As I remove the now hallowed out leg from my lips, I reveal the white meat on my tongue before bringing it into my mouth. Sitting there watching me, his eyes get big and his mouth drops as he drools at the sight of me eating the lobster. I continue to do this will each leg. As I do he struggles to get the meat out of his lobster legs fumbling with every move he makes.

After his third attempt I decide to help him out. "You know, it's easier to eat lobster with your hands than it is with those little utensils."

"Yes I know." He says in a shaky voice.

"Watch me and do as I do." I tell him hoping he will mimic me.

I repeat what I have been doing only slower so he can do what I do. When it comes time

for him to suck out the meat he acts like he can't muster it. "I can't do it like you but I got it." Then he sucks on his to get the meat out.

Now holding the body near the tail end steady with one hand, I pry the shell off the top of the lobster with the other revealing its rib cage. I pick the meat away from each rib ensuring that each piece is saturated with butter before placing it into my mouth.

As we continue to eat our dinner in this fashion, the waitress comes over and asks if we can tell her our story. Asking what she means, she explains.

"We hear many stories of how couples meet," she says, "and how their love for each other grows. The cook told me he knows you and said I need to hear your story."

Craig smiles and tells her to have a seat. I try to see who the cook is, but can't. "Shall I start, or do you want to?" he asks me grinning from ear to ear.

I let him saying I will butt in if he misses anything, laughing as he begins.

"Well, we have only been together for about a week and technically speaking," he pauses for a moment, looks at me and smiles, "this is our first date."

I sit here for moment thinking about what he just said. He is right, although we have been together and done many things together in such a short time, this is our first real date.

"We met last Friday and it was a meeting for the record books. I saw her walk out of Carmines and it was an instant attraction, at least it was for me."

"And one that almost got all of us killed and you in jail." I mock.

Nodding in agreement he explains how he followed me and my aunt. "The rest of that afternoon we were working getting ready for the truck rally that weekend. That's where and when we officially met and I couldn't take my eyes off her the entire time."

The waitress speaks up and says she heard of that truck rally and was supposed to attend but ended up working. Craig adds, "She was so sexy in those jean shorts and tank top, the first day and being dirty from the mud we made just made her sexier."

"And he said so, without even realizing it was me he said it to, until after the fact and he blushed." I added.

He tells her how messed up I was and the rough time I was having and without saying the reason why. "All I wanted to do was hold her and tell her everything was going to be okay, but I couldn't. So I did the next best thing."

"What was that?"

"He spent the night on the couch and then treated me like a child the next day."

He then explains what happened with Eric. "I just needed to know she was alright and only left her side when I had to."

She is smiling. "That's so romantic. He is there for you even when he doesn't know you."

Nodding in agreement Craig continues.

"We spent that day together. I made her lunch, she rode with me in my truck during my race, and we sat together at dinner."

"Awe, that's so sweet."

He pauses asking her for another bottle of wine and more butter for our lobster. She takes care of the other two tables, we finish eating. She comes back.

"As I was saying," Craig says, "We then spent two hours lying beside each other in her bed talking. She had a rough spot that hit her hard and I wanted to be there for her. We kissed, and during that conversation I told her how I felt about her."

"It was now dark and there was a bonfire going so we went outside to sit with the others." I say.

"She is sitting in my arms in a lounge chair," he adds, "and to almost everyone's surprise, we learn she can sing. So we get her up to sing a couple of songs."

"Well how did she do?"

"It was like an angel singing from heaven and everyone there agreed with me."

"And your love grew from there?"

"Sort of." I tell her.

We then explain how he spent the night in my bed and what the next day was like. "It wasn't until we were away from each other that we both realized how we really felt about each other."

Craig tells her that he already knew how he felt and to prove it he describes what he did with the rose petals and gifts. Now she is crying. We tell her we reconnected Tuesday morning and haven't been apart since.

She gets up and clears our plates asking us if we want any desert. Craig orders a chocolate chip lava cookie cake to share with a blend of Irish Whisky and Gerber Coffee topped with whip cream to drink. She wipes her tears and goes to get our order.

When she returns, the cook is with her, it is Hunter. After saying hi to him he tells Amanda, the waitress, some of the things we did not say. "These two were meant to be together." he says. "They only just meet and you would swear that they had been together for years."

He tells her how I was the rider on the bike the first day and how it was Craig and I both the second day. "Did they tell you about the singing?"

"Yes and I wished I didn't have to work that weekend."

"Well, she sang three songs the first night and the last song she sang had everyone there in tears. The second night, which by the way was Valentine's Day; she started to sing one of the most romantic songs ever. It was Don't Know Much originally sung by Linda Ronstadt and Aaron Neville."

"What song did she sing that brought everyone to tears?"

"Amazing Grace and I have never heard it sung like that before."

"And how did the duet turn out Sunday night?"

"Well you haven't heard that song either until you have heard these two sing it. She started to sing it by singing the chorus line. By the time she was done he was standing there asking for her hand and he sang Aaron's part as they walked up to the stage. She had no idea he could sing. They both took the microphones and by the time they were done the song, everyone there was holding someone close to them."

"Now that is magical." Amanda replies as she fights back the tears.

We have finished our desert and the story, so we say good night and thank them. As we walk out Amanda asks, "Can I use your love story to tell others? It is the best one so far."

We both nod in agreement and leave. I spend the night at Craig's apartment. It is our first real night together and I am a bit nervous.

It is a small yet intimate place with open concept. When you first walk through the door, the living room is ahead of you with a large screen television along the wall to the left, a coffee table in front of it and a couch alongside the table. To the right is a small kitchen with a counter separating it from the living room. Across the room behind the couch is a small dining table with four chairs and a dresser style hutch along the wall. The far outside wall has three windows that overlook the countryside at the edge of town. At the end of the kitchen is a short hallway that leads to the bathroom, master bedroom and spare room.

The evening acts as a continuation from dinner. I take a seat on the couch as Craig puts on some soft music and grabs a bottle of white wine from the fridge and two glasses. As he joins me on the couch, he leans into me and gives me a kiss. My heart is now pounding very hard and my hands begin to shake. I don't know why I am so nervous.

We cuddle on the couch just being with and feeling each other. We talk asking each other about likes and dislikes; history and past relationships. He then tells me about his late wife and how she passed away. I then tell him about my past relationships but don't say much about Josh and how he died because he already knows that story. We both are careful no getting into too much detail as neither of us wants the night to become a 'bash your ex' night or relive any bad or sad feelings. It is about us and getting to know each other more.

Craig gets up and puts in a cd of romantic love songs. He picks up a lighter and goes around the room lighting candles then shuts off the kitchen and dining room lights. We lay together on the couch, me between his legs with my back against his chest. As we sit here listening to the music sipping on wine, he wraps his arm around me and begins to kiss the back of my neck. I tip my head to the side enticing him to continue. I lift my left leg up and over his running my hands up and down his legs and hips. He turns my head to face his and kisses me with a romantic French kiss. Like one you would see in a movie.

He gets up, holds out his hand for me to take and pulls me up into him. We begin to dance to the music as though we are one, holding each other tightly close. As we move and gaze into the others eyes, our hands caress the other all over. As we dance closely together, our hips sway back and forth as one, as we kiss and hold each other, caressing the others' face.

After a short while he looks into my eyes. "God, you are beautiful Chloe. I could stay like this forever."

"I feel very safe in your arms and could stay like this forever too."

We kiss frantically as he guides me to the bedroom. When we reach the bed, he gently lifts me onto it. As he lays me back, he sits beside me. "If you aren't ready for this, we don't have too. I can wait."

Looking deep into his eyes, I cup his face with my hands and without saying a word, I kiss him pulling him in close to me as our lips lock. He knows I am ready and want this just as much as he does.

He kisses me feverishly as we begin to tear off each other's clothing. I sit up. He pulls my dress up over my head and I let it fall to my hips. I unzip his pants tugging until he stands letting them fall to the floor. Pulling me close to him he unclasps my bra letting my breasts spill out in excitement. I tug furiously at his shirt pulling it off revealing his hard, sculpted body. My nipples are hard and I get lost in his insistent embrace. How many times I have fantasized about this. Wondering how it would be or what it would feel like. Now it is happening and I plan on enjoying every minute of it.

I lie back down. Lifting my ass, he pulls my dress and panties all the way off. We are now both naked and I am lying in his bed. He looks at me running his hands all over me feeling every curve, every muscle, every imperfection, looking at me like he wants to remember this moment forever. He leans in and kisses me; first on my forehead, then the tip of my nose, to my chin and then on my mouth.

Exploring each other we get lost in the wonder of our passion. He slowly moves down my neck, then between my breasts, down my stomach to the inside of my thighs. I feel my stomach tighten as he separates my legs.

His lips are now in my clit and I can feel his tongue exploring my horizon. After a few minutes just before I am about to explode, he releases my clit and crawls over me. As I grab his tight ass, his staff of life penetrates my pussy as deep as he can. Consummating all of our previous maneuverings, his thrust increases our heart rates and the excitement intensifies.

He rolls onto his back pulling me on top of him. As I sit his penis pushes its' way in deeper until he can't go any further. As I grind clenching my stomach he cups my breasts before pulling me excitedly against him. He kisses me as he thrusts in and out. My body begins to tingle all over. He works his magic, slowly and precisely. We move against each other as we build to a climax I have never reached before.

He then rolls me onto my back and is once again on top of me. Clasping his hands around my wrists he holds them down against the bed beside my head, he guides his penis into my vagina. As he thrusts he is fast and furious. He kisses my neck and nibbles on my ears and I am now breathless, breathing more heavily now. My vision gets blurry and all at once my body feels lights, as it moves in unison with his.

He looks at me, as he kisses me, my body begins to shake uncontrollably like a volcanic eruption. Almost as if timed, he thrusts one last push and it's like a wave of hot lava filling me inside. He collapses beside me on the bed. We are both breathing heavily barely able to catch our breath.

After a few minutes we look at each other and he asks if I am okay. I nod my head. "I am more than okay, I am great. That was amazing."

"I agree. It's been a very long time since anything that great has happened to me."

We lay beside each other trying to catch our breath and relax after that workout. After a while he rolls onto his side and looks at me with a bewildered look. "Do you have any regrets?"

"No, absolutely not. Why would I?"

"I just didn't want you to feel bad. I wasn't sure if you were ready for this yet."

"I am good. No worries, no regrets. I am glad I did not stop you. I wanted it just as bad as you did. Do you have any regrets?"

"Of course not. It was great and to me very special. It is something I will never forget and hope that there are many more nights like this to come."

We end up spending the weekend together acting like teenagers. Everything we do, we don't keep our hands off each other. When we are not beside each other to where we can touch the other, the sultry looks across the room and sexy stances take place.

CHAPTER 37

EVERYTHING LEADS TO the most, hot and steamy sex two people can have. We have literally rock each other's world. It was the best weekend I have had in a very, very long time and I wouldn't change it for anything.

The next week is spent working on papers, going through the accountants two years' paperwork mostly at Craig's apartment and getting Bryce the two workers he needs to help him out in the garage. Things are looking up and quick. Jobs are getting completed and out the door, customers have paid their bills, and Craig and I are doing great. I am almost done going through everything and have come up with payment plans as promised.

I am a week ahead of schedule and with today being Thursday afternoon, I decide to do some work in the shop. Bryce has shown me a few things here and there when I needed a break from the paperwork and I have spent some time with my uncle in his shop during the weeknights. I have learned a lot this past week.

Bryce and Craig have gone into town and his workers are at school today for testing. I need a break so I drop the papers I am working on, go into the garage and put on a pair of coveralls. I put a salsa music cd into the cd player and begin to work on the car. As I tighten plugs, change the fan belt, and check the fluids I move to the beat of the music and singing along to the words I know. When I am done with this work, I decide to put the tires on their rims that Bryce has waiting at the far end of the garage.

I dance around to the music on my way over there. As I do this, I act as though I am in a spot light. I use the tire changer wheel as a partner and a lug wrench as a baton. When I am done, I find myself sweating so I unzip my coveralls to my waist, take my arms out and tie the sleeves around my waist. I remove my t-shirt revealing the black sports bra I am wearing.

I put on the song, Sexy Latin Nights. It is a slow salsa song and one that I have danced to many times when I was younger. It is generally a partner song but being by myself for so long, I have adapted and created my own dance for it. I begin with the standard legs apart, shoulder width, arms crossed in front of you and head down stance.

The music begins and I sway my hips back and forth then in circles to the rhythm. Slowly I raise my head then unfold my arms moving them with my body and hips to the music. I dance around mambo style as it is a bread and butter dance that can be done with a partner or single.

Mixing it up I do a combination of right and left turns with the Guspea move thrown in. All of the motions use the walking motion as your hips carries you through your moves. The salsa dance is a very sexy dance on its' own and with the presence of the human body, that is what makes the dance so irresistible. Whether or not you can dance the salsa, it is enjoyed by everyone. The beat gets your legs and feet moving and sometimes hands clapping. As I dance and move about I really get into it. About half way through the song and coming around again in a turn, I notice that Craig and Bryce are standing there by the door watching me.

Bryce drops the bags he had in his hands standing there with his mouth wide open and eyes as wide as can be. He looks as if he is in shock. Craig on the other hand, is grinning from ear to ear as he kneels down to set the box that he is carrying in front of him. The entire time, neither of them can take their eyes off of me.

I stop and look at them surprisingly. "You scared me. I didn't know anyone was watching."

"Don't stop, that was amazing." Bryce muffles.

"And she's very sexy!" adds Craig who is now walking towards me.

"Sometimes I wish you weren't my cousin."

"Well I am so no more thoughts like that Bryce!" I say not sure how to take that.

Craig stops about two feet in front of me, holds his hand out for me to take. I do with a puzzled look and smile on my face. He turns me into him and before I know it, he has his left hand on my lower back with his right hand in the air as my left hand rests in it. Shocked, he tells Bryce to replay that song, looks at me and says, "Shall we salsa the right way!"

When the music begins he asks, "Are you ready?"

He begins to move. Nodding my head, we begin the mambo style salsa dance but this time as partners. It's as if we are the only ones in the room and nothing else exists. My hands are all over him from his neck to face, down his shoulders and body to his waist, to holding his hands. His hands

Raging Desire

go from my neck to waist to holding my hands and my leg when I lift it. Our hips move in unison with our legs as though they are one.

It is a sexy and romantic dance that can be very hot, in more ways than one. I can hardly breathe yet I am captivated. We move together as one like a precision instrument, gliding across the floor like we are on air. It is with ease like we have been doing this dance together forever. I didn't know he could move like this but it makes sense with what he does in the bedroom!

As the song ends, so does our dance. He kisses me then lets' go, turns and begins to walk away. I grab his arm stopping him in his tracks. "Wait a minute, where do you think you are going?"

He turns with a smile. "What?"

"What do you mean what? How did you learn to dance like that?"

"When I was growing up, my mom and dad danced like that in competitions. I learned on the side lines doing what they did. When I became a teenager, my mom practiced with me when my dad wasn't there because I knew the moves."

"Wow, I am impressed and once again, shocked."

"How did you learn to salsa?" he asks in return.

"I learned in a class when I was in high school. I did what I could to stay away from home. Salsa, karate and gymnastics were my only choices where we lived. I ended up learning all three."

"Well, I am impressed too. You dance very well."

"Thank you. So do you."

Having to cool off, I go into the office leaving them to work on the car. I turn on the two fans in there and sit in front of them. I am physically hot from dancing but boiling hot from Craig's dance moves and how we fit together like a glove. It takes me almost an hour to cool off enough to get back to work.

I STAY AT Craig's place most of the week as it is easier for both Craig and Bryce to help me. It is also easier on my aunt and uncle because there are times when we worked until midnight and they are in bed early. This way we wouldn't keep them up.

It is now Friday morning and before going into the office, I get up early to finalize the paperwork. I have found a grave concern. I have gone over the numbers several times this morning, several different ways and come up with the same thing every time. The audit shows Ms. Baker has been taking money from Bryce for the past two years, making me think it's been happening since the beginning.

Asking Craig to join me, I call her and put her on speaker so Craig can hear the entire conversation. "All I need you to do is sit here quietly. I don't want her to know you are here with me, okay?"

"No problem. I'm going to enjoy this."

"Now, now be good."

"I will baby, I promise."

"I want to cover my butt so she can't say I said something or didn't say something, or she didn't say something that she did. I also want you to record the conversation so there is no question later of what was said by whom and how."

He agrees, and gets us both a cup of fresh coffee as I dial the phone with it on speaker.

She answers the phone as he sits down. "Good morning. This is Ms. Evelyn Baker, how may I help you?"

"Ms. Baker, this is Chloe. I have several questions for you and I need answers NOW!"

"Oh, hi Chloe." her voice is trembling. "I only have ten minutes so make it quick. What do you want?"

"There is a huge discrepancy in the numbers you have given me. You told Bryce that as of December 31st he was in debt almost $63,000. Correct?"

"Yes and?"

"Your own numbers show a lot less than that. Please explain the $20,000 discrepancy and where it came from?"

There is dead silence on the other end of the phone. After a few seconds she asks, "What are you looking at first of all that shows the error?"

"Are you at your computer?"

"Yes!"

"Open up Bryce's file and let me know when you are in there."

After a few moments and in a shaky voice she replies, "Okay I am there, where am I looking?"

"Your journal entries, your numbers and your work are all I am looking at right now. Go to the Trial Balance and tell me what it says on line 432."

"It shows a debt of $43,415."

"Okay, now open the Sales Journal and tell me what the amount says on line 129."

Raging Desire

She does telling me the same number she just told me that was on the Trial Balance. I tell her to go to one more place, "Now go to the Retained Earnings Statement and tell me what it says there, please."

After a few more seconds she says, "So what it your point!"

"$43,000 is $20,000 less than the $63,000 you told Bryce. Where did the extra twenty thousand came from?"

She hymned and hawed for a bit like she was trying to find the answer. After a couple of minutes, I ask, "Well?"

"I don't really know."

"Okay so lets' move to the next one, we will come back to this in a minute."

"Fine. What else is there?"

Craig is just sitting in the chair smiling with his arms folded over each other wondering where I am going with all of this. It is like he finds this very amusing.

Smiling at him, I maintain my demeanor to her. "Please explain the numbers on the invoice you send Bryce every year?"

"What do you mean?"

"Well, I have an issue with the amounts you gave me in the breakdown letter. According to the amounts your company charges for each of these lines you quoted in this letter, and the amounts you actually charged Bryce, there is a $1,500 discrepancy each year and I want to know why?"

She is very quiet. I give her a few minutes.

"Well? Time is ticking, what's your answer?"

"The numbers from the company are the minimum charges, we can charge more than that if we did more work and it warrants it!"

"Who do you think you are and just who do you think you are trying to kid? I have worked in this field for many years and worked for KMGP for six years before going out on my own. I know perfectly well that is not the truth. So tell me, why are you charging Bryce $1,500 more every year than what the actual is?"

She can't explain, so I give her one chance.

"Well, I will give you the benefit of the doubt. It is only 8:20 a.m. Be at our office today at 3:00 p.m. with answers that you can prove. If you don't show up I will take it as guilt that you are stealing from Bryce's company. If you show and can't prove your answers to my satisfaction, I will charge you with stealing."

"I don't know if I am free and able to meet with you today!"

"The way I see it you have 2 choices: one don't bother coming and not only lose your job but get sued and possibly end up in jail; or, two prove what you just told me and come to our office."

"I don't like being threatened!"

"Oh my dear, it is not a threat. I will do what I said. And be forewarned that if you are in fact stealing from Bryce, I will not only have your job but you will never practice in the U.S. again. See you at 3!" I hang up before she can say another word.

Craig sits there for a second and hands me my coffee. "That was amazing. You actually think she is stealing from him?"

"She definitely is. The only reason any accountant would charge more is because they feel they are worth more than what they are being paid and when their company won't give them a raise, they over charge the client but pocket the difference."

"I am amazed that you can tell all that just from looking at some numbers."

"The $20,000 difference she can't explain, it's because she was hoping to pocket that as well. Bryce never checks her work and just takes her for her word on everything, so she hid it within his reports and ledgers. If Bryce was less trusting, he wouldn't be in this mess."

I ask Craig to call Bryce and put him on speaker as I pick up my papers. Once Bryce is on the phone I tell him what I found and the conversation I just had with his accountant. "Do you know the accounting firm that Eric and Quentin use for their businesses?" I ask him.

"Yes, it is the same company but different people than me."

"Okay. We are on our way in. You and I need to talk before Ms. Baker gets there this afternoon."

"Okay see you soon." We hang up.

I then call both Eric and Quentin and tell them what is going on and ask them to get their accountants to fax them the same break-down letter I got from Ms. Baker and bring it to Bryce's as soon as possible. They agree and Craig and I get ready and leave for the garage.

We bring everything to Bryce's office and it's not long after we are there when Eric and Quentin show up. I look at their letters and compare them to the company's charge letter. Then I explain to all of them exactly what has happened with Bryce and what I believe she is doing.

"Eric, I will start with you first. By the look of this letter your accountant is on the up and up. There is very little variation in charges and where there is, it can be easily explained and verified."

"That's good." he says with a sigh of relief.

"Quentin, I am skeptical with yours. Like Bryce your accountant is over charging you, just not as much." I take a minute and check on the calculator very quickly. "Bryce's accountant is overcharging him each year by 35%. It looks like yours is overcharging you by 20%. Some of the numbers can be explained but only a few."

"Oh Lord, what do I do now?"

I tell both Eric and Quentin that they should be leery and if I were them I would look for a new accountant right away. I give them KMGP phone numbers and tell them of their history and how they check their employees.

"At KMGP they screen every prospective employee before even hiring them and double check every letter and reference they are given. They are then checked for bond-ability every three months for the first two years they are there."

Telling them how I worked for them, that I know this as fact, I explain that the company they are with now, does none of that. "I checked into it and all they do is call two of the five references you give them and they take the papers you give at face value. Anyone with a computer can make up those letters with letterheads to make them look believable."

It is now, 2:45 and Ms. Baker is supposed to be here in fifteen minutes. I ask all of them except Bryce to go in the garage while we meet with her but ask Quentin not to leave, "I need to talk to you when we are done."

"Okay, I won't go anywhere."

They all go out into the garage pretending to be working on the car. While we are waiting I print out a termination letter I drafted for Bryce to give her. "It doesn't matter what she tells us Bryce, she is stealing money from you. She needs to be fired. I can do your books until this is settled then we will go to KMGP."

"Okay, I trust you Chloe." He signs the paper and as he places it on the counter behind us, he sees her drive in.

"This should be good." I say looking at Bryce.

He nods and goes to greet her at the door. He leads her in and I point her to the chair in front of the desk telling her to have a seat. I sit in the chair opposite her and Bryce stands beside me. Both Bryce and I notice that the guys are standing close to the door trying to listen and see what is going to happen.

She hands me a file. As I open it and glance through the papers she brought I ask her, "What is this?" She responds by telling me it is the explanation I asked for.

"I don't have time to read through all of this. I don't want to take up any more of your time or mine for nothing. Explain to me what is in here."

I hand Bryce the file and he rifles through the papers.

"The amount of work I have had to do with Bryce the past couple of years is why I charged what I did. All the papers in there are the results of all that work."

Bryce questions her. "These meetings and discussions that you say has occurred, I don't remember any of them happening. I also have questions with some of this paperwork that you claim I verified. I never verified any paperwork from you except the year-end financial statements. I don't recognize any of this! I have never seen any of these papers before today so when did I supposedly verify them?"

"Every time you came into my office or I came here. You signed off on paperwork."

After ten minutes of the two them bantering back and forth, I look at her and interrupt them. "Okay that's enough."

I stand using my finger as a gavel on the desk. "I can't listen to any more of this bullshit. You are trying to cover your tracks and very poorly at that. I have been doing this kind of work for many years and I know when someone is taking money to better themselves."

She tries to explain. As she is I look at Bryce and nod telling him it is time. He goes to the counter behind us and picks up the envelope, she stops talking. He hands her the letter.

"What's this?"

"It is a termination letter. You are officially fired as his accountant. As we speak your boss is gathering all of Bryce's things and one of our delivery guys is one his way to pick them up." I tell her.

She stands up. "Well I've never!" she walks to the door.

I get up and stand between her and the door. "You're right because, you never got caught. That is until now. Trust me, I am conducting a full blown investigation, the police already have a report on file and I have already talked to two lawyers willing to take our case."

She huffs as I open the door and she walks through it. As she walks to the main door I walk beside her. "This isn't over. Trust me, you think you can hide but you can't. I know where to look and if there is anything in your past, I will find it and will use it against you."

She stops at the door, turns and looks at me. "I don't take too kindly to threats."

"Good because it wasn't a threat, it's a promise and I keep all my promises because I don't make ones I can't keep!"

"Try it bitch." she says, "I am ready!"

"Ya that's professionalism at its' best right there." I reply.

I can see Craig already walking towards us and he seems mad. I put my hand up to him as if to say, it's okay. I look at her and smile. "Well you finally have something right. I am a bitch and this bitch is the best! You haven't heard the last of me; your life is now going to be a living hell. I hope it was worth it for you!"

With that I close the door as I push her out, turn to the guys and laugh. Craig has now approached me and is pissed off because she called me a bitch but shocked all at the same time how I handled it. He puts his arm around me as we walk to Quentin and Bryce, who has since come out and joined the guys.

I look at Quentin. "If you still want me to help you like I am with Bryce, I will be glad to do it."

"Absolutely." he says with much excitement.

"It's like having the best lawyer who knows everything fight for you!" Bryce tells him.

I want so badly to stick it to her and that entire operation. I tell Quentin what I will need and if he can have it all to me by next weekend I will start then. "This weekend I am keeping free for Craig. He and I are going away and to be honest, I need a break from all this."

Agreeing, he leaves almost in a skip like a child who just got away with something.

Craig asks me if I am ready to go. "Yes, I just need to pick up the papers then we can go."

While I am in the office, I can hear them talking but don't know what is being said. As I open the door, I hear Craig whisper, "It's a surprise, she doesn't know."

I tell him I am ready to go. We say goodbye to Bryce and I ask him to tell his parents I will call them or come by and see them when we come back.

As we drive away I ask him what's a surprise. "You will see. Just be patient baby."

CHAPTER 38

WE ARE NOW in his SUV and on our way. It is late Friday afternoon so we stop for dinner at a truck stop along the highway. While we are eating, I ask him where we are going. This time he gives me an answer.

"It's my quiet place and I find it very romantic and beautiful there. I have never brought anyone there with me before, but I want to share it with you. No pressures or anything, just a get-away, have some fun and relax. I am hoping we get to know each other on a whole new level this weekend."

I nod my head and smile. "It sounds great!"

We are almost two hours into the trip and we have turned off the highway and are now on a back road, in the middle of nowhere. All I can see is trees, trees and more trees with the odd stream and small rock cliffs. I don't know where we are but I am happy. I am sitting here beside the man I love, hand in hand, riding along a back road, sun is setting over the trees and you can see the stars beginning to shine brightly in the sky.

As we arrive, I am shocked at what I see. Granted I don't know Craig all that well yet but this is impressive and I am beside myself. As you drive up the road it looks like a small clearing in the middle of all these trees on the left hand side. When you get to the clearing, there is a driveway only noticeable by the tire tracks left in the grass. Unless you know it is there, you would drive right by it.

We turn down this trail. As you drive, trees are growing into the path and the branches bounce off the windows and side of the truck. Not long onto this path, it opens up to a large clearing that, from the road you would never see. In this clearing sits a one-story, hand built, log cabin to the left and a matching ten-by-ten shed on the right. You can see logs and trees lying on the ground everywhere. About twenty feet from the porch is a fire pit with wood and sticks piled around it.

He stops the SUV by the porch as I am looking all around. It is dark out now but you can see everything. Looking to the sky you can see the brilliant lights from the many stars filling the night sky. Among these lights is the brightest, fullest moon. In town, you don't see the sky like this; everywhere you turn there is a different constellation. It is an amazing sight and one that I miss seeing. I haven't seen the sky like this in years and it is a sight for sore eyes.

He gets out of the truck and holds my hand as he helps me out. I close the door and look up as we walk towards the porch. I stop on the bottom step. As he unlocks the door I gaze up at the brilliant sky. I lose myself in its beauty; so much so that when Craig puts his hand on my shoulder asking me if I am okay, I jump.

Smiling I take his hand and reply. "Yes, I am fine. Just looking at the stars in the sky. You don't get to see them like this in town."

He walks me into the cabin, it is like a home. All the walls are made of logs. There is a kitchen to the right. All the cupboards, counters and even the table are all made from logs taken from the land. Through the kitchen is the bathroom which follows suit. The counter is a half log hollowed out at one end where the sink sits. The toilet seat is also made of wood.

The entire east side of the house is the living room and office. In the center of the wall is a large fireplace that burns wood, not propane, electrical, or fake like you see in town apartments. In front of the fireplace is a white bear skin rug. The bedrooms are on the west side of the house at the other end of the kitchen.

Craig gets a fire going as I walk around looking at the intricate details in the furniture. All the furniture within the cabin is made of logs including the couch, chair and bed frames. I then sit on the couch and watch him start the fire. As he picks up three or four fire logs at a time, his muscles bulge as he carries them in one arm. Once the fire gets going he goes outside to get more firewood, so he can keep it going. I grab some blankets and pillows from one of the bedrooms to set up a make shift bed in front of the fireplace.

He comes in, arms loaded, and muscles bulging everywhere. Noticing what I am doing, he smiles. "What are you doing?" he asks amorously.

Smiling I shrug my shoulders as I help him set the firewood down. Once his arms are freed I grab his hands and lead him to the makeshift bed on the bear rug.

"I love watching a fire with flames dancing around and changing hues. It is mesmerizing and peaceful. I want to lay here with you for a bit and watch it wrapped in your arms. Of course, if anything else comes to mind for you, well I am up for that too." I wink and smile hoping he catches my drift.

He does. He gets up, goes into the kitchen and gets a bottle of sparkling chardonnay and two glasses. He brings it over, sits with me on the blankets and pours us a glass. Telling me not to drink any yet he sets the bottle down on the coffee table and turns to look at me. He sits there for a second and takes my free hand in his.

"The hours I have spent with you these past few weeks have been the best. You and you alone make me feel alive. You are truly an angel, a blessing God sent just for me. I love you with all my heart. Here's to a great weekend and us!"

I hold back the tears; we clang our glasses together and take a drink.

He then stokes the fire and sits beside me with his arm around me as we sip our wine. I am lost in the fire's dancing flames feeling secure and at peace in his arms. After a bit, he pours us another glass then tells me, "You are very beautiful Chloe, and in the fire's light you glow like an angel."

If he keeps this up, he will make me cry. I smile and then kiss him as he holds me. Looking into his eyes I return the favor. "Craig, I love you too, very much. Not only for whom you are but for what I am when I am with you. As long as I have you with me, I am the richest woman in the world. I never want to lose you."

Okay so I made myself cry. As I tell him this, I think about all that I have lost. He is truly the best that has ever happened to me in my life and I don't want to lose him.

Craig has an inner urge that drives him to obtain the sensual pleasures of life. He is charming and magnetic, loves to make people laugh striving to maintain harmony with the cosmos. Spontaneous and enthusiastic, he never says no to an adventure with gifts in shamanism. Often, he surprises and shocks the people he cares about. He has many interests, if something proves of interest, he will not rest until he acquires a profound knowledge in that area.

I am a romantic and an eternal optimist who believes life is a gift. I try to achieve as much as possible and put this gift to best use possible. As an advanced soul, I am loyal to a fault to those I care about through thick and thin. I use every opportunity to forgive, learn and grow because I believe life is too short to do otherwise. I open my heart and spirit to the energy of unconditional love in all forms – self-love, platonic love, spiritual love and romantic love. I always take time to reflect on the abundance the universe has bestowed upon me. I am here to teach and to love and I do both well.

We spend the night in front of the fireplace, listening to a soft romantic cd Craig has put into the player, this is the best way to spend a night with the one person you love. The sex is slow, tender and most affectionate love making one could ever have. Our hands run over every inch of each other's body feeling every muscle, every curve, and every imperfection. Our bodies are soft, smooth and tender. The entire night is filled with passion, infatuation, and lust. We are very aroused by each other. Looking into each other's eyes and seeing the others' soul, we watch each other as we move our hands and our bodies with the other.

Moving to the music and in rhythm with each other, we roll around, enjoying how the other feels both in and out. The touch of his hand makes me feel weak and his thrust is tender creating arousal and delight. His lips are like sweet nectar you would get from a flower and he tastes so good. His kisses melt me as his lips touch various parts of my body. It is the kind of love making I have never felt; like ones you see only in movies thinking it is never real.

It lasts for hours. He then adds a couple more logs onto the fire, lays beside me and pulls me in close. We are facing each other as we gaze into each other's eyes and begin to kiss again. After a few minutes he lays down and holds me in his arms. It is so romantic. The only light is that from the fire, soft music in the background, and being held by the person I love the most in my life. It is a wonderful feeling and I never want this to end.

I don't know how long it took to fall asleep but waking up was the best way one could. His arms are still around me, my right arm is around his waist with my hand along his back, my leg is across his and my head is on his chest. My breasts are against his torso and our naked bodies are touching each other as though we are one. It is the most wonderful, loving feeling in the world.

The day begins with him making me his famous omelet for breakfast. I ask if I can help to which he replies, "No. This weekend I am looking after you. You have done for everyone these past few weeks and its time someone does for you. This weekend, I am doing everything for you, you are to do nothing except have fun."

The look on his face and the tone in his voice tells me not to argue so I don't. While he makes breakfast he can tell that I am not fully at ease with this so he asks me if anything is wrong. I tell him no but then explain,

"The only time anyone has ever done anything for me, I had to ask and even then I was lucky to have it done. This is weird for me because I am usually the one doing, not sitting."

He says he understands and can tell. "Don't worry, it will be fine."

I smile and we both chuckle as he cooks.

He is right, he makes the best veggie omelet I have ever had. After breakfast he tells me there are clothes in the dresser and closet for me to wear. "You need to wear jeans with a t-shirt."

Wondering why but not asking I oblige him and find some that fit. Putting them on, he gets dressed beside me. He isn't saying much until I am dressed, "You look good in those clothes."

"Who do they belong to?" I ask but he doesn't answer. He just smiles and winks at me. We then head outside and walk to the shed.

He opens up the door and asks me to help him pull off the cover. As we do, it reveals two motor cross bikes, the off-road kind. Smiling I ask him if he has helmets and before I could finish the question he has them in his hands. "Will this work?"

"Yes."

He tosses the one helmet to me then we walk the bikes out of the shed. Before starting them, he puts his helmet on his bike. "I will be right back. I forgot something." and heads back into the cabin.

After a few minutes he comes out with a couple of bags. Smiling he puts one bag under his seat and the other under mine, telling me they are for later. He tells me to follow him. "There is a place I ride to when I am here that I absolutely love and want to show it to you. It is peaceful and one of the most beautiful places I have ever seen."

"Okay, lead on McDuff." I tell him as I put on my helmet and start the bike.

We ride across the clearing to the other side then up through the woods on a path. The path winds through the woods. As we ride up and down small hills, over roots and over small bridges we stop along the pathway. The first stop is at the edge of a clearing where we get off our bikes and sit quietly at the edge. It's not long before a family of deer come out, two fawns frolic in the tall grass, a doe munches on the grass and the buck stays back with his head up and ears all over listening.

After a few minutes we get back on our bikes and we are away again heading down the path. About twenty minutes later we stop again. This time there is a stream nearby. Craig takes out the bag from under his seat and takes out two tin cups handing one to me. We walk up to the stream, "This is the best tasting water you will ever drink. And if we are lucky we might see a bear or two catching fish."

Intrigued as I love wildlife, we find two rocks that are side by side in the middle of the stream and walk out to them. The water is only a foot deep but rushing fast and very cold. Sitting on them we look downstream as we dunk our cups into the water and take a drink. It is very refreshing and the purest, coldest water I have had in a very long time.

When we are done and getting ready to stand up to leave we hear a splash from behind. Slowly we turn our heads to see what the noise is. There is a bear about thirty feet away trying to get a fish or two as they swim by. We slowly stand and walk back to our bikes trying not to disturb it. So far, so good. That is until we start the bikes. The bear stands on his hind legs and lets out a loud, ungodly roar. We release the brakes and we speed up along the path in hopes the bear does not follow.

He doesn't, thank God. We stop when we are at a safe distance, look back and laugh. It was invigorating with an adrenaline rush all at once and I love it. He puts the cups back under the seats then I follow him as he continues up the path along the stream. He stops about a half a mile up the path and tells me that we will be coming to an embankment soon.

"It is a bit of a climb as it goes high up. Just do what I do and you will be fine. When you crest the top, slack off on the gas as we will be stopping almost immediately."

Nodding my head in agreement, we go.

The incline is only minutes away. You can look up all you want; you don't see the top until you are about ten feet from it. It is hard to see because of all the trees, bush and rocks. To the left of the entire climb is a cliff and although you can't see the water you can hear it as it runs down the hillside.

He crests the top first and all at once he is out of sight. As I crest the top I stop in my tracks; it is the most beautiful oasis in the middle of nowhere. At first sight is the majestic waterfall followed by a beautiful arrangement of colors everywhere you look. I am breathless, taken in by its beauty. I take off my helmet and with it on the handlebars I start to walk the bike as I take in the most gorgeous sights God could ever create.

The lightest shade of green ever seen is the grass, hypnotic as it moves with the warm breeze; like ripples on a calm body of water. In the midst of this rippling grass are birch trees with one large shade tree. The tree, extremely fragrant is blooming with yellow flowers. It is known as the little-leaf linden and well known for its pyramidal canopy with dense foliage. This is where he is standing.

Craig's hypnotizing features only add to the seductive scenery, with his suit dangling at his waist and wife beater shirt showing his muscular build. He watches me. I am smiling. You can't help but smile, with the enchanting aroma and trance-inducing scenery. Everywhere you look there are many colors, floral's, wild life, and riveting scenes.

To the left of us there is a body of water edged with floral's of varying heights, shapes and colors. "This is the water that feeds the river we stopped at down below."

He walks to me. I park my bike beside his and we walk hand-in-hand to the waters' edge.

The water is the bluest shade, like blue food coloring in a glass of water, and just as clear. It is pooled in a small lake-type setting. On the other side you see many different trees and shrubs housing many colors in various forms. "Come with me and we will go there."

We then begin to walk along the lake-ponds edge.

At the far end of the lake is an alluring water fall as it flows from high above. As it gets to where we are it is less dense and misty. "When we get underneath it, it is like taking a shower, it is so gentle."

I gaze up at its majestic presence. We climb up on some rocks that lead us behind the waterfall. There is something unique about looking at the world through a curtain of water, as though you are on the outside looking in. I put my hand out and feel it's strength as my hand cuts through its path.

As we get to the other side, it is like a whole new world. It may be in the same place as the other side, but it is totally different here. This side is peaceful, serene, dense yet open. I am careful where I step not wanting to disrupt the nature of the area.

There are several small, low shrubs, consisting of lavender, periwinkles and small roses of varying colors. There are families of succulent orange and yellow marigolds, honeysuckle and daisies. The aroma is spellbound and alluring. There are birch trees among these floral arrangements.

As I am in total awe and in complete serenity, Craig asks me what I think. "Do you agree with me this place is beautiful?"

I nod my head, hardly able to speak as I am in awe of this beautiful place. "It is more than that, it is magical! It is nature at its' purest. Butterflies fluttering are about. Hummingbirds zip here and there. Rabbits are hopping in and out of the grass. Frogs sun themselves on the lily pads. Cardinals, blue jays and finches sing and fly among the trees. Bees buzz from flower to flower collecting their nectar. What could be more breathtaking?"

"You." he says as he puts his arms around my waists and leans in for a romantic, French kiss.

We spend the balance of the afternoon lying in the grass, skinny dipping in the pool and diving off the waterfall, walking from behind it then through it before jumping into the clear, crystal blue waters below. It is an enchanting, charming, yet slumber and I am very absorbed in everything, including Craig. I could not ask for anyone better to spend this day with.

As we lay here in the warm grass, the sun starts to dip behind the waterfall. Looking at Craig, we kiss again and then get ready to leave. Not wanting to leave this place, I look one last time, get on the bike, and we head back down the mountain. What seemed like forever getting to the top only took minutes to get back down.

Once we are back and the bikes are put away, he lights the BBQ and goes in to get the steaks. He is making me a steak dinner that he promises to melt in my mouth. As he does, I get a fire going in the fire pit. He tells me not to because he will, but I tell him I can and he doesn't have to do everything. Once the fire is lit, I go onto the porch, give him a kiss and go inside. First to use the bathroom, then to change my clothes into something a little more comfortable when we sit by the fire.

I grab two bottles of beer from the fridge for us. As I get closer to the door it sounds like Craig is either talking to himself or someone else has stopped by. I open the door and as I step onto the porch I chuckle. I give Craig one of the beers as he asks me what is so funny. "I thought you were talking to yourself at first."

There is a man and woman standing at the bottom of the stairs and he is talking to them. He introduces me to them saying they are his neighbors. "We thought we heard his bikes but wanted to make sure it was him and not someone stealing them." His name is Vance and her name is Clover. It is a weird name for me but then my name is not common either.

"Well Craig won't let me help him cook. Would either of you like a beer?"

Craig asks them to join us for dinner at the same time. They say yes to both so I go in and get them a beer as Craig gets a couple more steaks to throw on the BBQ. Clover and I sit by the fire letting the guys cook the dinner.

We spend the next few hours eating dinner and drinking beer while talking and getting to know each other. They are a great couple and I can see why Craig is friends with them. Around nine Clover and Vance decide to leave. "It was very nice meeting you." I say shaking their hand.

"It was our pleasure. It's nice to see that Craig has found someone who is down to earth and makes him this happy. It's been too long since he's been happy and it is nice to see." Vance replies.

They leave and I tell Craig I am going in.

"I already got the fire in the fireplace going. I will join you in a minute baby, I just want to make sure this fire is out first." he says.

I kiss him quickly and then hurry inside. I want to end the night feeling him and loving him. As he puts the fire in the pit out, I take off my clothes and put on a low cut, short, all lace black negligée I brought with me and stand in the doorway of the one bedroom waiting for him to come in.

When he walks in, his mouth opens, eyes get wide and he almost drops the bottles he carried in with him. He sets them on the table and saying wow he walks towards me. We embrace and immediately dive into the clawing, breathless, animalistic passion. The sex is hot and steamy, lustful and very intimate. It is aromatic, exhilarating and electric all at the same time. When we are done we are sweaty, flushed and enthralled.

It is now Sunday morning and it is time to head back home. As we get ready to leave, I thank Craig. "Baby, you have no idea how good this weekend has felt. There are no words I can use to describe it. I thought we were just going to be somewhere quiet to talk and get to know more about each other. Although we did this, it was much, much more."

He agrees. "What did you enjoy the most about this weekend?"

"First was this place, very retro, log cabin and making love to you that first night by the fireplace; it was incredible. Then yesterday, with the bike riding, trail blazing, watching the family of deer, fleeing from a bears' grip; made it more exhilarating. The Gods oasis, in itself was magical and then you made it even more special and enchanting. Then meeting your friends and having dinner outside by an open fire and the hot, steamy sex that followed. I can't remember the last time I enjoyed being with someone like this."

"Well, I am glad you enjoyed it. I too enjoyed every minute of it as much as you did. This whole experience was more than I hoped for. I learned so much about you this weekend just by doing these things than

Raging Desire

I would have learned just from talking. It is definitely something we will do again. I promise!"

We kiss then get in the truck and drive out. We stop for breakfast twenty miles up the road. While eating he tells me there is one place he wants to stop at before we head home, but won't tell me what it is. "I know you will enjoy it as much as I do. It only happens twice a year and it's been that long since I have attended plus, it's on our way."

I trust him so after breakfast, we are back on the road and headed for this place.

An hour into the trip he pulls into this little town called Howardwick. We drive through the town to the arena where a city of tents can be seen and a sea of cars. It is a vintage car show, "I absolutely love old cars." I state.

We walk hand in hand up and down the rows of vehicles featuring classic, muscle and collectible cars. There are GTO's, Road Runners and Olds 442s, each waiting for a new owner.

After a few hours we walk into a food court area where we stop and eat lunch, when we are on our way again. The vehicle's range from 1910s to 1980s models with price tags ranging from $28,000 to $2.4 million. We walk up and down each row looking inside some of them, looking at the different paint jobs and Craig looks under some of the hoods to see what motors run these cars. I stand up and that's when I see it, like an exotic show piece. It's my car, the one I have always dreamed of having. It a beauty all on its' own, a 2-door, black 1967 Barracuda Convertible with an A-body platform.

It's paint job is immaculate, black metallic with speckling of emerald green throughout. Red wall tires with red door handles and wipers deck out the outside, keeping in tune with the red striping on the hood. Solid dark green color up the center fades out into the black as it moves to the edge giving the illusion of depth and deviousness. The inside remains in theme with black leather seats, emerald green dash with green shifter and steering wheel. Dash lights, stitching and wording are in metallic red making this car even more alluring to me.

The roof is a red soft vinyl cover. Under its' hood, it sports a Slant V8 engine Hemi RB with a wheelbase of 108 inches. Design cues include a concave rear deck panel, wider wheel openings, curved side glass and I am absolutely in love; but, not with a price tag of $1.6 million.

After I stop drooling over this car and take several pictures, we continue our walk through. It is now after four p.m. and we have seen all the vehicles so we decide to go and get some dinner then head home. We get into his truck and he drives to the front gate. "I forgot to get their card and brochures for the next event, I will be right back." he says as he gets out of the truck.

A few minutes later he comes out with brochures and pamphlets grinning from ear to ear. "What is so funny?" I ask him.

"Nothing is funny. I am just happy, that's all."

The car show was the perfect ending to a perfect weekend. We stop at a small truck stop on the side of the highway for dinner then head home. It's after ten p.m. when we arrive so we unload the truck, settle in and go to bed.

CHAPTER 39

IT IS NOW April and payment schedules for both, Bryce and Quentin's creditors, landlords and suppliers have been approved with first payments already made. Both have workers needed to get jobs completed and every customer have fully paid their bills. After further investigation, charges are made against Ms. Baker, Mr. Hunt (Quentin's accountant) and J.G. Accounting, the firm they work for. We have secured a lawyer who is now in the process of filing court proceedings against them.

I have proven Ms. Baker pocketed over $6,000 in the past four years and tried to hide money within Bryce's financials so she could pocket over $20,000 in the next year or two. Mr. Hunt pocketed almost $9,000 in the past five years and hid almost $30,000 in Quentin's financials. We were ordered not to pay them a dime until the court case has been settled and a judgment made.

The next week is spent working on changes for both to implement with training so they become profitable and remain as such. I have five months left to get them debt free and it's looking like I may be ahead of schedule.

Neither of them has a website so I have enlisted a student from the local tech college to create one for each business. On the site there will be a feedback forum and a satisfaction rating page as well. I am also working on customer feedback cards; early payment incentives; certificates for free oil changes; $25 of the next $120 spent; one-hour free service on next $150 or more repair call; free estimates, etc. They will also learn inventory control, ordering processes, rules and regulations and how to keep costs down.

Both Bryce and Quentin are breathing sighs of relief. It has been three months since I began Bryce's overhaul and almost two months for Quentin; with fantastic results thus far, for both. They are working well with me and do everything I ask and Quentin and I seem to be getting along well too.

So far the results show: Bryce's debt reduced from over $63,000 down to $18,000 and changes made to reduce the interest rates he is being charged. Quentin's debt has been reduced from $46,800 to $26,500 with changes also made to his interest rates.

We make plans to pay amounts owing at bare minimum right now due to the litigation we are in. If all goes according to plan, our lawyer says they should both receive enough money to pay off their debts in full and have some left over in their bank accounts. Both Bryce and Quentin have employed KMGP to be their accounting firm and next month Eric will be with them as well.

A few weeks have now passed and we receive word that our court date will be June 8th. It is now almost May 4th leaving us one month to get ready. I work with our lawyer Mr. R. Hennessey during the month making sure that every basis is covered and no loop holes catches us.

Everything is going great between Craig and I as well. I no longer have nightmares and life couldn't be better. These past few months I have been back and forth between Craig's place and my uncle's. Weekdays are usually spent at my aunt and uncles house where Craig sometimes stays but only the odd night. Some weeks there are two to three days we go without seeing each other because of our jobs and it is hell. The weekends are our time and we are inseparable from Friday night through Monday morning.

The weekend is coming and we are attending a party at his friends' mansion across town. I have never felt closer to or more in love with anyone like I am with Craig. It is a feeling I have never felt before. I can't describe it and I wouldn't change a thing.

Friday is now here and the weekend is upon us. I am excited yet nervous. We wake up to a beautiful Saturday morning as we head for the mansion. When we arrive it is as I had expected a mansion to look like. Interlocking white and grey brick driveway with gates you need to be buzzed through to get in begins the experience.

As we drive up we go around a center garden. The center garden has a three-tier stone fountain in the center of it with red, blue and white lights on each tier. Circular in shape, the tiers range from one-foot in diameter as the top tier which flows into the second two-foot diameter tier; which in turn flows to the third four-foot tier. All tiers cascade down into a ten-foot diameter pool like base. Each tier is painted pressed blue and black marble with a finished edge of pendant drop motifs. This fountain is surrounded by a myriad of yellow and white daffodils, pink and orange lilies, red and yellow roses, blue and purple tulips all edged with pink and blue alyssums and geraniums. A grass pathway leads to the fountain from three directions.

I look up as we stop to see a tall, three-story, two-tone grey brick home. The front of the house has three peaked roofed windows, one with a balcony. The Grand entry has two pillars with covered panels and faceted designs give rise to the Eastlake 1820s style stair case. It all gives rise to the front porch entry way. Either side of the entry, are long colored glass windows with molded painted wood designed with Roman and Greek themes.

As I enter the interior of the house I am awe struck, like I am meeting a famous person. It is the most beautiful place I have ever seen. It is like something out of a fairy tale. First to meet us at the door are his friends, Ariel and Joe, the hosts of the party. As we walk down the hall I move slowly taking in all the exquisite detail and décor.

The interior of the house is focused around a large central hallway which flows into a large, wide staircase that provides the main means of egress from the entertainment area of the house to the private rooms on the second floor. Four formal rooms with sixteen foot ceilings, pocket doors, fireplaces and tall windows form the main block of the building. On the first floor, the hallway and front parlor possess classic Anglo-Japanese asymmetrical designs and exotic motifs. Adjacent rooms approximate the original paint colors and add class to the overall décor.

As you enter through the front door, you pass into a grand hallway with Roman and Greek themes on the ceilings and walls. The predominant colors are dark with tan and gold highlights, and pale blues with black detailing are repeated throughout both floors of the house. The tall, heavy, varnished wood doors have colored glass panes of amber, blue and pink, in a geometric design. On either side of the main doors are smaller, longer versions of the colored glass windows. The doors and windows have molded painted wood with bulls-eye corner blocks and decorative accents. The door knobs, plates, and hinges are brass with raised Eastlake style ornament.

Off the main hallway, to the right, is a small sitting room with a fireplace, situated on the interior wall and has a tall mantel of Birchwood with turned spindles flanking a rectangular mirror supporting a tapered hood. The hearth is set with dark patterned tiles of Eastlake designs with light blue and black marble tiles surrounding the firebox. The ceiling is painted pressed metal with a curved crown molding. The tall windows are of the Queen Anne style, banded at the top by a panel of colored lights (blue, white, purple, red). The height of the window is emphasized by a dado panel of wood with molded trim beneath each window. This style of window is repeated throughout the main block of the house.

On the south side of the hall is the large front parlor. This room contains a fireplace with a mantel similar to the one in the front sitting room; including, dark tiles of geometric designs with lighter colored tiles around the firebox. This is where I meet Craig's mom, Winter. She stands five-foot eight inches tall, slender in build, plain looking yet elegant. She is sixty-two years old and doesn't look a day over fifty. Her long radiant auburn hair bounces gracefully past her shoulders. She has a narrow face with angular cheekbones, defined thin lips and a sturdy jaw line. Her dark eyes are small yet evenly spaced sitting below pencil thin eyebrows. A medium build body type with long legs and arms sporting glamorously finished and polished nails. Her dress is long with slips up the side to the top of her thighs with the front v-shaped to mid-thigh. The back flows to her ankles while the top has a low v-shaped cut emphasizing her thirty-eight D breasts and hugs at her waist.

She stops suddenly and turns. She is now standing three feet in front of me. Facing me, her smile makes me nervous. She hugs me like we have known each other for years. "So, how do you like the place?"

Very nervous yet enamored with all of it I reply. "I love it. I have never been in a place like this before, it's gorgeous."

"May I join you for the tour?'

"Sure, we can get to know one another at the same time."

Agreeing she walks with us hanging off my arm, as Ariel and Joe continue with the tour.

Continuing down the hallway, a center arch of decorative painted columns and molding with ornamental keystone designs with the haunch of the arch angular shaped rather than curved. The arch is formed by two freestanding columns flanked on either side by a smaller arch with engaged pillars. The side arches form decorative surrounds for the classic statuary that was placed in this area and serves not only as a support for the upper floors, but as a visual break to make the main hallway feel less imposing.

Past the archway is a large 30' x 20' kitchen with large casement doors that open onto the deck that wraps around from the front of the house. The doors are of the same design as the front doors with the top panel of geometric colored glass. The room is done entirely in painted pressed metal, with dado, walls, crown molding and ceiling of different patterns.

Across the hall from the kitchen is the formal dining room. The fireplace is located on the east wall of the room and is of wooden moldings with a large mirror over the mantel, bracketed by electric candles and tiered over mantel. The dining room has panel doors on the west wall, one of which opens to the verandah that runs the length of the house and wraps to the back.

A large post with carved panels and faceted design serves as the introduction to the cherry staircase done in the Eastlake style that rises to a landing, turns and then continues to the second floor landing where the private rooms are located. Attached to the side of the risers are the balustrades, the lower portion of which are finished in a faceted pendant drop motif with moldings and turned designs.

The corner newel posts are also of substantial size with the drop design reaching below the staircase. The staircase is open to the second floor ceiling and upon reaching the second floor landing, the balustrade forms a balcony overlooking the staircase. Above the stairway landing, is a set of paired windows with multi-colored panes of glass and when the sun makes its western descent, Dante colored light is produced filling both the main and second floor hallways with shades of green, purple and blue.

As you reach the second floor landing, there are bedrooms to the north and south. To the east, is a small room that serves as the entranceway to the second floor balcony. The second floor has four main bedrooms, a bathroom, a tower room, and two servants' rooms. The doors to the rooms are carved with an eight panel design and the windows are the same Queen Anne style. Door and window surrounds have the same moldings as on the first floor with polychromatic paint schemes. There is a large floor to ceiling mirror of dark varnished wood mounted on the east wall.

The tower room is entered directly off the landing by a doorway to the left of the large mirror. It is a small room, possibly used for a sewing room, with a set of four wide steps leading up to casement doors that open out to the second story balcony of the tower. The doors are set under a fixed transom of various sized rectangular panels of colored glass. There are triangle colored glass inserts in the middle of the door with a large pane of clear glass above.

The bathroom is on the west wall of the main block and can be reached from a small hallway that runs between the bathroom and the master bedroom. The hall ends in an entrance to a bedroom. The master bedroom is at the other end of the hall which has a door in the northwest corner that opens to a second story balcony overlooking the pool and grounds. Off this hallway is the staircase to the attic and the third-story tower room.

The south side of the second floor has two bedrooms: i.e. one in the southeast corner of the main block and one on the south side. The south bedroom is accessed through an ancillary hallway. This hallway also serves as the access to the servants quarters, down a set of stairs and a narrow hallway to the second floor of the west wing.

The third floor is the attic space which is finished and used as a meditation room. Like the tower room below, this room also has doors opening onto a small balcony, which overlooks the eastern side of the valley.

The basement houses the pantry with cupboards and shelving on both sides. A small sink and drain board are set on the south wall of the room. There is a small work and supply room, as well as a laundry facility, cold rooms, storage rooms and a utility room. The basement can be reached from the interior by a door under the main staircase and a set of steps in the northwest corner of the kitchen area.

The back yard houses a large in-ground pool with a marble deck surrounding it. The pool is a fireplace berth shape with lights throughout the bottom and sides of the pool. The lights slowly change color from white to yellow to green and red. You can walk into the pool from either side down the lit stairwell. They gradually deepen from three-feet to six-foot in depth at the far end. Where they are connected the depth gradually gets to ten feet deep in the center with a water slide that curves into this end. There is a square section at the center of the back length with a depth of fifteen-feet and has a diving board in the center. The water is a clear blue and I can't wait to dive in.

Around the pool there are several patio tables with chairs and umbrellas as well as many lounge chairs for sunbathing. There are many people sitting about all around the pool with several swimming and sitting in pool chairs in the water. Kids are splashing in the shallow end of the pool and some are going down the slide or diving off the board at the deep end. There is a shower house on the left side of the pool where we can get changed and take a shower before or after swimming. The shower house also holds the pool toys and cleaning supplies.

I am wearing a light summer dress knee length and sandals to match. I didn't realize swimming would be involved. When Winter asks if I swim,

I answer, "I love to swim but I didn't bring my bathing suit. I didn't know we would be swimming."

She smiles and turns to Craig. "Take her to the shop and let her pick one out."

Okay so now there is a shop where you can pick out clothing? I am really shocked because I didn't see a shop anywhere.

As Craig and I walk back into the house, he asks, "So what do you think of the place?"

"It is huge and magnificent, like something out of a fairy tale book."

He walks me through the kitchen to a door that is on the far wall. I thought the door went to a storage room or pantry, however I was wrong. It is the 'Shop' as Winter called it, and what a shop it is. It has dresses, shoes, sandals, swim wear, sunglasses and short sets.

Curious I ask, "Why do they have this in their home?"

"They always have parties like this and not everyone brings this stuff so they make sure they have it available so everyone who comes here can take part in everything."

"How do they know what sizes to carry?"

"They have the most common sizes. If anyone is smaller or larger than the norm, they have their workers go and buy it from the store up the street."

I guess this is what rich people do, I think to myself.

"Go ahead pick out a bathing suit!"

I look through them. They have so many different ones from one piece suits to bikini's. I want to dive into the pool off the diving board but can't in a bikini but I also want to wear a bikini. Then I find it, the perfect suit for both.

It is a one piece but looks like a two piece all rolled into one. It is two-tone blue; the top ties around the neck like a bikini and covers the boobs the same way. It then has a thin piece of material down from mid breast on both sides that come together below the navel in a V-shape. It gathers around a gold washer then into the bottom which goes under and attaches around the waist. The top also ties around the back from the boob base like a bikini keeping it on your body. I pick this one and also take a light blue wrap for my waist to wear as I walk around the pool and a pair of sunglasses.

"Wow, I like that one. Put it on, I want to see what you look like in it."

I go to the bathroom near the staircase and change into it. I put the wrap on and lay the dress over my arm. I walk out and under the stairs but that is as far as I get. Craig is standing there with his mom looking at me. "Well?" I ask.

They both really like it. "You couldn't have made a better choice." Winter says adding it is one of her favorite suits and she likes how it looks on me.

Craig asks me to take off the wrap, so I do and I turn so he can see. He really loves it. I put the wrap back on as his mom takes my dress and puts it in the front room.

As we walk out to the pool a waiter comes over with a tray of drinks so I take one. It is a White Russian and it tastes really good. Craig tells me to find a seat wherever and he will be right back. "There is someone I want you to meet but I have to find him first." He kisses me then leaves.

I begin to walk towards the lounge chairs as I love the sun. Before I can sit, four women walk up to me all giddy like school children. "Are you with Craig?"

Nodding my head I sit in the lounge chair. They sit with me on the same chair. After a minute or so I ask them who they are and what they want. They introduce themselves, Arianna, Demi, Trinity and Uri and they are on a diving team. After talking to them for a bit, Demi gets up as she sees someone she knows.

"So do you swim?" Trinity asks me.

"Yes I do." I tell them how I grew up around water with a pool in my schools, being careful not to tell them of my swim meet or diving years.

Uri then asks me if I know how to dive. Telling her yes most people can, she further explains to me the type of diving she is talking about.

Hesitant I tell her I used to when I was in high school and college because they had a pool and we did that during our gym classes but proceed to tell her I haven't done any since then. They try to convince me to dive with them but I stand firm and eventually they stop.

There are two diving boards there, one that bounces and is at pool level. There is another one they wheel over which is six-feet above pool level and they secure it to the cement pad. They have done this before and it shows. I sit in a chair that is close to them to watch their dives.

The five of them put on a show for us doing various dives from both platforms. They all start with easy one flip, summersaults and backwards dive from the pool level board. Then they move to the higher one where they do double flips and summersaults, twists, and backwards half pikes. They also provide an aquatic aerobic demonstration in the shallow end of the pool. The entire exhibition lasts about an hour and is quite impressive.

When they finish and climb out of the pool they all gather around me, this time in their own chairs. Sitting and soaking up the sun the girls share memories of competitions they have competed in over the past few years. Everything seems to be going good as they share different things that happened to them in training and competitions.

After a while, Demi and Arianna, who have been whispering among themselves back and forth, get up and without saying a word, seem to be on a jog towards one of the tables. There is a laptop on one of them and that is where they end up. While on the computer they keep looking at us, smiling and snickering. Trinity yells to them, "What are you laughing at?"

At first they don't answer. It isn't long before Arianna comes running over saying, "I knew it! I knew it!"

"Knew what?" Trinity asks, "What are you and Demi laughing at?"

"Come with me and I will show you!" she says tugging at them to follow her.

They all follow rather quickly while I walk slowly behind them. They are ahead me quite a bit and Demi hollers to me, "Are you coming?"

I nod my head but don't pick up my pace. I'm not sure what they are doing but have a feeling it's about me. Arianna recognizes me from my earlier years and seeing that Demi has a laptop on the table, my guess is my diving days are on the internet.

Craig meets me part way. "Baby, what's going on?"

"I'm not exactly sure but I don't have a good feeling about this."

We are now at the table and Demi has turned the laptop around so everyone can see what they supposedly knew and about who. As they are watching the video, it is of me during my swimming competitions. Demi says, "Arianna thought she recognized Chloe but couldn't put her finger on it from where. Sitting by the pool she put two and two together so we checked it out."

"Okay so what's the big deal about what Chloe did when she was younger?" Craig asks.

Trinity looks at me and in a high pitch tone says, "I thought you said you didn't dive?"

"I never said I didn't dive." I reply curtly. "What I said was it's been a very long time since I have and didn't want to do it anymore!"

I look at Craig then to Demi and walk away almost in tears. I go back to the chair I was sitting in making sure not to look back as them as I do. I take a seat and it's all I can do not to cry. I am pissed off that all this stuff is on the internet. First I find out my singing is there, then my bike riding years and now this. Computers never existed when I did these things so how they got put onto the World Wide Web is beyond me. I am now left wondering what else is on there.

Minutes go by before Craig and Cora come over to see if I am okay. Responding that I am fine Craig gives me a kiss saying he will be right back. Cora sits with me and begins to chat.

"You know I thought I recognized you but I couldn't place you either. Our coach uses your videos for our team training. We've won several competitions following your lead."

Now I am not sure how to feel. "Thank you, I guess." is all I can say.

Just then the other girls come back and join us. Trinity apologizes for saying what she said and Demi and Arianna apologize for bringing it up like they did. I tell them it's okay and it gets dropped.

Another round of drinks is brought over on behalf of Craig. I look over to him and he smiles blowing me a kiss. He puts up five fingers as if to say he will be done in five minutes. I nod, smile and blow him a kiss back. I turn back to the girls.

A couple of hours pass and things seem to be going smoothly between me and the girls. Craig has introduced me to a few people but mostly I am left with the swim team. After a while the conversation begins to change and I am starting to get an uneasy feeling, again.

The discussions have turned from happy-go-lucky to a superficially deep tone. Whispers begin to take place among the girls leaving me to wonder what they are saying and wondering what else they think they know about me.

The dialogue has gone from general every day chit chat to a more serious one with innuendoes thrown at me. It is like they know something from my past and are trying to get me to tell them. I have gone from smiling to frowning as part of the conversation makes me close up, talk less and try to ignore the questions. Now my thought process is one of worry.

They keep at it one after the other and are now questioning me about my teenage years. It's not long when they ask, in a round-about-way, about the rapes. Uri left a few minutes ago and is now coming back with the laptop in hand. She hands it to Demi, who has brought up an article regarding me and my step dad and another article where I put my first husband in jail.

I can't believe they would bring these things up and request I give them answers. My past is my past and I don't see how it is any of their business what happened to me or why and how I did what I did. Trinity threatens that she will tell Craig these things if I don't answer their questions.

After an hour of them trying, I get fed up and tell them I have to use the bathroom and will be right back. "When I return, I will answer your questions. It's going to be a while so I want to make sure there are not interruptions."

They all agree and I head inside.

I have been emotional with everything I have been through in my life and with the most recent events, it is all causing me to be over sensitive and all I want to do is cry. I am extremely upset and pissed off all at the same time and not really sure what I want to do. I do know I am not telling them anything.

As I stand inside under the stairs, I decide that I'm not going to take any more from them. Craig has left me with the girls knowing I was not comfortable after what happened, and all they have been doing is badgering me into telling them things about myself that I made clear I did not want to do. Now they are digging up my entire past and questioning me over and over about things that are none of their business.

I grab my dress from the front parlor, put it on over the bathing suit and walk out the front door, telling no one I am leaving, not even Craig.

CHAPTER 40

I DON'T TELL anyone I am leaving, I just walk out. I am so upset, angry and aggravated over what occurred that I walk to Craig's apartment which is four miles away in under two hours. It seems like I just left the party and here I am, already at his apartment. I get the spare key he has hid outside and let myself in.

I lock the door behind me, lie on the couch and begin to cry. After a few minutes I make some coffee and sit here wondering how I get myself into these jams. On my second cup, I walk over to the window and look outside. I can see the mansion from here and am now wondering if I did the right thing.

What is Craig thinking? Is he wondering where I am? Does he even notice I am gone? Should I go back? There are a million and one questions running through my head and now I feel bad about leaving without telling him.

I stand here for a minute just staring out the window. Before I know it, I am talking out loud and crying. I ask myself, *'Why do you do this to me? Why can't my past just be that, my past? Why does it have to follow me everywhere I go? I try to move on but you keep putting people in my path or have things happen that bring me right back to that place. Why?'*

It doesn't matter what I do, where I go, or what I try, I just can't get away from it. Leaning against the wall, I set the coffee cup on the window sill, wrap my arms around my waist and cry as I slide down and sit on the floor. With my back to the wall now and eyes closed I ask out loud the questions again only this time out loud.

"God why do you punish me like this? Why did you have to put them in my path today and have those girls know who I was or what I did? What is the purpose? I just want to leave it all in the past. Things were going so good and now because of this, it is totally messed up. This time, there won't be any recovery."

Just then I hear a voice from out of nowhere. "Nothing is messed up."

Even though I am sitting I jump, my heart is in my throat. I stand up. Craig is standing at the end of the couch in tears. I just stand here, looking at him wiping the tears from my face. "I am sorry for running off without telling you." Is all I can muster to say to him.

"It's okay. I was frantic looking for you and even had the staff looking." He slowly walks towards me. "One of the waiters told me he seen you a few hours ago walk out the front door. At first I thought you were just walking the grounds so I walked them too hoping to find you. It took me an hour and you were nowhere."

I don't know what to say or do. I just stand here, waiting for him to yell or scream or question me or something; but he doesn't. He wipes the tears from his face and continues to walk slowly towards me. He says what he went through looking for me thinking something seriously happened to me.

"I'm sorry." I say over and over.

It doesn't seem to do anything and understanding what he went through I cry even more. I turn away and look back out the window grabbing my cup. By now he is behind me.

He puts his arms around me and holds me really tight, "Was it something I said or did? Was it because I left you alone?"

"No it had nothing to do with you."

"Then what was it? What was so bad that you walked out on me?"

"I didn't walk out on you. At least it wasn't my intention."

"Then what caused you to leave?"

"I was really upset and so aggravated that I really didn't think. I walked all the way here before I even realized where I was or that I had even left. I thought about going back but then I got nervous and worried. Not knowing if I should or not I came in here. I didn't call you because you have my cell phone and I don't know your number by heart, it's programmed into my cell."

He takes out my phone and hands it to me then takes out his and calls him mom to tell her he found me and where I am. He tells her I am alright, briefly explaining what happened and why I left. Facing him now, he hangs up, puts his arms around me again and walks me to the couch.

He sits beside me with his arm still around me. "So tell me what upset you like that?"

Looking at him now I have tears in my eyes. "I don't know if I can."

"Please try. I would like to understand what happened."

"If I do it will take a while because it is a long story."

"Well, I have lots of time, two days in fact. Please tell me."

"You will now absolutely everything about me making me 100% vulnerable to you, if I do. No one in this world knows all of it, only some know parts of it. In the past when I told people parts of it, it was used against me and things went bad." I stand up and walk to the table to pick up my cup.

I face him standing beside the table as he looks at me. "I won't force you but I really need to understand. Right now it does not make any sense to me what could be so bad that you would leave without saying a word to anyone, including me."

"Craig I love you. I really do but, I am scared. I don't want to mess this up, that is if I haven't already."

He stands up, walks to me, takes the cup out of my hand and sets it down. He places my arms around his neck then puts his arms around my waist. "You haven't messed anything up. I love you and want to be with you. I won't pressure you into telling me but I do ask that you trust me. I won't use anything you say against you and there is nothing you can say that will change the way I feel about you!"

He kisses me with passion to show me he means it.

"Before I decide to, I need to apologize to you. I am really sorry that I ruined your day and the party for you."

"No apologies. Things happen. Besides if anyone should apologize it's me."

"You. Why?"

"For leaving you there, and putting you into that position. I am sorry for that."

"It's okay, it wasn't your fault. You don't know much about my past, my life or what I went through and neither of us knew they would be there or that this would happen."

"That is true. Okay so will you tell me?"

Craig is immensely annoyed, you can see it in his eyes and by the expression on his face. He wants me to be open with him and tell him everything. Fearful of the fallout based on my past experiences, I am hesitant. After a few moments, I give in and tell him I will tell him everything but tell him how I am leery about it and why.

"Let me get another coffee and I will tell you. However, it is long and it's going to be very emotional for me."

"It's okay. I am here baby. Nothing is going to happen, I promise."

I get myself and him a coffee and sit on the couch. He is at one end of the couch so I sit at the other end with my legs crossed facing him.

I begin by telling him about the rape by the four guys when I was in grade ten. I go through all the emotions as I tell him, the hatred, the guilt, the shame and wanting to kill myself. I even tell him how I tried while I was in the hospital. I state how Josh left me that same year and about my step dad and what he put me through right after that.

"It was during this time that I took Jui Jitsu lessons to learn how to protect myself so it wouldn't happen to me again." I tell him what was said as I was held at gunpoint and what happened that got him caught.

I then pause because I need to calm myself down. Craig gets up and gets a bottle of wine and pours both of us a glass. "I think we both need this instead of coffee."

I get up to go to the bathroom and he orders Chinese for dinner. While we wait for the food to arrive he asks some questions. "Did they ever find the guys who raped you?"

"At this point no because not too many knew it was me and I could not describe them as they were wearing dark clothing and ski masks. All I had was their build, strength and voices. The police tried to put together something to identify them with but there wasn't enough."

The food is now delivered. As we eat I tell him that I know the whereabouts of two of the four guys. I explain to him how the first guy I ever lived with learned of these rapes and how he used it against me by trying to force me to have sex with him. I even tell him about the knife he held to my throat and the punch where he hit the wall, just missing my head by inches.

I tell him every detail on everything. If I am going to tell him, and if he truly does love me and it is going to help me and us, then I am going to tell him everything and leave nothing out.

Then I talk about the guy in college and how he learned of my step dad and what he did. "He decided that if it is what I was used to, then he will treat me like that too, and he did!" I am now very angry as I begin to feel the emotions I felt when I went through it.

"It lasted a year and during that time is when I took up swimming because it gave me some time to myself where I could escape the world I lived in. I also got my blue belt in Jui Jitsu that same year and used it on him. That is how I stopped him and he too got jail time."

"Well that's good. Is he still there?"

"As far as I know he is."

"Good. So what happened after that?"

Now it's time to tell him about my first marriage. "Well after a few years passed, I started dating again. That's when I found my first husband."

I explained how well it went before we got married. "I loved him but because of the life I had, I thought it was true love simply because he wasn't like the others were, or so I thought. I didn't have any other kind of love to match it against other than Josh, so it made me naïve and stupid."

I then summarize the details of our wedding. "Then came the wedding night. At that point I always thought that the wedding night was to be special, one where you celebrated as a married couple your love, the passion, etc. you have for each other. I could not have been more wrong."

Looking at me puzzled he asks, "Why were you wrong? That's how it's supposed to be."

I hesitate. "I thought so too. I went into the bathroom and changed into the negligée I bought for the occasion. When I came out he didn't even notice what I had on. He grabbed my arm and threw me on the bed, pulled out the marriage license from his pocket and told me that he now owned me. I could no longer go out with my friends. I had to quit my diving team and motorcycle racing. I wasn't allowed to go anywhere or do anything unless it was with him or I had his permission."

As I say this I am pissed off again and I can tell that Craig is a little upset himself.

"He pointed his finger at me almost to my nose and told me that now I had to do everything he told me and if I questioned him I would regret it."

"I'm afraid to ask."

"Ask what? How I would regret it?"

Nodding his head yes I tell him how he turned overnight from a soft gentle man to a bear.

"He had me followed by him or one of his friends when I went for walks. Said he couldn't trust someone like me because I was so popular with everyone around. He would hit me if something wasn't done to his exact specifications. He said that anything I wanted to do was to be considered a privilege and I had to earn them."

Now I have gone from angry to scared because I know what is coming next. I stop for a minute, look at him with tears in my eyes, stand and walk towards the window.

"Are you okay?' he asks.

I look back at him then back out the window. "Yes but this is very hard for me. I thought I left all this behind me, that it was dealt with and over. Here I am reliving it!"

"I am so sorry, I didn't realize you went through all this. You don't have to tell me anymore if you don't want to baby, it's okay."

"No. I think maybe I need to do this. Maybe this is why it keeps coming back to haunt me no matter what it is I do. I never told anyone so even though I thought I dealt with it, maybe I didn't and this is how I will be able to finally move past it and truly put it all behind me."

He asks me to come and sit back down on the couch with him. I turn and sit beside him. Then I tell him what my husband did.

"Brace yourself because you haven't heard the worse of it yet."

"What? Being beaten and left for dead and almost killed and raped by everyone else and now held hostage isn't bad enough?"

"You would think so but no, there is more and it is worse."

He shakes his head in disbelief. I tell him how he decided one day that I wasn't worthy of any privileges. "He took all my clothes and his out of the bedroom and put them into the spare room. He then locked me in there with nothing to wear telling me I was a bad girl and had to be taught a lesson. For a week he would unlock the door to give me food or something to drink or because he wanted sex. He was a lot stronger than I was and would force me to do things to him and in positions that almost broke a few of my bones."

I am now fighting back the tears and it looks like he is too but I can't tell for sure. "Wow, that's the kind of shit you see on television and in movies, not in real life."

I nod then proceed to tell him how a week later he came in and decided to change things. "He told me that I haven't learned my lesson yet so he was upping the game. He said I have no clothes for a reason. I was to be ready for him or anyone else that came into the room. He didn't care what time it was or how tired or how sore I was. If any of his friends or him wanted it, I would give it or they would just take it! The choice was mine."

Craig leans forward and latches onto me wrapping his arms around me tight. I am crying by now and I think he is too. I pull back and sit away from him a bit so I can continue.

"This went on like that with friend after friend after friend coming in and out every day. Some days it seemed like there was no break and then there would be days where it would only be once but rarely none. Sometimes there would be three or four on me at once. This went on for over a month."

"Oh My God!"

"I don't know which was worse for me, the rape by the four guys in high school, my step-dad or this."

I can feel the pain I felt then just like it is happening now. Even though it isn't, it feels like it is. I didn't notice it but at some point while telling him this, I have put myself in a crouched protection position at the end of the couch. I look at Craig and he has tears rolling down his face.

He starts to move beside me but I guess I back away trying to get into a tighter ball. He stops. "Baby, I won't hurt you I promise."

Realizing what I am doing, I let go of my legs and sit letting him beside me. "I'm sorry I didn't realize what I was doing or how I was."

He puts his arms around me crying trying to stop me from crying. It is very emotional for the both of us and I am only half way through the story. I am not sure how he will handle the rest but I need to say it all now.

After a few minutes he says, "I am so sorry you went through all this. I don't know how you even like men after this, or how you are even here."

"Thank you but you don't have to be sorry. You didn't do it and you weren't there. I didn't like men for the longest time. But that's not all of it."

He looks at me shocked. "How much more could there be?"

"Well, believe it or not, quite a bit."

"First how did you get away from your husband?"

I tell him how one day there was no noise for almost two hours. "I wrapped the towel around my fist and broke the window in the bathroom. I was skinny enough that I was able to fit through that small window. I climbed through it scratching my back and hips as I did then I slid down the snow bank wearing only the towel he had left me with. It was so cold and the wind was blowing so bad I could hardly see and I was very cold. I fell into a snow bank and almost froze to death there."

I explain how the couple driving by in a car saw me and brought me to the hospital barely alive.

"When I got to the hospital they weren't sure if I was going to live or not at first. When I started to get better, their fear was that I might lose three of my toes and my one thumb to frost bite. Thankfully I didn't."

I then tell him what they did at the hospital and the reports the police got and that within two days, all of the men who did this including my husband not only got jail time but they will never get out.

"This was when I found out that one of the guys who raped me then was one of the original four who raped me in high school. His first day in the pen he bragged about it and it wasn't long before it got out."

"That is incredible. I really don't know what to say."

"There is nothing you can say, but it's okay. After a few years pass and thinking that I had finally put that life behind me, I ended up in a relationship that proved me wrong once again."

He sits there like a young boy enthralled in the most captivating story waiting to see what is going to happen next.

"Why did it prove you wrong? What happened?"

Not wanting to disappoint him, and telling him everything until now, I figure I might as well lay it all out there. I continue telling him what happened.

CHAPTER 41

"I WENT SEVEN years before I could trust another man again and even then, I was very skeptical and scared. That is when I found my second husband, my son Dylan's dad Zak."

I pause. I look at him with an inquisitive look. "What's wrong baby?" he asks.

"I have to ask you something before I continue with this next part of my life."

"Okay, you know you can ask me anything."

"Well, I need you to be honest with me no matter what the answer is."

"No problem. What is it?"

"You know how you felt about me before today right?"

He nods.

"Hearing and knowing what you know now without me saying anything else," I pause not sure if I want to ask because I don't know how I will react to what he might say. What if he tells me what I don't want to hear? Will I be able to take it?

"What is it?" he asks a bit irritated.

I look at him with tears in my eyes. "What are your feelings for me now? Have they changed at all?"

He looks at me, leans towards me pulling me close to him and kisses me. Then he says, "No. My feelings for you have not changed. I am still very much in love with you. I am very sad and sorry that you went through all this and I now know why you got upset this afternoon. This makes me understand you better and will help me when I plan things for us in the future, but that's it."

I am extremely relieved because I thought he was going to tell me they have changed and he doesn't know how he should feel or act around me, just like the others did. I decide to tell him about my life with Zak and how I suffered twelve years of physical, mental, emotional, financial, and sexual abuse.

"Life was never a picnic with Zak, but it wasn't bad until Dylan was two years old. He decided that I needed to find a job and he should be the one to stay at home. He never left the house and from what he told me, he couldn't work because of a back injury. It wasn't until ten years later when I found out that he never had a back injury. He faked it so he didn't have to work."

I proceed to tell him what he put me through. As I do, I show him the scars I have from the things he has done to me like putting out cigarettes on my body, cutting me with a knife and stabbing me in the stomach with scissors, etc. With each one I show him, he winces, says ouch or fights back the tears.

I tell him of how he prevented me from talking to most of my family for twelve years; how I lost my job of fifteen years because of him and what he did for that to happen. "I was in court suing for wrongful dismissal when it came out that he had my keys duplicated, went into my office after hours and read my files."

"How did they know that?"

"Thinking that I was stealing or doing something I shouldn't have been, the board put a camera all over the office to see what I was doing. That is when they caught him after hours."

"Wow, that's just crazy. Why would he do that?"

"I don't know. He then went around telling people what he knew about them to make it look like I was breaking confidentiality."

"So what did you do?"

"Well, when they first approached me telling me he was breaking confidentiality, I didn't believe them. I couldn't understand how he even knew what he said he did because I knew very well I never said a word. Work is work and home life is home life, I never confused the two or brought the other into it. To prove this, they said I had to disbar him from the office with a trespass warrant and everything, so I did."

"What happened then?"

"Well not much because I was let go shortly thereafter. When this came out the judge charged him $20,000 for his part in it. I did win my case and got $30,000. The judge said that even if I broke confidentiality, the way they let me go was wrong."

"Wow. How could anyone do that?"

"I don't know. I had to pay his fine from the money I was awarded which left me $10,000. I hated him for that."

"Ya I can see why. I would have too."

I then tell him two years later is when I found out that Zak started doing a lot of this stuff to Dylan, when he no longer had any effect on me.

"Oh My God. What is wrong with him? What did he do to his own son?"

"He did everything, except the sexual abuse. He imposed emotional, financial, mental and physical abuse on him. It was his eleventh birthday party when I found my son hanging from the rafters trying to kill himself." I try to hold back the tears as I tell him how I found him after his birthday party.

"I had him hospitalized for it and it was during this time that he told me and the doctors he couldn't handle being around his dad anymore and if I was staying with him he wasn't."

I am now crying almost uncontrollably. "That's when I sold everything I could, Dylan moved to another province to go to school with some friends and I moved to Florida. That is where I found Josh again. You know that story because I have told you some of it and so did my family."

"Yes that is true but I don't know it all. Is there anything else I should know?"

"Well, he was the first one in my life and until you, who actually loved me and treated me right. During our initial years together we were at one of his son's football events when we found out that the second one of the four who raped me in high school was found dead. DNA deciphered that one. The other two are still out there somewhere."

By now he is crying, as though he is going through it as I am. He hugs me tight and after a few minutes I pull away and finish.

"It wasn't long after when Josh became a truck driver. He drove for a year and when he was three days from coming home and being home for good, his truck slid on some ice and he went over a cliff. He died on impact."

"Wow, I am sorry you went through that."

"It's okay, it wasn't your fault. That's what brought me here. I tried to drown myself in the ocean but failed epically so I decided I needed a new start."

"Okay and I know it from there."

"Yes you do. So now that you know everything about my life and what I endured, I have to ask again, has anything changed?"

He shakes his head, stands up and grabs my hands to stand me up. He brings me to the bathroom. Standing in front of the mirror and tears running down both of our cheeks, he stands behind me, puts his arms around me and says, "I want you to tell me what you see."

Standing here for a minute all I can do is look at the both of us in the mirror. "Well, what do you see?" he asks again.

Trying to calm down I look at him through the mirror and attempt to give him an answer.

"I see a person who is broken. I see someone who has suffered a lot in life, and just can't seem to get away from it. I see a woman who doesn't deserve someone like you and can't understand how someone like you could even be with someone like me. I don't see much more."

He then tells me what he sees.

"Well here is what I see. I see a woman with beauty. I see a woman who is smart, intelligent and very strong. You have a will power like no other I have ever seen. I see a woman who has a big heart and even though she should not want anything to do with men, forgives and acknowledges that we are not all the same."

I am still crying, and he is holding onto me very tightly. I don't see what he does, at least not at this precise moment. He turns me to face him.

"Others may have treated you badly or differently or used this against you, but Chloe, I would never do that to you. I love you. You telling me everything tonight, opening up to me like you have, makes you vulnerable yes, but no one has ever done that before with me."

He pauses for a moment. Looking at me as he wipes away the tears that are flowing down my face, then says, "You asked me twice tonight if any of this has changed how I feel about you. I told you no, that there was nothing you could say that would change how I feel about you."

I look at him and am now a bit worried. *Has it changed now and if so, how?* I think to myself.

He smiles. "Everything you told me only makes me love you all that much more and I feel closer to you than I have ever felt towards anyone in my life. I lied when I said my feelings for you would not change because they have. They got stronger and I didn't think that was possible. And to answer your other question, how someone like me would want to be with someone like you; well, it's easy. You are what every man should want. A strong, self-sufficient, caring, loving and beautiful woman and I am proud you are mine."

Now we are both crying. I hug him not wanting to let go as I tell him I love him.

He picks me up and carry's me into the bedroom. Setting me on the bed he says he will be right back. "I'm just going to lock the door and shut everything off." he says with a kiss.

I lay here while he is doing that trying to settle myself down. I have told him everything, opened myself up for the very first time in my entire life. Besides me, he is now the only other person on this entire earth who knows absolutely everything of what I have gone through.

What's going to happen now? Are the thoughts going through my head. It's not long before he comes back in. All night long we lay here cuddling, kissing, making love, feeling each other, and just being together. It is one of the best nights we've had together and certainly a better one than what I thought it would end up being.

The weekend is now over and I for one am glad. Although it turned out to be fine, it was a rocky one for me. Now, this week will follow suit as we will be getting ready for court, which is next week.

IT IS THREE o'clock Tuesday afternoon and Craig comes into the garage. He sits in the chair in front of my desk. "Chloe, there's something I want to ask you."

I stop what I am doing, lay my pen down on the desk and look up at him. "What is it baby?"

"Well, I was going to ask you this past weekend but with everything that happened I wasn't sure if it was a good time or even the right time."

"Well, the weekend is over, I thought we were past that."

"We are but it got me to thinking."

"Okay, so what is it?"

First he tells me that he spent the morning with his mom and told her what happened. "I only summarized what you told me though. I didn't tell her any details."

I'm shocked. Why would he tell her? So I enquire and ask him that question.

"I hope you aren't mad that I told her but she would understand because she went through some of what you did."

I shake my head. "I guess it's okay."

"I told her what I wanted to ask you and she said I should ask you anyway. But, if you don't want to or if you feel it's too soon I want you to tell me. I won't be mad but I think I need to ask you now rather than later."

I give him my wonder look not sure what to think. After a few moments of him not saying a word I am the one now getting a little irritated. "Ask me already."

He takes my hands in his and looks in my eyes before he gets it out. "Chloe, you know that I love you and I know you love me. I can't handle being away from you at all. Two to four days a week without you is becoming harder and harder for me. I want to see you and be with you every day. I want you to be the last person I see at night and the first one I see when I wake up, in the flesh, not just in my head."

Okay, so I am bracing myself thinking he is going to ask me to marry him and that I don't think I am ready for, at least not just yet. I wait. "Okay." Is all I can get out before he stops me.

"Will you move in with me and live with me at my place?"

I sigh slightly a bit relieved as his question wasn't what I thought it was. Hoping he doesn't notice me sighing in relief and not saying a word, he says he has a way for it to work.

"If you are not sure then we could do it on a trial basis. Do it for two weeks and if it's not what you want then you can move back to your aunts' house."

I look at him and smile. "Well, you are right. I do love you and I know you love me. Like you it is very hard for me to not see you every day as well and I too am tired of having to see you in my head rather than in person. Are you sure this is what you want?"

He nods his head. "Absolutely I am sure. I have wanted it for the past month but I didn't want to push anything on you and I certainly didn't want to rush you. My mom said she could tell you wanted the same thing that is why I am asking now. I want this, us, to last and be perfect for the rest of our lives."

"Well then my answer is yes but only on one condition."

"Okay and what is that condition?"

"If I move in, it's not a trial basis. It is for good. We make it work knowing that we have no one else but each other."

He agrees as he walks around the desk and gives me a kiss.

We are both happy and excited. Even though we are both in our late forty's, you would think we were in our twenties with the excitement we are showing.

After I am finished my work, he drives me to my aunts' and uncle's house. We have dinner with them telling them that I am moving in with Craig. We also summarize what happened this past weekend and how it brought us closer together rather than break us apart.

They tell me that if I need to come back their door is always open to me. I thank them and hug them telling them the condition I imposed on Craig if I was to move in with him. I pack my things and move to his place.

IT FEELS DIFFERENT going home to Craig's' place; however, it is a good different. I don't feel as tired because I am not going back and forth between work, Craig's house and my aunt's. I also feel better and different since I have told Craig everything. It's like a weight has been lifted off my shoulders and I no longer am carrying a burden with me anymore.

We spend the rest of the week with the lawyer getting ready for court. We go over game plans, how to speak, what words to use, how to sit and even how to answer every question that could be thrown our way.

It is now Friday afternoon and Mr. Hennessey says we are ready. We finalize the paperwork and leave for the weekend.

Ready or not we have no choice as court begins Monday morning.

CHAPTER 42

THE WEEKEND IS now over and being Monday morning, court is about to begin. On our side sits me, Bryce, Quentin and our lawyer, Mr. Hennessey. Behind us is Craig, our family, some friends and even our workers have joined the group. They asked us if they could attend, we are caught up with work and all bills are paid so we closed the shop for the week and let them join.

On the other side sits Ms. Baker, Mr. Hunt, Mr. Kinsley – the rep from J.G. Accountants and their lawyer Mr. Sloan. Behind them is their family and friends. They also have some of their co-workers, whom I recognize from when we went to get Bryce's papers, along with a few of their high paying clients. They wasted no time making sure we knew who they were.

Everyone in the courtroom is there because they want to know what will be said and what is going to happen. Cases this big aren't usually held in the courts here in this small town.

We state our case first because we started the proceedings. It takes us a good part of three days to present our side. We lay out our findings and what I did that led me to the results. It's late Wednesday afternoon and we are done so the judge adjourns until tomorrow morning at nine a.m.

It is morning now and it is their turn to present their case. They try to deny everything we said and brought out papers that say different. By Friday afternoon the judge breaks for the weekend to be reconvened Monday morning at nine a.m.

The weekend is spent planning for July 4th celebrations which will be here in two weeks. A much needed break from the court case, for all of us. My uncle will be hosting the annual truck rally this year and we will be helping him to get ready. It is Craig and mine five month anniversary of when we met and we want to celebrate it doing what we were doing when we met. There will be a few changes with this one as it is a rally rather than competitions, and half time shows. The weekend is long but we got a lot done and all that is left is to get the yard ready.

It is Monday morning once again and we are back in court. The other side is continuing to present their case to the judge. It takes them until late Wednesday afternoon before they are done. They gave the same papers that we did to the judge but tried to explain it all away.

The judge adjourns for the day reconvening the case Friday morning at 9 a.m.. Everyone leaves saying they are going to pray for a victory tomorrow.

As Craig and I enjoy a candlelit dinner at Rosy's Formal Dining Lounge, we discuss our upcoming weekend. "These past two weeks living with you have been the best two weeks of my life." he says.

I agree with him then he says, "I really don't want to lose you, ever. I have learned a lot about you, good and bad. You have told me everything and opened up like no one has to me ever before." He stops as desert is brought to our table and the waitress pours us a cup of coffee.

"Why are you saying all this to me?" I ask him.

"I want to do the same for you. There is one thing about me that I haven't told you yet and I so badly want to. I have held back not knowing how you will react but I don't want any secrets between us."

"Okay, should I be worried?"

He tells me it is more of having to show me rather than tell me. "Next weekend is going to be the events at your uncle's house for Independence Day and I want it all out before then. This Saturday I will take and show you, then everything will be in the open. Hopefully, we will be able to move forward as one and build our life together from there."

"Okay but you should know that I am a little worried and nervous about it."

"I understand. I am nervous as hell but it needs to be out. If you can take a chance like you did last weekend, so can I."

The next two days will tell all for me. Friday, we will know what will happen with the lawsuit. The next day after will tell me if Craig and I will remain together or will no longer be. At least this is what I am getting from what he said. Hopefully Sunday will be one huge celebration on both counts; we win our case in court, and Craig and I remain together even closer yet. However, I am worried about what he has to show and tell me.

It is Friday morning now and I did not sleep at all last night. Worrying and being anxious about today and tomorrow kept me awake, most of the night. Craig was restless as well, I think I kept him up. Quiet and not saying much, we have our coffee and get dressed. All morning all I can do is pace and fidget. I can't sit or stand still as I am nervous. Craig tries to calm me down but it doesn't work.

"I love you baby. But it's not working. I am just too nervous about today. What if they only get a slap on the wrist and Bryce and Quentin don't get much? Or worse, what if we lose completely? Then, what?"

I really don't expect him to answer me, but he does. "You presented a great case baby. It will work out and you might be surprised at the results."

Hoping he is right I give him a peck on the lips as it is time for us to leave. We meet Mr. Hennessey and the boys outside the courthouse and we all walk in together.

The three of us are very nervous but Mr. Hennessey tells us we have nothing to worry about. "I have presented many of these cases before and to this judge. I have won many of them with a lot less than what you had."

It does help to settle us down but we are still worried and very nervous.

Everyone is already in the court room waiting as we walk in. We get to our table just as the judge walks in. We all stand until she tells us to be seated. Now all we can do is cross our fingers, hope and pray we win and win big. I so badly want to prove them wrong and I don't want all of our hard work to be for nothing. It's not long before she begins her findings.

"Well, I have heard many cases in my life." she begins, "But this one ranks up there with intrigue and genius."

I look over to the other table as the judge is talking and they all have smirks on their faces like they already won. I do hope they are wrong but it makes me nervous because they all look so confident. The judge continues with her findings.

"Usually it takes weeks for the clients to prove their case and only days for the company to prove their innocence. This case was the opposite."

She then goes on summarizing what we both presented and how she sees it. After what seemed like hours she says, "I reviewed everything carefully, heard both sides for a week, and deliberated over the case for the past two days, and am now ready to render my verdict."

Now their faces have puzzled looks and they seem almost as nervous as we are. For some reason, this makes me feel good. I smile at them and then look back at the judge. Mr. Hennessey is sitting closest to the aisle, then Bryce, me and Quentin. We are all asked to stand.

As we do, the three of us hold hands praying it is what we want to hear. Looking back on the crowd everyone is on the edge of their seats waiting to hear the verdict. In this town very few have won cases over companies so if we do, it will be big. The judge begins.

"I find that there was an erroneous wrongdoing here. I commend Mr. Hennessey and his clients for their stance and courage. It isn't easy taking on a company as well known and successful as J.G. Accountants."

Nodding our heads in agreement, my heart has almost stopped and I can't swallow. Bryce and Quentin are holding onto my hands so tightly that they are starting to lose their feeling. We all hold our breath as the judge continues.

"I find J.G. Accountants guilty on all counts."

Oh my god, we won. I am crying and everyone behind us is hooting and hollering and clapping and we are all hugging each other. Everyone on their side is shocked as the four of them sit in disbelief. They are asked to stand.

"I've never seen such blatant wrong doing by a company and its employees in my life. Therefore, I am imposing the highest of penalties as possible. They are as follows: Ms. Baker, you are personally held liable for your client and will pay Mr. Bryce Bream $150,000, your license is hereby suspended for 10 years and you are to serve 2 years in jail."

I think everyone is shocked as you can hear them gasp. I for one am elated. She looks at Mr. Hunt. "Mr. Hunt, you are being held personally liable for your client and will pay Mr. Quentin Bream $150,000, your license is hereby suspended for 10 years and you to sir, will serve 2 years in jail."

Wow, they both are being sentenced for their wrong doings, I love it.

The judge then turns to Mr. Kinsley. "Mr. Kinsley. I am fining J.G. Accountants to pay each of Mr. Hennessey's clients $500,000. All fines imposed today must be paid in full to both Mr. Bryce Bream and Mr. Quentin Bream within sixty days."

Unbelievable, even the company has to pay damages and what a payout. Everyone is clapping and cheering and we are getting pats on the back from those directly behind us. The judge is slamming the gavel down several times as the bailiff shouts for everyone to settle down and be quiet.

As everyone settles the judge continues. "Furthermore, I am suspending J.G. Accountants license to practice until further notice. All of their clients will be sent to an accounting firm of Mr. Hennessey's discretion."

Our lawyer then raises his hand and asks the judge if he may speak to that. She grants it to him. "Your honor, Chloe here is the one who found these issues and brought it to our attention. I believe that she has the perfect firm to handle all of their clients."

The judge then looks at me and asks me to speak. "KMGP would be perfect and I recommend them to take on their clients." I explain my history with them thus explaining why I recommended them.

"Okay then, it is granted. Mr. Kinsley, you have two weeks to have all your clients forwarded to KMGP of which Ms. Chloe Bream will oversee. I am placing your firm under investigation and if comes forth that these dealings are occurring with other clients, they will be awarded the same judgment as those here today and, you will never practice again in the United States. Court is adjourned." She hammers the gavel down.

Mr. Hennessey congratulated us as we thank him for his help. "No thanks needed Chloe. You did all the work and it was your dedication and findings that resulted in the judgment today."

I thank him for the kind words as everyone hugs us and shakes our hands congratulating us for winning. It is unlike anything I have ever felt or experienced. They each got $650,000, much more than I expected. Now I need to show them how to run their businesses successfully and they will be set for life.

I sit down as I am weak in my knees. I can't believe that everyone got what they deserved. As I look over I see Mr. Hunt and Ms. Baker being taken away in hand cuffs and led out the side door. Craig comes up to me and asks if I am alright. I look at him, smile and nod but can't speak. I really don't know what to say as tears of joy roll down my face. We not only won our case but we won it for all the other clients they had and hopefully help others throughout the country.

As I stand up, a woman and man dressed in suits carrying briefcases walk up to me. They ask to speak to me, Quentin and Bryce so I pull them back. They introduce themselves.

"I am Mrs. Britta Vaughan and this is Mr. Reuben Glendale and we are with KMGP's corporate office."

They tell us how their corporate office heard of this case and asked them to come and see what the outcome would be. Mrs. Vaughan says that they are impressed with us and the results then ask how many clients J.G. has.

"I'm not 100% sure. However, I do know that it's more than 100." I reply.

Seemingly happy with this Mr. Glendale gives me a card and paper saying, "We have ten offices in this area. This paper lists their addresses and contact information. If you wait until Monday to contact them, I will make sure they have the number of clients they each can take, with the names for you to connect their clients."

I agree to wait until Monday.

Mrs. Vaughan then says, "We would also like to help you all out as well."

Mr. Glendale nods and looking at Bryce and Quentin says, "We will do all that is required

for both of you. We will do your books and help you with financial aid and answers for the next five years, free of charge."

They are both really happy with this, shake their hands thanking them and then head out the door, almost in a skip high fiving each other as they walk through the door.

Mr. Glendale and Mrs. Vaughan now turn to me and Craig as Mr. Glendale says, "As for you Chloe, you seem extremely smart. We would like to hire you to oversee the investigation in the J.G. Accounting firm and in turn we will pay you $30,000 a month for each month that it takes until completed."

Well I am surprised. I did not expect this. I tell them I except their offer but make it clear to them I still have work that needs to be done with Bryce and Quentin. "I have a home life too and won't do it if it interferes with any of that." I tell them.

They agree to it saying they understand.

Mrs. Vaughan adds, "We have one other offer for you. Because you have brought us all these new clients, we would like to extend our services to you personally as well. Should you ever own your own business, we will gladly do everything we can financially to ensure its' success. This will be free of charge to you for the life of your business. This will include us doing your books and investing into the business to ensure its' success. You helped us remain successful and we want to return the favor."

Wow! I don't know what to say other than, "Thank you so much. I will definitely keep it in mind should I ever need it."

I shake their hands and tell them I accept their offer. They tell me they will draft up the contracts for all three of us and send them to my email before the end of today. I tell them I will ensure a signed copy is faxed back to them with the original in the mail Monday morning. They leave as I turn to Craig. I think he is shocked as much as I am. Today could not have gone any better and is much more than I ever imagined.

Craig hugs me telling me how happy he is for me and how proud of me he is. We then walk hand-in-hand out of the almost empty courtroom and out the main doors to a whirlwind of people. Bryce and his family, Quentin and his family, our lawyer, my aunt and uncle are all standing at the top of the stairs waiting for us. Bryce, Quentin and I clasp hands and hold them up high to say we won. Every possible media outfit is here with microphones and cameras in our faces wanting to know how it feels.

We stop at the bottom of the stairs and Mr. Hennessey speaks on behalf of all of us. "We are ecstatic at the results. We hope this is the beginning for others to take a stand, have more say and get involved with their own accountant. We did this hoping to help others to not be afraid to speak up. It is your money and they work for you." He then says thank you and we all get into our respective cars and drive off.

We have agreed to meet at my uncle's house for a small celebration. We all have fun partying, singing, dancing and drinking having a great time. We won not only for us but for everyone else too. Luckily it is Friday because the celebrations continue on into the wee hours of the morning. Everyone crashes at the house as we all have had too much to drink to drive.

It is almost noon Saturday before we are all up and ready for the day. Slowly, as everyone leaves for their homes, Craig and I follow suit but not for home; which still seems odd for me to say. "Remember the other day when I said I had something to show you?" he asks as we drive out of the driveway.

"Yes. I remember."

"We are going there now."

"Okay but I am still nervous about this."

He says he is as well but it's now or never. I have just gone from being overjoyed and hung over to really nervous again. *Maybe if I am this nervous, it will turn out like it did yesterday*; I think to myself.

During our drive he tells me how much he loves me and says that he wasn't forth right with me when I asked about his job. "I told you I worked from home and only went into the office if I got called in; but, I didn't tell you what I did or why!"

Okay so now I am not so nervous because it is about his job, this I can handle, I think.

As we get through town he is holding my hand and has pulled me close to him. It is like he is holding onto me worried that I am leaving and he doesn't want me to. The further we drive I notice that we are headed towards the mansion that we attended the party at. He calls someone on his phone. "We will be there in ten minutes." and hung up the phone.

He holds my hand even tighter now. "You know that I love you very much right?"

"Yes."

"I hope you still love me after this." We have now gone through the front gate and his arm is around me holding me tightly until we are at the front doors.

Two guys dressed like chauffeurs come out and open the doors helping us out of the car. "Good afternoon sir." says the one, "Would you like me to park the car or will you be staying long?" he asks.

Craig tells him to park it for now because he's not sure how long we will be here as he looks at me. As we walk up the stairs a maid is standing at the door. She smiles and says, "Master, your mom is by the pool waiting for you."

"Ah, very good then. That will be all for now."

Okay, wait a minute. Sir? Master? That will be all? It is like this is Craig's place and they work for him; but, it can't be. It was his friend's house three weeks ago so how can it be his now. Something isn't adding up.

"I can see you have questions." he says putting his arm around me. "My mom will help me answer your questions and explain things."

As we walk out onto the deck, his mom is sitting by the pool in a lounge chair waiting for us. As we get closer, she gets up and is now walking towards us.

"Hello dear. It's nice to see you again." she says as she hugs me.

I say hi back then apologize to her for walking out at the party. She tells me not to worry. "Craig told me what happened and I had a talk with the girls. They won't bug you anymore and have agreed to let your past stay there. They promised not to bring any of it up again."

She then turns to Craig. "Did you tell her anything yet?"

He shakes his head telling her he was waiting until we got here. "I told her on the way here that I wasn't fully honest with her when she asked me about my job way back and that I want her to know everything. I also told her you were going to help me explain."

She looks at me then waves over a waiter who brings us a wild berry sangria drink. She hands one to me, one to Craig and takes the other for herself and we all sit down. She then starts.

"Well, I have to ask you this first Chloe."

I just look at her trying not to spill my drink. I am shaking so bad that even with two hands on the glass it still rattles the ice in it. Noticing this she asks, "Why are you so nervous?"

"I don't know what is going on." I explain what Craig said about this, then add, "He hopes that after I know whatever it is you are going to tell me, that I will still love him. I can't figure out what is so bad that it would stop me from loving him so I am nervous."

"It's not that it's bad. It is not what he does or where he is at, it is the fact that he wasn't totally honest with you up front; so, he is worried you will leave him because of that."

I tell her I understand that then ask what it is.

She begins, "Well, have you noticed anything unusual about Craig or his lifestyle or things he may have done or said?"

I sit here for a minute and think about her question before responding.

"Well I did wonder how he paid for everything that he has without a second thought or even worried about costs. That is when I asked him about his job. It wasn't because I cared how much he made or didn't make, I just didn't want him spending all his money on me."

She totally understood and then asks, "Is there anything else? You must have noticed something wasn't right."

Thinking for a moment of everything that has happened that may have triggered something, it's like a light bulb went off. "Well, yes there is."

Smiling she says, "I could tell just by the look on your face that something clicked."

"I often wondered what he did because it seems like he is with me a lot, no matter the time of day or day of the week. Not that I didn't like it but if he had a job, I wondered how he could be away from it so much and still have money like he seems to have."

"Okay has anything else happened that you might be questioning?"

"There wasn't until today." I explain how the staff talked to Craig like he was their boss when we arrived. "Which didn't make any sense because only a couple of weeks ago when we were here for the party, this was his friends place, not his."

She smiles as I stop to take a drink. Craig gets up off his chair and comes and sits beside me on the lounge chair I am sitting in and puts his arm around me.

"Baby, please keep an open mind about this. What we are going to tell you, I didn't tell you simply because I had to know one thing. When we are done I will tell you what that thing is but right now, please listen and try not to judge me too harshly."

Looking at him, I give him a kiss and respond to him. "Look, you all have me really nervous right now but there is nothing you could tell me that would make me not want to be with you. Unless you killed someone and you are living under an assumed name, I don't see it coming to that."

He says he hasn't killed anyone and it is nothing like that. Telling him he then has nothing to worry about, Winter begins. She first tells me about her late husband and how he owned a diamond company that made him millions of dollars. She tells me the companies they owned in their life together, how he was killed and what she was left with. She explains that when all was said and done she had over eight million dollars. With three kids at home she opened up savings accounts for each of them with a million dollars.

Craig's sister, Farah is three years older than he and was fourteen when their dad passed away. Craig is the middle child and was eleven at the time and his brother Grayson who is the youngest was nine. She then tells me that when they each reached 18, these accounts would be signed over to them to do what they wished. However, they were told that if they gambled it away or became broke, they would be on their own. This money was theirs but they would get no more.

Craig then spoke and told me how his sister spent almost half of her money buying a business that was going under without any investigation into it and less than a year lost it all. He says that before she spent the money, her million grew to almost a million and a half in just four years. When all was said and done she had just under $250,000 left. She bought a house and invested $100,000 which helped her to recover some of her money but she is still trying to get it back.

I am then told about Grayson and how his million dollars was almost $2.6 million by the time he received it. They tell me that he got in with the wrong crowd at school and spent all of his money on drugs and alcohol then rehab. He is now living far away working at a job he hates just trying to make ends meet. Winter sends him money every month to try to help him but refuses to support him. I can't say I blame her. Who spends almost three million dollars on drugs and alcohol and becomes broke in less than three years?

"Why did you skip over Craig?" I asked curiously.

They look at each other smiling then Winter explains. "Craig was different. He was fifteen when his sister got her money and at sixteen seen how she was losing her money. Craig asked me then if he could invest his money saying that he knew of some things he has been tracking and said he would make money before he was eighteen. He was sixteen at the time and I was skeptical at first."

I asked her how much he wanted to invest and she said $125,000 divided into three companies. "I made it clear to him that if he lost it he would have that much less money when he turned 18." She said he agreed to it and she signed so he could invest it.

"By the time I was 17, the $125,000 made me over $750,000." he adds.

Okay so now I am impressed but still not understanding why I would be mad or upset enough to leave. I guess I am still missing something so they continue with their story.

"When I turned 18 I had over $3.5 million. I bought a business and then invested some of it. The rest I kept in the bank, lived with mom and finished school."

"That was smart." I said.

"Agreed." says Winter, who then continues. "The business Craig bought ended up being a very bad deal. He found out that the people he was dealing with were crooked, so he got rid of it. He then decided to spend his money and time on regular people."

"What do you mean by that, regular people?"

"Well, even though I had money I wanted a normal life." answers Craig. "I didn't want to have friends or girlfriends or people around me because I was rich. I wanted people around me because they liked me and wanted to be with me, not because of the money."

Well that I understood because if it were me, I would probably be the same way and want the same thing. Telling him this he looks at his mom and says, "I think I was nervous for nothing."

She tells him, "Don't count your chickens before the eggs hatch my boy. She thinks it but it hasn't sunk in yet what we are telling her."

I stop her and tell them exactly what they told me for what I understood. "I think I know exactly what you are saying and if I am right then it explains so much."

Looking at me baffled, she asks me to explain what I think I know. I oblige her.

"Well it seems to me that unlike his siblings, Craig is smarter and was able to not only retain his money but make money with it as well. If I have to guess, this mansion actually belongs to one of you. Craig, you didn't tell me when I first asked you because you needed to know if I loved you for you and not for your money. Because of this, you kept it under your hat so to speak until you knew for sure that I loved you for you. This you know I do because I knew nothing of your money."

They both just sit there bewildered that I figured that out. Nodding their heads yes Winter says, "See my boy, she is much smarter than we gave her credit for. You made a fantastic choice when you picked her."

"So are you mad at me or does this change anything with how you feel about me?" Craig asks.

I look at him, then at Winter and smile. "Hmm, I have to think about it for a minute." I make him sweat a little bit before I say, "No baby, nothing has changed. I still love you and I don't love you any more or any less because you have money. I totally get why you didn't tell me

when I asked you but, if I am to think about it, you did hint around about it since the first day."

Looking at me surprised Winter asks me how. So I tell them.

"The first day we met he was wearing clothes that seemed a little too, shall we say, good, for making mud pits and getting ready for a truck rally. The second day when he walked away with me and the girls asked him why me, what did I have that they didn't it was his response, that had me thinking."

I look at him and ask him if he remembers what he said. He nods saying, "I told them that they were all gold diggers looking for sugar daddies to care for them and give them what they wanted and you weren't like that."

Nodding my head in agreement I add, "That was the first real clue that you had money but I didn't put two and two together. If they were looking for sugar daddies and they wanted you, then you must have had money."

"Very true." says Winter. "If you know this now, why didn't you pick up on that or some of the other hints?"

Craig tells her that I was in a bad place when we first met and that the reason I was here to begin with was because I lost the one man in my life that loved me. She said okay and told me that she knew a bit of my past because Craig told her. She asked me if it was okay. I said yes I had already told him that it was fine.

"Now I have a question for you." I tell them both.

Taken aback a bit they look at me and tell me to go ahead and ask.

"Well, I get why you didn't tell me that first week, but why the charade with the apartment? I mean, when you asked me to move in with you, don't you think you should've told me this first?"

They look at each other and Winter says, "Okay my part is done here. Son, you are on your own now. I can't answer why you say or do what you do, only you can."

She looks at me and says she is happy that telling me this did not deter me away and she will see us later. She gets up and walks towards the bar at the other side of the pool.

I look at Craig and say, "Well?"

He turns so he is facing me then answers. "The same reason I didn't tell you in the beginning. I wanted to know for sure you loved me for me and not my money. I know it seems stupid seeing as it has only been two weeks but I want total honesty, and you had just told me about your past. I didn't want to spring this on you during that same time. I had every intentions of telling you that weekend we were here for the party, but then things happened and you left."

"So why were you so nervous telling me all this?" I ask him.

"I know you said before it didn't matter how much I made or what I even did because you love me for me. I do know from past experiences, that what is said and done are two different things."

Agreeing with him he continues with the reason. "You are different from any other woman I have ever known. You're upfront, straight forward, yet open, honest and compassionate. Not things most woman have all at once."

I just sit here for a minute not sure what to say. He grabs my hands, looks at me in the eyes for a moment and holds his gaze. Then he continues with what he wanted to say earlier.

"Chloe look. I know it is a lot to take in but, I really want us to live here. This is my home and I want to share all of this with you. I know you don't want me for my money but,"

I interrupt him there. "I never had any money of any kind in my life, you know this. I wouldn't know how to act or be if I had money. I know I moved here for a new life, a new beginning, and if I didn't find it I was moving on, possibly not moving on at all."

Craig says he knows this and tells me that I don't have to worry about it. "We can all help you with that and I don't want you to change a thing. I love you just the way you are."

I hesitantly nod saying all I can do is try. He kisses me. "Do you know how happy you have just made me? I could not be any happier. You now know everything and I am relieved. I really thought that you would be mad at me for lying and leave. I am glad that I was wrong."

I reply saying he technically never lied to me, he simply didn't answer the question when I asked it. "Evading a question and lying when you answer are two different things and you evaded, you didn't lie to me."

He spends the afternoon introducing me to his staff and telling me what they do and where things are. His mom doesn't live here but, is here all the time. "She owns the mansion three blocks away." he tells me as we look out the west window of the master bedroom pointing to her estate. Their yards actually link together but because of the woods between them. The only access is by the road.

We spend the rest of the weekend at his estate giving me a feel of what it is like to be rich. I am not sure if I could ever get used to asking people or telling people to do something for me all the time. Even more so, when it comes to things I can do for myself. However, at the end of the weekend he asks me if I would move onto the estate with him. I agree and he has his chauffeur pick up our things from the apartment and move them here.

I ask Craig why he keeps the apartment and he tells me it is a getaway for him. He likes being rich but he also likes to live as normal people do, so he keeps it so he can do just that when he wants to.

"If you are business savvy, why didn't you help me with Bryce and Quentin's businesses?"

He tells me he wanted to see what I could do and if I could do what I claimed. I ask if I held up to his expectations.

"There was no question and even if you lost the case, I would have still asked you to move with me and told you this was my place. To be honest, it was fun watching someone else do that for a change."

Now it is my turn to get back at him so to speak and make up for all of this. "Well, I am glad you enjoyed it!" I say telling him he can now help me to train them next week so they will learn how to properly run a business successfully. "I would hate to have done all this for them to blow through all that money and end up where they started."

He agrees with me and says he will help. "I would love to be on your team and work with you side by side. I think it would be lots of fun."

MONDAY IS HERE now and we spend the morning signing contracts and sending them back to KMGP. Craig and I go over papers, ideas and plans of what they need to do and what would help them best. We tell both

Bryce and Quentin to meet us Wednesday morning so we can go over our ideas and plans with them.

The next day goes by quickly and it is now Wednesday morning. Both of the boys are here waiting for us as we arrive.

We go over our ideas and explain our plan and how it will all work, including end results. Now that we have an agreement in place and everyone knows what their roles are, I spend the next couple of days at KMGP helping them to connect with their new clients while Craig begins teaching the boys what needs to be done. All goes well and the next couple of months is spent training Bryce and Quentin and helping KMGP with the investigation into J. G. Accountants.

Results prove that more than eighty percent of J.G.'s clients were being taken for more money than they should have. In total it is over $300,000 taken from 90 of their 112 clients. The company is fined $500,000 payable to each of them and has to close their doors permanently, declaring bankruptcy.

CHAPTER 43

IT IS NOW Labor Day weekend and Craig is taking me to the Nascar race at the Texas Motor Speedway. He got us great seats, up in the bleachers on the second level where we can see most of the race track. I love car racing and Dale Earnhardt Jr. and Danica Patrick are my two favorite drivers. Everyone who knows me knows this, including Dale and Danica as I am a life time fan and longtime friend of both.

We are now sitting in our seats and they have just brought out all the drivers as they do before every race. We are standing for the national anthem. As the singer finishes, they clear the stage and before they yell, 'Drivers Start Your Engines', Craig says he will be right back. My guess is he wants to get a beer before the race begins so he doesn't miss anything.

He is gone about five minutes, when the drivers start their engines and take their place on the track for their starting positions. Once they have all taken their place, they turn off their engines, something that is not usual for this sport. For no reason, Dale Jr. drives his car from his starting position and drives up to the winners circle. He gets out of his car and takes the microphone.

Everyone in their seats are wondering what is going on because this never happens. The drivers are now all sitting on their window ledge as if they are waiting for something. Dale then says, "Attention everyone. Before we begin today's race we have a very special presentation for you."

This is very weird and unusual and everyone in the stands is now looking at each other in wonderment. Then Dale asks, "I am going to say a name and when I do can you please stand up and wave your arms so we can see where you are."

We all wait to see who he is going to call and why.

"Will Chloe Bream please stand up."

Shocked and wondering why he wants me to stand, I also wonder where Craig is because he has not come back yet. I stand and wave my arms so he can see me. Pointing to me, I am now on every television screen and jumbo tron in the stadium. He tells me to go with the ushers who will bring me to him. Now I am wondering, as is everyone else there, what is going on and why I am being called out in front of everybody here.

While we walk down the stairs and across the track to the winners circle, Dale is telling everyone how I have done some work with his and Danica's team for a few years now and how I am a person with a kind soul who is always helping others yet asks for nothing in return. I am looking around wondering where Craig is and if he has any part in this.

As the two ushers and I approach him, he says, "Now it is time for us to return the favor and give her something back."

He then stops talking and gives me a hug. As we hug I ask what is going on but he just smiles. Over the microphone he tells me to get up on to the roof of his car and have a seat. Still trying to figure out why, I am helped up onto the roof of his car and I sit facing the crowd. He asks me to turn and face the drivers, so I do.

"Will everyone please look up in the sky straight above the grandstand?"

As everyone looks to the sky, we see an airplane, a sky writer, and all watch reading as the plane writes the message in the sky. It says, "Will you marry me Chloe?"

I look at Dale confused because he is already married and his wife and I are good friends. Everyone in the bleachers gasps and is now looking at us wondering the same thing I am. He says, "No, that message is not from me."

Then from the start line Danica leaves her place in line and begins to drive towards us, but slowly. She has something on her roof but she is in the twentieth position and is too far away for me to see what it is. Very faintly we hear music, soft romantic country music with no words. As she gets closer the music gets louder and everyone is watching as she drives towards us. Almost to the front of the line now we can see that it is a person on the roof of her car but still unclear who it is.

Then the person begins to sing 'I Love You Always Forever'. As she gets closer I now see it is Craig singing and he is dressed in a full tuxedo. As he gets half way through the song, I am brought to tears as he sings is beautifully. Danica pulls up beside Dale's car and Craig and I are now side by side. He stops singing and faces me.

"Chloe, you and I have been together for nine months now." he begins as he reaches one hand out for mine. "It has been the most magical time of my life. I have never loved anyone or cared for someone like I do you."

I have to let go of his hand because I am crying and I need to wipe the tears. He gets down on one knee, pulls out a small box from his inside pocket and opens it. "Chloe, will you make me the happiest man alive and become my wife?"

I am taken aback in disbelief. It is the most romantic proposal I have ever seen and heard and here it is, for me. The ring is extremely gorgeous too, like something I have never seen before. In a vintage setting it is a fourteen Karat white gold quarter inch round diamond with Marquise Sapphire Ring.

Nodding my head and crying I say, "Yes!" He puts the ring on my finger, stands up and jumping over to the car I am on he kisses me, as we embrace.

Everyone in the stands and all the drivers are now all standing and clapping. I look up and can see that we are on the jumbo tron and every screen around. I try to stop crying but I can't, it is the happiest moment of my life and I can't believe he put all this together.

We are helped down off the car and Craig picks me up carrying me off behind the winners circle. Dale and Danica congratulate us and we thank them for being a part of this wishing them luck in their race. They get in their cars and drive back into their respective starting positions.

We are led to the upper deck where we are given champagne and fruit platters to watch the entire race. When we enter into the circular deck I am in shock. How he did this I do not know. First he gets the sky writer to ask the question, then the entire Nascar circuit for today's race to go along with the proposal, and now this.

My mom, son and youngest sister, his mom and sister, my cousins, and some of our friends are all inside waiting. They are crying too, as they are happy for us. "My first born, my little girl." my mom says hugging me, "You have been down this marriage road before. This one is the one you have been waiting for and I could not be happier for you. You have truly finally found your soul mate."

I have never been hugged and kissed so much in my life and to my surprise they all know Craig's money situation because he told them. They tell me how Craig called introducing himself to them and how he told them what he wanted to do.

"Your other two sisters and brother could not make it and I never did get in touch with your dad." Craig tells me.

"It's okay. The fact that you went through all of this just for me is beyond belief. I think I am in shock."

Throughout the race we have Nascar people come in asking us questions about how we met and how we got to where we are. We tell them the same story we told the waitress a few months back. Our story is now worldwide and everyone who knows us and even those who never met us, know of us now.

I can't help but cry on and off the entire day. I hug him and kiss him and keep looking at the ring and am in awe of everything that has happened. Everything he does and says right from the minute we met, he has shown and proven to me not only that he loves me, but is in love with me, completely with his whole heart, body and soul. I have never met anyone like him and I couldn't be happier that I am spending the rest of my life with him.

CHAPTER 44

THE LAST TWO months have been the happiest ever for me. I am living in a mansion and I am going to marry the man I love more than anyone else in this world. Thanksgiving is now approaching quickly. It is this coming weekend and I want to make an announcement during dinner. Craig is aware of what I want to announce and he is going to help me.

It has been several months since we won the court case and Bryce and Quentin have received their money. Both businesses are thriving now but seem stuck without a way to move forward. That is until I make my announcement, I have a way they will both benefit and possibly triple their existing profits.

Thanksgiving is here and we are at the estate. Everyone is here – my aunt and uncle, Bryce and his family, Quentin and his family, Eric and his girlfriend, Dante and his fiancée, my mom Lee, Craig's mom Winter, his sister Farah and her family, are all here. Everyone is having a great time drinking, eating and swimming.

Dinner is now being served so we all take a seat at the very long table that has been set up by the pool. The staff has done a fantastic job getting everything ready and together for this dinner. Once dinner has been served, we give the staff the rest of the afternoon and evening off to spend with their families. Shocked but happy they all leave saying thank you.

While everyone is eating Craig stands and tells everyone he has an announcement to make. He takes my hand and has me stand beside him. "Chloe and I have set a wedding date. We have been talking and we want to celebrate our one year of living together with our marriage. We will be getting married on Saturday, May 30th."

Everyone is happy as they take out their phones and PDA's and puts the date in their calendar. We tell them we will be sending out invitations soon then sit back down.

Almost finished dinner, I stand and cling the side of my glass with a spoon to get everyone's attention. Now that everyone is looking at me I begin.

"As you all know, these past nine months have been very grueling with many changes for most of us here."

They all nod in agreement.

"I want to state where everyone is at and then I have another proposal for you."

I begin by stating that Bryce in six months is now out of debt with $450,000 in the bank and running his business successfully. Then I state how Quentin in five months is also out of debt with $340,500 in the bank and he too is running his business successfully.

"Continuing at this rate you will both be okay with your business and home life. However, that is all you will be doing, living."

By now the kids have now gone back swimming in the pool while the rest sit drinking their drinks curious of what my plan is.

Craig is now standing beside me and hanging on my hand. "The idea she has is a great one. Most of you know how I made my money and you all know I too am business savvy. We both worked on this idea to fine tune it and I hope you are all as excited about this as the two of us were when we were planning it."

We sit down and tell them our plan hoping they agree to it. "If the two of you meld your businesses together and move to a larger space, you will be able to triple your money. What it means is this. Right now you have combined about $800,000."

Craig adds, "If you combine your individual businesses into one, you will be able to provide every service possible for small engine repair. This is something that no one around here is doing so you will hold the monopoly on that market."

Asking us questions, we answer them and explain how it would work. We also tell them of a place we know they could use as it has everything they need, to do all the work they want to do. "You both have said that you want to spend some money on lifts, putting oil change pits in and upgrading your equipment, right?"

I ask looking at Bryce and Quentin. They both nod agreeing with us.

"Well, this new place has five lifts with six pits and all the equipment you will ever need, and nothing is more than five years old." Craig says.

We explain to them in detail what each would be responsible for and how well they could work together, if they combine their efforts. We also give them figures comparing to how much they are making separately now and what they could make if they joined forces.

"End result is this, the $800,000 could easily become almost $2 million in less than one year. You would never worry about your businesses, and neither of you or your families will ever have to worry about money again for anything. The choice is yours. We realize that it is a lot at once and you both have to be okay with working together as equal partners."

We tell them to think about it and talk it over with their wives and families and let us know. Craig tells them that they have until the end of December to decide because the owner of the building has a prospective buyer. "He is holding them off until Christmas to give us time to respond."

We spend the rest of the evening swimming and diving and drinking and eating and talking. It is a party that lasts into the early morning hours. Around midnight all the children have fallen asleep and are bunked in sleeping bags in the upstairs eastern bedroom. We put them there because it is closest to the bathroom.

The rest of us are by the pool sitting with our loved ones on the lounge chairs or on the steps in the pool. We are talking and having a nice, quiet evening. Before long, Bryce gets up and walks over to Quentin. In minutes they both walk over to Dante and talk to him. It isn't long before the three of them walk over to Craig and me.

"We have been talking about your idea and we have a question." Dante says.

Craig and I sit up in our chair and ask them to sit down. They do then Bryce asks, "Could your plan include the three of us if we all combined our forces into one?"

We tell them it is a great idea and it in fact was something we had discussed. They all say it is what they want that they have been waiting for something like this for a long time. We agree to discuss this further next week and will start putting things into motion, then.

Slowly everyone is passing out around the pool, some have gone inside to crash in the bedrooms and Craig and I go to bed around three a.m. It seems like I have just gone to sleep when I hear the kids running around and whispering. Craig gets up to see what's going on to find that they are all awake and want to go outside but no one else is up. Some of our staff have come in and inform us they are there. They take them outside and feed them breakfast watching them until some of the parents get up. He comes back to bed.

It is now eleven a.m. and we decide to get up. As we head outside to the pool area everyone is already there having coffee. We grab a cup of coffee from the bar and join the rest of the group. Soon we are told that breakfast is ready; the cook has made us omelets with sausage patties and toast.

When everyone is finished eating, Craig calls over Daryl, one of the waiters. "Tell Devon to bring it out front please. We will be out there in fifteen minutes." Daryl nods and leaves. Ruby and Sophie, the waitresses begin to clean off the table when Craig stands and asks everyone to hold up one minute. He looks at me, smiles, and then tells everyone he has something he would like to say. Everyone quiets down including the kids.

"First, I would like to thank all of you for celebrating Thanksgiving with us here in our home. It feels good to not have to hide this part of my life anymore."

He pauses and looks around for a moment, waives Sophie and Daryl over who have small gift bags. They hand one to each kid that is here as they have toys with candy and gum in them.

"As you all know Chloe's birthday is coming up in two days. Because you are all here, I would like to give her my gift now."

He takes my hand and asks everyone to follow us to the front of the house. As we walk down the hallway to the front door Winter puts a blindfold on me so I can't see what it is. Now I have to rely on Craig, total trust is in him now. As we go out the door I can hear them all gasp with ooh's and aah's.

Now I am curious, "What is it?" I ask.

He walks me down the stairs telling everyone, "This is something that she seen a while back on one of our weekend excursions and she absolutely fell in love with it. I lied to her before we left this place because I really went in and bought it on the spot to make sure it would be hers."

Now I am trying to think about what we have done, where we went and what it is I saw. We have been many different places over the past year and I can't think of what it could be.

"Are you ready?" he asks me.

Telling him yes he takes off the blind fold. I am in shock. Sitting there in front of me with a very large bow around it, is my car. I look at him in shock, "Are you serious?"

He says yes it is mine. It is the 67 Barracuda convertible we seen this past summer at the car show. I walk around it slowly taking in it beauty. I am in disbelief, "Its' really mine?" I ask again looking at him.

Everyone is walking around looking at it. As I come back to the drivers' side, he hands me the keys and says, "Get in baby." I take the keys from his hand, give him a kiss and unlock the door. I open it up, and open the other doors so everyone can see the interior. I get into the drivers' seat and press the button to open the roof. I really can't believe it; the one car I have always wanted since I can remember, I actually have.

"Oh my Craig, you have outdone yourself." my mom says. "Since she was five years old, we seen a car very similar to this but in red and she fell in love with it. She has said since then, this was the car she would someday own. You have made her one life-long dream come true. It is truly unbelievable and very romantic." She hugs him in tears.

I am already crying, still astonished that I am actually in this car. "Baby," I say looking at Craig, "Get in!" He climbs in the passenger seat, I lean over to kiss him then I thank him. "It is the best gift I have ever gotten. I love you very much."

I look at everyone else there and tell them that we will be right back. "When we get back I will give everyone who wants one a ride." I say smiling.

Driving this beast is even better than looking at it. You can feel the power, the strength and the roar of the engine telling me to go. The wind in my hair, the love of my life beside me, and the most exquisite car ever made is what I now have. It is the best feeling ever, so great that I can hardly describe it.

When we return, I give everyone a ride. When we are done, everyone leaves to go back home except our mothers. My mom is staying with us for another two days before going home and Winter lives next door. I wash the car then dry and wax it until it shines, like it is still in the show room before letting Devon put it in the garage.

CHAPTER 45

CHRISTMAS IS ONLY three days away now and my cousins have combined their business into one and are now celebrating their new found riches. Things are looking up for them and they don't need me anymore.

Christmas this year will be a lonely one for us because there will only be Craig and myself. My mom will be in Costa Rica with my sister and her family, his mom will be in Dubai with his brother and family, my aunt and uncle will be in Canada with my dad, son and brother, and his sister has moved out of state.

Craig gets an idea and for once tells me what he is thinking. "We are going to have a great Christmas. It is our first one together and I want it to be a romantic one."

"Sounds great, what do you have in mind?"

"I want to take you to Maldives. It's a very romantic place with lots of fun and relaxing things to do."

Having never heard of Maldives let alone been there I am excited. "I have never heard of Maldives. It sounds perfect."

"I also have something for you, my love."

Asking him what it is, he tells me there is a package on our bed waiting for me. We go inside and I skip steps as we go up the stairs to our bedroom. I am excited. I love surprises and Craig knows this. On our bed sits a large clothing box with a green and red bow on it. I look at him inquisitively as he sits me on the bed and hands it to me. I take off the bow and open it up.

Inside is a beautiful, mermaid style, blue snowflake on white dress. This gorgeous floor length, sleeveless, embroidered drop waist hugs my curves. The beautiful embroidery around the bra flares down to the tulle drop at mid-thigh. It is a sleek and feminine style dress that follows my silhouette to the mid-calf before flaring out at the bottom. It is very elegant and stylish and I love it.

As I am getting dressed, I hear him talking on the phone. When I am done I walk out of the bathroom to find that he is now dressed in his navy and white suit. "It fits me perfectly, as always." I say twirling for him to see it.

Craig is absolutely enamored with how I look in it. He takes my hand and we walk out the front door. There is a limousine waiting for us at the bottom of the stairs which takes us to the airport. Craig owns his own plane, this I did not know until now. We board it and sit in a double seat that looks and feels like a leather sofa. It is soft, comfortable and reclines, unlike any seat I have seen or been on any airplane that I have ever been in.

We are only in the air for an hour before landing at yet another secluded airport and another limousine awaiting us. The Maldives is officially known as the Republic of Maldives. It is an island country in the Indian Ocean and lies west of Sri Lanka.

As we drive along the roads to the resort where we will be staying, I am in awe of its' beauty. You can see the ocean along one side of the road and on the other are lush tropical forests full of color. The homes here are like our mansions at home.

"These are where the Maldivians live. It is the poorest part of the country." The chauffeur says as we drive through.

I think to myself, *if this is the poor part, I can't wait to see the rich part.*

Craig tells me some of the things about this place and what we will be doing. "We will be on a secluded lagoon. We can bathe in the warm sunshine on the endless beach. We will go snorkeling and take in the sights of the underwater coral gardens they have. There are palm trees and sand dunes everywhere."

"It sounds beautiful."

"It's not as beautiful as you." he says making me blush. "I can't wait until you see the resort we are staying at. It is called the Ocean Water Villa and it stands up to its' name."

I am now Intrigued, and can't wait either.

As we drive up to the ocean, we are greeted with a large cruiser boat and I am hooked. The resort is a paradise all on its own, an island away from prying eyes. Once we sign in at the main hut, we walk across two sand dunes before walking onto a boardwalk. It is a half a mile long yet beautiful. As you walk over deeper waters, the boardwalk turns into glass so you can see the fish and plants in the underwater oasis that is underneath you.

The water is crystal blue in color and as clear as the water is from your tap. At the end of the boardwalk is a hut, the one we will be staying in. There are ten boardwalks with huts on the end jutting out from the main hut where you sign in.

The hut is single story with a solid wood floor. In the middle of the hut you walk down a set of stairs which leads you to underneath the hut. When you are in this space you are literally under the water and with its' full glass surround, you can see all the beauty their underwater world holds.

I didn't understand why we are dressed as well as we are until evening comes. After we are settled, a large cabin cruiser pulls up. Craig smiles and leads the way to the boat. He shakes hands with the driver as though he knows him but no introductions are given. We get on the boat and are then driven across the turquoise waters to a large, personal showboat cruiser.

As we board Craig introduces me to the owners, "Chloe, this is the Callums, Lord Frederick and Lady Ambrosia."

I shake their hands as I am told that they are long-time friends of Craig's family. "It's a pleasure to meet you both." I say.

We have dinner on their cruiser with live entertainment as we cruise along the Indian Ocean. We pull into a lagoon that is tucked out of everyone's view where we anchor and watch the beautiful sunset. As we sit on the bow of the cruiser overlooking the calm waters of the ocean, and holding hands with Craig I close my eyes.

Relaxing, I inhale deeply taking in the odors of the oceans' water. I can smell the salt in the water, musty smell of the sea-weed and the crispness of the impending night air. The waters are tranquil and crystal clear, soothing any anxieties that I may have felt.

I open my eyes to see the magnificent blue expanse reflecting the last of the warmth radiating from the setting sun. It has cast an orange haze over the horizon, as if lighting the sky in a ring of flames. The sun, like a concave gold plate, emits its' last crimson rays of light, before embracing its' sweet slumber. Clouds in the distant sky, with their various shades of pearly white fluff to deeper purples, surround the setting sun bidding it farewell. The ocean however, has now opened its arms to welcome its guest as it sinks lower casting the reflection of a pale, mirrored pathway of shimmering light over the rolling waters. The sky appears in a mixture of yellow and deep mauve which further descends into a dull, brown as it disappears under the distant horizon. The moon, reflecting the bright light of the sun, is now bright orange as it rises higher into the sky shining its path of fiery light over the waters.

As we take up anchor and begin to cruise back towards our hut, I watch the moon as it rises higher into the dark sky, turning into a bright white light, lighting up the sky to show the starry night sky. It is breathtaking and beautiful and ever so calming. We are almost back before I realize that the air has become cooler and Craig is now trying to wrap himself around me to keep warm.

We arrive back at the hut, thank Lord Frederick and Lady Ambrosia for a wonderful evening and step off. The night is spent making love to each other and gazing at the stars through our endless windows.

The rest of the vacation we walk the island, take in the fantastic sunsets and sunrises over the Indian Ocean, sip on island drinks, and admire the sights this island getaway has to offer. We take surfing lessons, and I find out that surfing is not my thing. I can't stand on the board without falling.

We walk hand-in-hand along the endless beach, float on tubes in the blue and turquoise waters and have even done some snorkeling. We spend a week here and it is the most romantic time I have ever spent with anyone.

Craig was right, it is the most romantic place in the world; at least the most romantic place I have ever been to, and all the time spent with him allowed me to fall in love with him all over again.

CHAPTER 46

A FEW MONTHS have now gone by and our wedding is less than two months away. Craig has surprised me with a trip to Belize for Valentine's Day. Upon our return home from this trip Craig surprises me with a bookstore. It's the one I have been involved with since the Christmas holidays and knowing I have always wanted to own one, he bought it for me.

While we were in Belize, he told me how he wants to plan our wedding leaving me to relax and enjoy my time being pampered. Although I am hesitant, he has done very well with everything else he has planned including our trips, so I agree to let him plan it.

As the weeks pass by, I have spent a lot of time at the bookstore while Craig plans the wedding. He tells me what has already been done and where he is with the wedding plans. The colors are going to be royal purple, pearl white and emerald green with gold and silver accents. I ask him why those colors.

"I know it sounds like an 'odd' mix of colors but trust me, it goes well with the wedding I am planning. You will need to know the colors for your dress; which, by the way, I have people who will help you get it together. They know the theme and the color scheme, all they need now is what style you want and your size."

He then proceeds to tell me when and where I have to be. I guess he has it all under control. "I feel weird that you are doing all of the planning for our wedding. It is usually the woman who does this because the man doesn't want to be involved." I say to him.

He acknowledges this as fact but then says we are not traditional people. Our love is unique as we are, so why not have a wedding to match. I agree and am getting nervous yet excited all at once. I can't wait to see the end result and how it will turn out.

Our wedding day is only a couple of weeks away now and although I am busy with the store, I am starting to get really nervous. My life with

Craig this past year has been great, the best ever. We love each other and have shown it making sure to say it every day. We do not let one day go by where we don't let the other know this. It is amazing and I can't believe that I will soon be spending the rest of my life with the one man who means more to me than any other in the world.

The next two weeks pass by very quickly and before I know it, the day is almost here. I wake up after a night of restless sleep. Both of us have tossed and turned all night keeping the other up and barely sleeping a wink.

Tomorrow is our wedding day and for me, I still have a wedding dress with accessories to get together. So far, all I have done is answer questions from all kinds of people who have either called or visited me at the store. Some have taken measurements, other have shown me samples of dresses and after a few days I was finally able to get a rendering of the dress style I want to wear. Other than the colors and theme that they already knew, nothing else has been done, that I am aware of. I decide that today I am going to make some calls and see if I can find out anything.

As per usual, I get up and walk out onto the pool deck to see Craig reading the morning paper and a cup of coffee waiting for me. We sit by the pool talking about the days' events eating breakfast. We get ready and leave in our own cars going about our day separately waiting until we can be together again that night.

Today though, things are a little different, not like our typical morning. Craig is by the pool reading his paper and my coffee is there waiting for me but he is dressed and ready to leave. "Good morning my love." he says, "I have a lot of last minute preparations to do for tomorrow so I won't be able to have breakfast with you."

"I understand baby, it's okay."

He gets up, bends down and kisses me, then leaves saying he will pick me up for lunch. I put the behavior off as nerves of tomorrow's events and trusting that he knows what he is doing. I eat my breakfast and drink my coffee before heading out myself.

Around ten a.m. I tell my employees that I will be in the back making some phone calls if they need me and I head to my office. I am not in there ten minutes when Brooke knocks on my door telling me that there are two guys dressed in tuxedo tails wanting to see me. "They say it is urgent and only want to see the owner." she says.

I tell her to show them in. She says okay and goes back to the store. She comes back quickly saying, "They say they need you out there and won't take no for an answer."

"Did they say who they are, where they are from or what they want?"

She shakes her head saying that all they said is they need to see me and asked for me by name. Not impressed I follow her into the store.

Annoyed, I walk up to them. "Okay so what is so important that you couldn't talk to me in the office?"

"Are you Chloe Bream?"

"Yes I am. What can I do for you?"

The one grabs my right arm and tells me I have to go with them. I pull my arm from his grip and tell him I don't have to do any such thing. Brooke is standing between us and the door and Brandon and Alexis are standing at the counter. Alexis has the phone in her hand.

The guy grabs my arm again and tells me very harshly, "It is in your best interest Chloe to come with us." he says as he rushes me out the door.

As we get closer to the door I yell to my staff to call the police and give them their description along with the car they are driving.

By now each of the two men are on either side of me dragging me by each arm to their stretched limo. I am pissed off and a bit scared because I don't know what is going on or who they are. After they push me into the car, the door slams shut and immediately locks. I am screaming to let me out and try to unlock or open the door but to no avail. Nothing works.

I start pounding on the window that is between me and the two men in the front seat but they ignore me. After a few minutes I notice there is a phone on the wall below the window so I pick it up. As I put it to my ear I hear it ringing so I wait.

The guy in the front passengers seat answers it and before I could say anything he says, "Don't worry Chloe, this is all part of the plan. You will understand very soon. It is not what you think is happening."

I start yelling at him asking what plan and who is behind it. He does not answer he just turns to me, smiles and hangs up the phone. I pound on the window and door for a few minutes only to make my hands sore. Nothing I do works so I sit back on the seat and look out the window to see if I can tell where we are, any landmarks I might need to take note of and where we are headed. The more we drive and the further from town we get, the more nervous and scared I become.

I look around and see nothing but trees, rocks and the odd small building. I don't recognize where we are and we have not passed a road in a while. I try to look out the front but have a difficult time as the window between me and the front of the car is frosted making it hard to see out of. The side windows are tinted very dark allowing me to see outside but not clearly.

The only window clear enough is the back window and the sunroof on the ceiling. It's like I am being kidnapped but I'm not blind folded or bound or gagged, so I am not sure what is happening to me or why.

Almost forty-five minutes into the ride, I can see a clearing. As we drive further the clearing gets bigger and longer. There seems to be a paved road running along the clearing in the same direction as we are. It is another ten minutes before I see a small building and an airplane, realizing we are at an airport. Where this airport is and why it is in the middle of nowhere is beyond me but, it seems to be where we are headed.

The car is driven onto the tarmac and stops beside a personal jet that has the name, Hawker 400xp along the side under the windows. On the back wing there is a logo with a large CF. I have never seen a logo like that and have no idea who or what company it stands for. The two men help me out of the car and lead me to the plane.

As I walk up the stairs and enter the cabin it is nothing like any other plane. The floor is flat however the entire space is oval in shape. There is seating for seven people with a bar and bathroom at the back of the plane.

As I look around I notice there are four people standing there, in different uniforms, with a smile on their faces. "Welcome Chloe." they all say almost in unison.

I nod my head and take a seat in the front row. I don't know any of them nor do I know why I am here or where I am headed. The two men leave, the stairs are pulled up and the door gets closed and locked. I look at the other people who are still smiling and still not saying a word. They too take their seats.

"You had better buckle up." the tall thin man says.

Within minutes a voice comes over the radio, "Welcome Chloe. Please make sure you are buckled in. We will be taking off in just a few moments."

Now I am dumb founded and nervous. I don't know any of these people and have never seen them before in my life; so how do they know my name? As we take off I look to my right and ask the woman who is wearing a smock. "How do y'all know my name?"

"The person who planned all of this told us. We were told to address you by your name or we would be fired."

"Who planned all of this? Who is your boss and how does he or she know my name?"

They won't tell me. All they say is that they were told to do a specific job and nothing else.

As we level out the pilot comes back across the radio saying we can unbuckle our seat belts and move about the cabin. I leave my seatbelt on thinking to myself that I am only going to get up if I have to use the bathroom; otherwise, I am not leaving my seat.

Well, I could not have been more wrong. The woman with the smock comes over to me and undoes my seat belt asking me to stand. I ask why and she stands me up, waves the other three over and they tell me that they are here to do my hair, nails and make-up while we are in the air.

"Why?"

"Because it's our job and we were paid to do this."

"Craig is going to be picking me up for lunch in an hour and when he doesn't find me there, he will be looking for me!"

Snooky, the name of the woman in the smock, talks to me. "Everything will be okay. It's not what you think it is." as she leads me to the back of the plane.

By this time I decide to go along with them because going against them has gotten me nowhere so far. There is nothing I can do and if I am going to get made up like a spa day then why not enjoy it. What I thought was a bar is, but only in part. It is also set up like a hair salon which is where she seats me. I am laid back as she washes my hair like they do in a beauty parlor. As she finishes, she asks me to sit at the desk with the mirror. I oblige her as I try to calm down.

She puts stuff in my hair, blow dries it, and works with it. As she does this I get turned in the chair to my right and there sits another woman with a tray filled with all kinds of things. She is going to give me a manicure then do my nails with gel. I sit here, close my eyes and try to relax letting them do what they need to do. As I do, they talk to me with idle chit chat asking me about my wedding.

There is not much I can tell them because Craig did all the planning and has only told me a few details. "He said that what I know is all I need to know and the rest I will find out when the time comes." The puzzle pieces are now starting to fall into place.

Cassidy, the nail lady, says, "That is so romantic. I don't know of any man who wants to be part of the wedding plans let alone plan the entire thing."

I nod in agreement and Winston, the man waiting for his turn to do my make-up adds, "Nor a woman who would allow a man to plan the entire wedding without her being a part of it." They all snicker.

I tell them that I trust him and why I trust him explaining all the trips and celebrations he has planned on his own thus far for me this past year. They all agree that if they had someone like that, they understand why I have no issues letting him make all the plans. By now my nails are done so Winston sits in place of Cassidy and starts applying foundation and make-up to my face while Snooky finishes my hair.

By the time they are finished the pilot comes back across the radio telling all of us to buckle up as we will be landing momentarily. We do and I look out the window to see if I know where we are. I don't recognize anything but then again, I don't see a whole lot either. More trees everywhere but they are different than those in Texas. These trees look like Cypress, Ginkgo and largely over grown plants. I ask where we are but Cassidy, Snooky and Winston tell me they can't say.

When we stop, I am led off the plane to yet another limo. I get into it and the door closes behind me and like the other, it locks immediately. I decide not to scream or bang on anything or even fight it. I will go with the plan because by now I am thinking that maybe Craig is behind all of this as part of our wedding plans; at least I hope he is.

As we drive I notice that we are in an old place. It is like something from the early 1900's. As we drive into town I notice a sign that says, 'entering the Province of Sergovia'. Having never heard of that name, it gives me no clues as to where we are. However, I do know that we are no longer in the U.S.

Throughout the town there are many different architectures and land sculptures. There are Royal palaces and cathedrals, many different civil architectures and monasteries with churches. All are mixed with urban sculptures which pay tribute by depicting illustrious figures that are linked to the city. The town is also home to many fields, parks and gardens paying tribute to the founders of the place, and to those who are respected both in the past and the present.

As we drive into the heart of downtown we pass through a white brick archway which connects two large towers made of the same brick. The road changes from paved to interlocking grey stone in circular patterns. The limo stops in front of the largest and tallest building standing on the block.

As I exit the limo I look up and see the name of the motel; Hotel Don Felipe. This elegant downtown hotel is a large red brick building placed in a stunning location among the hills located directly above the sea. A sign inside the door says, the chic soundproof rooms come with free Wi-Fi, a mini bar, city or garden views, and flat-screen TVs with satellite channels. It also says that the rooms offer views of the Alcazar. The polished suites add a living room and Amenities include a cafe, a walled garden and a terrace with city views. There's also a bar and a Massage parlor in the motel.

My room is in the penthouse on the top floor. As I get off the elevator, I am greeted by my mom and son who have been waiting here for me for three hours. Now I know that this is part of the wedding plans by Craig. I don't know of anyone else who would or could pull something this elaborate off.

The three of us sit talking and I ask them if they know what is going to happen or any of the details. My mom says she knows almost everything and promised not to say a word. "I will tell you that this is one wedding that no one will ever forget."

Dylan adds, "It will be one for the record books and if everything goes according to plan, everyone will know about this wedding and what was done for it. Like grandma said, everyone will remember it for a very long time."

They won't give me details or any further explanation other than my mom telling me to relax, sit back, do what I am asked and enjoy it.

We spend the night talking, telling jokes, and eating from the various trays of food that keep being delivered to our room. We also have a few drinks to loosen up and are in bed by eleven. They tell me that we have an early yet long day tomorrow. Tomorrow is my wedding day and we are supposed to get married at four p.m. that is if Craig hasn't changed the time.

Now knowing that all this is definitely about the wedding and that Craig is behind all of this, I will have no problems doing as I am asked, sitting back and enjoy it. Now, I can't wait. I am excited and nervous at the same time.

CHAPTER 47

IT IS THE morning of my wedding and I only slept last night because of the drinks I had before going to bed. My mom and son are getting ready to leave saying they have things they need to do before the wedding. They give me a kiss and tell me that they will see me later today before I walk down the aisle. I say goodbye and sit and wait for the days' events to unfold.

Not knowing what is on the docket I do know one thing, my dress still hasn't been made and if it has, it hasn't been fitted to me yet. I really hope that it is one of the first things they do. I also need my hair and make-up redone because my hair messed up from sleeping and my make-up is off.

As I sit here waiting for what is to happen next, I look back on my life. As I think about what has happened to me, the good and the bad, I remember the newspaper article I read many years ago and the one thing that Eric said to me when he picked me up from the airport when I first landed in Texas.

WHAT WILL MATTER……

Someday it will all come to an end. All the things collected will pass to someone else. There will be no more surprises, minutes, hours or delays. The wealth, fame and power you have will shrivel to irrelevance. It won't matter what you owned or what you were owed. Your hopes, ambitions, plans, dreams and to-do lists will expire. The wins and losses that seemed important will only fade away. It won't matter where you came from or what side of the tracks you lived on.

What Will Matter:

- --it's not what you bought but what you built
- --it's not what you got but what you gave
- -- it's not what your success is but your significance
- --it's not what you learned but what you taught

Every act of integrity, compassion and sacrifice that enchants, empowers and encourages others in your life is what will matter. How many people will feel a lasting loss when you are gone is what will matter. The clarity and care at which you loved those in your life and the positive influence you had on them is what will matter.

> Living a life that matters doesn't happen by accident and it's not a matter of circumstance. Living a life that matters happens by choice.

Looking back on my life, I realize just how true it is and how it all makes perfect sense to me now. When I was younger I lived my life according to everyone else and it was horrible. Recently, I started living my life by choice, to live one that matters to me, the way I want. My life has turned around for the better and I am living a happier, much more enjoyable life now.

Out of nowhere, there is a knock on the door and I jump. There are two women dressed in a Victorian Corset Dress with Incredible Needlework standing there. They ask me to go with them so I do. They lead me to a ballroom on the fifth floor where soft music is playing and several people are standing around with tape measures, fabric and lace all in various shades of purples, gold's, whites and greens. In the far right corner I can see a beautiful dress hanging on a Cobblestone Metal Accessory Dress Form.

They usher me in the door and have me sit in a large, reclining chair. A couple of the women drag the dress form over to me and begin to tell me about the dress. It is a Vintage Medieval Wedding dress lavishly trimmed in frills, lace, braid, fringe and embroidery work. It is very ethereal yet delicate looking.

The main dress is a Royal Purple renaissance Victorian fairy style with white embroidered design lace pattern along the top then drapes down outlining the cleavage. The dress is strapless, tight fitting from the breast to waist down in a V-shape to the naval. The skirt is full with white embroidered edging along the bottom.

The back of the dress is button up from the nape of the lower back to mid-back. The buttons are emerald green in color. The sleeves are three-quarter from mid bicep to a V-shape on wrist and back of hand. The edges are both embroidered in the pearl white to match the front of the dress with emerald green sequins throughout the sleeve. Attached to the bottom of the dress back is three-yards of Royal purple silk with an emerald green charmeuse that will flow behind me as I walk.

It is one of the most beautiful dresses I have ever seen and this is my wedding dress. I stand and they help me to put it on. Surprisingly it is not as heavy as it looks. The material is lightweight and the layers are minimal, making it look like more than what it actually is. With it being 102 degrees outside, I am thankful for this. Once the dress is on, there is very little that needs to be done for the fitting. I am just as surprised as they are that it fits me so well right away.

As the seamstresses make the final adjustments, the make-up artist and hairdresser work on fixing my face and hair. It only takes about an hour for them to be done. I put my dress back on and am asked to sit back down in the recliner.

As I do six men walk in with tons of boxes on trays with rollers. Each box has a different pair of shoes for me to choose from. There are several, some solid colors of each purple, greens and whites; there are some with two or all three of these colors mixed as well. After going through all the shoes and almost two hours later I decide on the emerald green, trance-bow pointed pumps with white crystal-accented buckle ankle strap and two-inch heel. It is a stunning satin upper, royal purple leather lining with royal purple leather soul.

Two other men now walk in with glass cases. Each case holds several necklace and earring sets. It's not long before I see the perfect set. It is an art deco sterling marcasite necklace, emerald green in color with matching earrings. It has sterling silver panels with tantalizing marcasites. The rich green onyx stones add intoxicating enhancements and decorate the fancy framed centerpiece and side accents. Between the onyx stones, there are gorgeous marcasites. The necklace is a comfortable 18 and 1/4" long and closes with a hidden box push clasp.

As I am fully dressed with my hair and make-up done, I am led to the elevators where a man dressed in a tuxedo with tails waits for me. I am taken from the ballroom and led to the main lobby then outside where there is a horse drawn carriage waiting for me. There are two midnight black, majestic Clydesdale horses at the end of the reins and a man dressed in black tails and a tall top hat at the helm.

I am helped up into the coach of the carriage and we are on our way. We ride through some of the most beautiful parks in the world and I am getting extremely nervous now. It won't be long before I marry my soul mate. Although I am ecstatic and elated I am still nervous yet I can't wait until I get to see him. I haven't seen him since yesterday morning and last night was the first night without him in a year; I really miss him.

CHAPTER 48

ALTHOUGH IT IS a slow ride, we are finally here. Just outside of town where rock cliffs, valleys and woods are more prominent, we pull up to a castle. The driver says it is the Segovia Castle, one of the most royal places this town is home to. It rises out of a rock cliff that sits between two rivers flowing around the mountain. It is the first Royal Palace of the province.

The exterior has six square towers framing a protective barrier around the castle and are connected by solid walls made of brown and red stone. "This is known as the curtain wall of the palace." the driver tells me.

A yette iron gate with broad metal doors leads the way to the castle. The castle walls are made of red and grey rocks with vines and plants growing from the cracks and climbing up the sides. There are well kept gardens of fragrant and colorful flowers, gorgeous trees and many bushes decorating the outside as we drive up. A draw bridge is lowered for us to cross as we enter the circle entrance of the castle.

As we stop, there are four men waiting to walk me up the stairs. Two men are on either side of me as the other two carry my three-yard train. At the top of the stairs stand my mom, son, aunt and uncle, and Brooke. They all look at me with jaws dropped, eyes as wide as they can get, and shocked looks on their faces. As I reach them I ask what's wrong. They all reply nothing, "Mom, you are very beautiful." Dylan says.

I thank him as he hugs me and we walk inside. The interior is more beautiful than the outside. It is decorated with delicate pendant ornaments. You first walk in to the Great Hall which leads up to the other rooms on the main floor. Along the walls of the Great Hall are displays of crowns of all the kings and queens of this castle; each surrounded by Latin motif extracts. Each room has a name plaque above the doors. I look at them but don't pay too much attention to them as we are busy talking moving through the hall.

About half way down we stop. Brooke, my mom, son and aunt say they have to take their places inside leaving me in the hall with my uncle. As we stand here I ask my uncle, "How long have y'all known about this?"

"Almost everyone has been in on the planning with details since y'all came back from Belize."

We then hear the music start. Craig has chosen CANON in D by Johann Pachelbel. It is one of the most romantic wedding songs of all times and one of my favorites. My uncle looks at me. "Are you ready?"

Nodding, we stand arm in arm in front of the grand double wood doors carved in medieval Latin style design. Two ushers open the doors showing the interior of the Throne room. There are chairs with people down both sides of the room creating an aisle leading to the throne stage at the front of the room. A royal purple carpet lined with white, orange and black rose petals channels the passage strip for us to walk on. Everyone is dressed in 1850 to 1900's dress including Craig.

He is standing at the base of the steps that lead to the two thrones atop the stage. He is wearing a pearl white tuxedo with royal purple and emerald green accents. His shirt is a royal purple spread color, bib front fit. It has French cuffs with mother-of-pearl button strips and white and emerald green knot cuff links. The shirt is a tight fitting, slim look to his chest and body. His pants are white pleated front tailored hugging his hips. They are slightly relaxed in the leg with a royal purple satin stripe from the waist along the leg seam to the hem. He is wearing a white tuxedo jacket that has impeccable tailored and embroidered purple and green lace design on the lapels. The jacket buttons are royal purple and has a lengthy luxurious drape at the back. He looks really handsome in this suit; and, when I see him I can't take my eyes off him.

As we get to the front, there is a clergy man dressed in royal gowns of purple and white standing beside Craig with a crown in each hand.

The Kings' crown is extravagant, brilliant in color plated in gold. It has a royal purple velvet trim with metal rhinestones of sapphires, emeralds, black rubies and sterling facets.

The Queen's crown is just as extravagant, brilliant in color and plated in gold and platinum. It has an emerald green velvet trim with sapphires, rubies, emeralds, pearls and diamonds. Both are extremely beautiful and look really heavy.

The clergy man places each crown on the table that is front and center at the bottom of the steps. He then steps down in front of the table, motions Craig to step down to his left then motions me to step up to his right. He takes each of our hands and places mine into Craig's and then has us turn and walk up the steps to the thrones. We each stand in front of the thrones waiting for the clergy man to tell us to be seated. My uncle takes his seat beside my aunt in the front row.

The clergy man then turns and faces the crowd, raises his hands and as he lowers them he tells everyone to please be seated. Everyone including Craig and myself sit. The next half hour is spent us listening to the clergy man talk about love and respect. He then turns to me and Craig and asks us to stand and face each other. As we do he says, "It is my understanding that the groom has written his own vows."

Craig looks at him and nods then looks back at me, grabs my hands, looks into my eyes and begins.

"Chloe, you are the most beautiful woman I have ever met, inside and out. From the moment I laid my eyes on you I knew you were the one for me. I could never have dreamed how rich my life would actually become until you came in it. I make only one promise to you today, all your troubles, worries and past issues will remain there. I will never hurt you in any way and promise to protect you from harm loving you for the rest of our lives. I will do everything I possibly can to make and keep you happy forever. Today I declare my love for you. I will always be there to support you, to catch you when you fall, to protect you, to pick you up when you are down, to take care of you and I will love you to the end of time. We will always be together now in life, and even after in death. You are truly the only one for me, forever."

I am fighting back the tears and in doing so have removed my right hand to wipe away some of them. I look at him and taking his hand in mine, I take my turn. "Well I haven't written anything but there is something I would like to say."

The Clergy recognizes me saying, "The bride would now like to say her own vows." I nod and look back at Craig.

"Craig, you are a man that most woman only dream of having. Until last year, I was one of those women. You have made my life worth living again. You were my salvation, my life line when I truly needed one. Now, you are my rock, my lover, my soul mate. My only promise to you is to love you forever supporting you in every way one person can. Today I too declare my love for you. I will always be there for you, loving you, standing by you, taking care of you and I too will love you to the end of time. I not only love you but I am in love with you with every fiber of my being. We are soul mates destined to be together here in life and after death living as one forever. I truly do love you."

The clergy then asks if we have the rings. Craig looks down to my son who brings him the rings. They are eighteen carat white gold platinum rings with an inscription on the inside that says, 'soul mates 4ever – Chloe and Craig'. They are beautiful. The clergy has Craig place my ring on my finger and repeat after him, 'with this ring I thee wed'. He then has me do the same to Craig.

We are then asked to come down to the bottom of the steps. He then explains to the congregation, "In the 1850's when a king married his queen they placed a crown on each other's head to signify their acceptance of power and partnership they both share. It is a bond that is never to be broken."

He turns to us and picks up the kings crown handing it to me and then the queens crown handing it to Craig. He then tells Craig to place the crown on my head which he does. It is now my turn. Craig bends down slightly so I can reach and I place the kings' crown on his head. They are heavy but not as much as they look.

The clergy then says a speech. As he finishes Craig turns to him and says, "Can we hurry this up please, I want to kiss her."

I smile and so does the clergy as the congregation chuckles. The clergy then tells Craig, "You may now kiss your bride."

Craig gives me a long, most romantic, French kiss. We smile as we look at each other, turn to face everyone and we clasp our hands together and raise them as everyone claps. We are then introduced by the clergy man, "Let me introduce to you Mr. and Mrs. Craig Forrest."

We take our first steps together as husband and wife and walk down the aisle to the door. We stand in the hallway being congratulated by everyone as they walk out. We then walk outside to have pictures taken in one of the gardens. After all the pictures have been taken, we go back in the castle into the Torre Juan II room just to the right of the Great Hall.

There are platters of food from every food source; Italian meatballs, scallops, shrimp, scampi, lobster, different kinds of salads, rolls, chicken, ribs, mashed and baked potatoes, baked beans, every kind of pickles and olives and cheeses. The food is sitting on rolling trays and tables along the far wall.

There are several tables each with eight chairs along the one wall and far side of the room and there are two bottles of champagne on each table. The tables each have a royal purple cloth table covering with white embroidered edging with the emerald green with white embroidered corners cloth napkins. There are green vases of white and purple roses on each table as well. The floor covering is a plush carpet in medieval Latin motif design in dark burgundy, purple, green and blue.

We all sit down at our assigned seats. Once we are seated the food is served to us in a four-course style meal and champagne is poured. First a tray of rolls, pickles, olives and cheeses are placed on each table. Then we each are served with a plate of different salads. When these plates are taken away we are served meatballs, chicken and the baked beans with our choice of mashed or baked potato. Once this course is finished they serve us a platter of scallops, shrimp, scampi and a lobster tail.

We are then given a break from all the food, which is good because we are very full and I don't think anyone could eat another bite. During dinner romantic music was played low key in the background. Now it has changed to more, fast paced, dancing type music. There is a mix of country and old style rock and roll. The kids are the first to get up and dance while the adults sit back to let our food settle.

The lights are now dimmed and candles are lit for a romantic atmosphere. Craig and I dance our first dance as husband and wife to, 'Me and You' by Kenny Chesney. Half way through this song the best man and maid of honor along with our parents join in. Then Craig and I decide to sing a song for everyone so we both take a microphone and sing 'Greatest Love of All'. We bring everyone to tears including myself.

After a few dances, deserts are brought out. They are all set out on the long tables and we can get what we want as we want it. There is everything from candied fruit to cookies to cakes to muffins to brownies and different fudges.

The celebrations continue on into the night. Everyone has changed throughout the night into more comfortable clothing. It is lots of fun, romantic and this day has been even more than I could have planned. Craig has proven that he can plan anything, can be trusted and always has my best at heart. He knows what I like and what I want and does a great job at it.

It is now midnight and I am sitting with my family talking about the day and the past year when Craig stops the music. He walks over to me and has me stand beside him before saying, "I want to thank all of you for coming and help us to celebrate this very special day for us both. It has been a long time for both Chloe and me to find true happiness. Having said that, I am sorry to say, we need to bid our farewells as we have a plane to catch."

Everyone says their goodbyes to us as we walk towards the doors.

"Where are we going?"

"On our honeymoon, of course." he says with a smile.

CHAPTER 49

LIKE USUAL HE won't tell me where we are going or what he has planned but I go along with him. We get into the limo and are driven to the air strip where we board the plane. It is a beautiful sunny Sunday morning as the plane lands in Tahiti, French Polynesia.

The eight-hour flight seemed quick as most of the trip was spent with Craig and I hand-in-hand or arm-in-arm, embracing and caressing each other in between the bit of sleep we do get.

"We will be here for two weeks my love." Craig says as the plane lands and comes to a stop.

We are staying at the Ocean Water Villa where the honeymoon suites are single-room, thatched roof, bungalows overlooking crystal blue waters of the lagoon. There are many tropical beaches secluded from the population as well as three coves they call 'paradise cove'; 'lovers cove'; and, 'sweetheart cove'. "While we are here we will be taking excursions and swimming in their breathtaking waterfalls. Ones much more enormous, extreme and beautiful than the one I took you to." he says to me as we settle into our suite.

The bellhop brings in our luggage. "Will you be joining us at the Tranquil Emerald Lagoon tonight for our romantic sunset dinner tonight?"

"Yes I believe we will." Craig answers.

After finding out what time and where, the bellhop leaves. Although we have been together for a year, I want the ceremonial sex to sizzle. During the entire plane ride we both flirted with each other giving each other a wink here or there, and touching each other in certain places on top of the clothing. When I ate the popsicle, I licked and sucked on it in provocative ways or sucked on an ice cube in an erotic way to entice him but I would stay far enough away from him where he couldn't touch me. He would walk by me and rub up against me as he stood behind me or passed by but only long enough to get me going then he would be on his way. We would talk to each other using sex words such as banging, oral, swing, vixen, woody, etc. every chance we got.

Walking with him hand-in-hand to the suite and having to wait for the bellhop to leave was torture, at least for me. All I want to do is push him onto the bed, jump him and consummate the marriage. For now it will have to wait a few more minutes. Although he took the liberty of packing everything there is one thing that I had his mom call ahead and hopefully is waiting for me in the bathroom. She did it in such a way that he does not know about it.

I step into the bathroom telling Craig that I will be right out. "I have a surprise for you now." I tell him.

I can hear him moving around as I close the door, making sure to leave it open ever so slightly. As I stand in the bathroom I position myself where he can see me changing through the mirror reflection. I slowly take off the dress that I am wearing.

I begin by lowering the spaghetti straps off my shoulders and letting them fall down my arms. I then unzip the back of my dress slowly as I glance into the mirror to see if he is watching. When he sees that I notice him watching he smiles and moves away. Seconds later I hear music playing; so I continue.

I lower the dress past my hips and let it fall to the floor. I then unclasp my bra and slowly let the straps fall down my arm making sure that the cups stay on my breasts until my arms are fully out. Then all at once, I let the bra drop to the floor revealing my naked breasts; which are right now, hard and perky.

Taking two steps backs I glance in the mirror and notice that he is sitting on the edge of the bed trying to see inside the bathroom. I place my fingers into the edge of my panties and as I slowly pull them off my hips and down my thighs, I bend forward until they are at my knees. I then stand up, let them fall to the floor and kick them off to the side. I move out of his view leaving him wanting more.

I walk over to the tub which is where the negligee I want is hanging. It is a full black, lace with rose print, two-piece outfit. The straps are quarter-inch gold chord. From the strap, the front goes down to the naval in V-shape form with edge barely covering my nipples. It is held together with three-gold chains – one ties it together at the base of my breasts, a second one inch down and the third another inch down. The back is a scoop style mid-back length. It is a pull over style top and when on fully, it is just below my hips thus showing my panties. The panties are the same black full lace with rose print tied on my hips with thin spaghetti ties.

Taking it off the hanger, I bring them back to the counter in front of the door to give Craig something to look at. I stand with my back to him but he is able to see the front of me as well by looking into the mirror. Spreading my legs shoulder width apart, I put on the panties tying them onto my hips. I lean forward bending at my hips slightly and pick up the top, pull it on over my head, and down barely covering my panties. Then I adjust my breasts.

Picking up the thigh high nylons, I sit on the edge of the tub which is just to the right of the door. As I do this, I can hear him moving around on the bed in the other room. Sitting on the edge of the tub I slowly put on the nylons one at a time. I have them rolled in my hand and beginning at my pointed toes, I slowly roll them up my leg, over my knee onto my thigh. As I glance out the door I see Craig is lying back on the bed watching every move I make.

Now fully dressed, I open the door fully, lean against the door frame and look at him. He is fully undressed with the blankets covering the lower part of his body, and he is looking at me in anticipation. I stand here running my hands down my body, onto my hips then to my thighs and back up again. Moving slowly towards him, I run my hands up and down my body as I walk moving to the music.

As I get to him he sits up and opens his mouth as if to say something. I put two of my fingers on his lips and shake my head, "No words, just enjoy." I tell him as I lay him back.

I lean over him, almost laying on him but suspend myself. I put my hands on his chest and run them all over his body. Then I lean in and softly give him a kiss on his lips, then his cheek and his chin.

Now I kiss his neck to the shoulder then onto his chest. He is moaning with excitement and his body is buzzing almost in vibrations. I stop, get up, sit beside him and looking into his eyes I asking him if he would you like me to stop. Shaking his head he says, "I love this. No, I don't want you to stop."

I smile, kiss him with a lingering closed mouth kiss then stand. Stepping back, I do a little dance turn. As I do I ask him if he likes it. "Yes, very much so." he replies as he pulls back the covers and stands in front of me, wearing only a tight pair of underwear.

He puts one hand on the lower part of my back and the other behind my neck. He then leans in and French kisses me like never before. Both of our hands are all over each other's body. He then lowers his hands to my hips, lifts up the top and unties my panties letting them fall to the floor. He bends down to pick me up and lays me on the bed.

As I move to the middle of the bed and lie back, he climbs on top of me coming at me like an animal in heat. For the next few hours we have the most passionate, animalistic, powerful love making a newlywed couple could have. We do it in every position keeping our bodies as close together as possible.

We lie down but rather than be in each other's arms, we lay side by side on our backs just looking at each other. After a few minutes he props up on his left elbow facing me. He leans in and without saying a word he runs his hands over my thighs, across my belly and along my bare skin.

He studies me caressing my breasts for a few moments. After a few moments, he licks my nipples, then moves his lips slowly down my stomach as he his hands move my panties slowly down my legs.

He is now kissing me just above my pubic bone slipping two of his fingers inside me. I move into his hands as he kisses me on my stomach, until he stops suddenly. He removes his fingers as if he'd thought better of the whole thing and lays back down beside me, still propped on his left arm.

I take my hands and looking deep into his eyes, I wonder why he stopped suddenly. As he lies onto his back, I lean over and kiss his chest rising to straddle him like I am going to ride a horse. Sitting on him now, he enters me. As he thrusts upwards I push my hips down onto him.

His hands are holding my hips helping me to move up and down on him as I place my hands onto his chest for stability and leverage. Still no words are said but they don't have to be; we both know what the other is thinking and feeling.

All at once he sits up, puts his arms around me and gives me a sloppy French kiss turning our gentle love making into a hot and heavy session; and I love it. I get into it quick as he rolls me over onto my back. He slides his hard cock into me again as we passionately kiss each other like it is our first time. On the lips, neck, nose and even a little nibble here and there on our ear lobes and nose.

I wrap myself around him as he makes mad passionate love to me. I allow myself in that single moment to be carried away. "Cum with me." he whispers to me with his mouth at my ear. He then kisses the nape of my neck as his hands float all over me. The sum of all acts unite us, the pure calculus of love. Then as if in unison and on cue, we cum together and it is a great release for us both, like a volcanic eruption.

We are sweat covered and visibly rocked yet fully and completely satisfied. I lay back onto the bed as he draws the water in the Jacuzzi. I am weak in the knees, watching him as he moves about to make sure the water is just right. When he turns the water off, he comes back to me, feels my body and its warmth, leans in and kisses me gently as he helps me out of the bed.

As we enjoy a nice relaxing, Jacuzzi together there is a knock on the door. It is the bellhop reminding us that the romantic sunset dinner is being served at the Tiki beach in a half an hour. Craig thanks him and we get ready.

The rest of our time here is spent making love whenever and wherever we can; swimming in the paradise coves; and taking in the majestic views. The tranquil emerald lagoons, breathtaking waterfalls, romantic sunsets and moonlit walks complete the experience.

This is the perfect way for us to begin our lives. In love with each other totally enamored with each other in everything we say and do.

Love has bit me twice and this time, it will be forever!

EPILOGUE

FIFTEEN YEARS LATER and it is now my 65th birthday. Craig and I are as much in love with each other now as we were when we first met.

My step-daughter Paige is now happily married with her second child on the way. She and her family live in Ohio where she owns her own clothing design business and her husband is manager of a major marketing company.

My son Dylan and his wife Kiara have three children and still live in Canada living a happy life. Both Dylan and Kiara are language teachers, her in French and he in Spanish. At times they teach abroad in other countries. During these times, we get to have my grandchildren with us.

My step-son Ethan is divorced with two kids and now has a second girlfriend. He is an airline mechanic working at the local air base in California, where they now live.

Craig's son Nathan and his wife Chantal have three children and one grandchild. He is a computer genius and works for the government while she stays home taking care of the home and children. They are living a happy life in San Antonio, Texas, not that far from us.

His daughter Elisa and her husband have two children with their first grandchild on the way. She has a home based Interior Design Company while her husband is a CEO of a legal firm in Oklahoma.

Together, we have five children, four in-law children, a total of eleven grandkids, and one great grandchild with a second on the way. Everyone is happy with their lives and things are going very well for everyone.

My uncle has passed away a few years back and my aunt is in a group home and very ill. The doctors say she only has a few days left and can pass anytime. With my birthday here and Christmas just around the corner, we are all sad by this news. Although we know it is coming, you can never be fully prepared.

My cousins are enjoying life with their families in a lap of luxury. Their business is booming and they have opened up another garage site and will be hosting an open house for their third one within the next month. Their children are in the best of schools and they are all doing very well.

Craig's sister Farah is happily married with four children and one grandchild on the way. They have moved back to Texas and now live in their mother's mansion.

His mom, Winter passed away last year with C.O.P.D., and left the mansion to Farah.

His brother Grayson has smartened up and is now on his way to regaining his riches. He has recently moved to Houston, Texas with his wife and they are expecting their second grandchild in a month. They now only live three hours away from us.

Both are around more often now and doing very well.

Craig as usual is planning an elaborate birthday celebration for me at our mansion and has invited everyone to join us. My mom and her new husband of two years along with some of our friends are also invited and will be here. It is going to be a birthday bash no one will ever forget.

Sixty-five years of life, finding the love of my life, finally happy and celebrating it all with everyone that means the most to me in my life; what could be better?

Life is wonderful. Craig's love for me only makes me more of who I am. We are happy together, share our life together, and are inseparable, just like teenagers still. I can't believe that not only did I get a second chance at happiness, but I found my one true love, my soul mate, my twin flame. It is Craig.

He is truly my happily ever after. I could not ask for better and would not change a thing.

www.ingramcontent.com/pod-product-compliance
Lightning Source LLC
Chambersburg PA
CBHW052012070526
44584CB00016B/1715